Guide to
Lump Sum
Investment

The Daily Telegraph

Guide to
Lump Sum
Investment

**TENTH
EDITION**

Liz Walkington

**KOGAN
PAGE**

First published in 1985
by Telegraph Publications
Author: Diana Wright

Tenth edition published in 1998
Author: Liz Walkington

Kogan Page Limited
120 Pentonville Road
London N1 9JN

© The Telegraph plc 1997, 1998

British Library Cataloguing in Publication Data

A CIP record for this book is available from the British Library.

ISBN 0–7494–2695–0

Typeset by Saxon Graphics Ltd, Derby
Printed in Great Britain by Bell & Bain Limited, Glasgow

Contents

UNITED TRUST BANK LIMITED

Founded in 1955

STERLING DEPOSITS

(Minimum Deposit — £5,000)

FIXED DEPOSIT ACCOUNTS

The choice of 1 Year, 6 Month or 3 Month periods

Excellent rates of return

NOTICE DEPOSIT ACCOUNTS

A choice of either 90 days or 180 days

Superior rates of return

*Our sterling deposit facilities are designed to provide competitive
rates of return with flexibility, whilst providing and maintaining
the highest standard of customer care
and service.*

For further details please contact:
*Sally Johnson — Manager, Sterling Deposits
United Trust Bank Limited
1 Great Cumberland Place
London W1H 7AL*

*Telephone: 0171 258 0094
Facsimile: 0171 262 4273*

Authorised under the Banking Act 1987

EXPLODING THE MYTH

"Stockbrokers only deal for the very rich". Wrong! Around 18 million people now own shares and many more know something about the stockmarket through the privatisation programme and building society demutualisations. Stockbrokers are far removed from the stereotyped images often portrayed in the popular press and above all are approachable, friendly and accessible.

Almost all of the firms who look after individual investors are members of the Association of Private Client Investment Managers and Stockbrokers (APCIMS).

What makes APCIMS members different?

Direct Access to the Market - the majority of our firms are members of the London Stock Exchange and are therefore unique in having direct and immediate access to the stockmarket for buying and selling shares. The computerised systems used mean that brokers do not have to be located in the City of London - they can be in your local high street.

Professionalism - the breadth and depth of investment experience and knowledge which APCIMS members make available to their clients contrasts with that of many other financial advisers whose expertise is limited to the selling of a handful of "packaged" products offered by the big insurance companies.

Genuine Independence - APCIMS members are truly independent unlike other financial advisers many of whom are "tied" to a particular company. The advice given by our members is completely impartial and their charges are disclosed to you in advance.

Tight Regulation - all APCIMS members are regulated by either the Securities and Futures Authority (SFA) or the Investment Managers' Regulatory Organisation (IMRO). They are subject to demanding tests of their financial resources and are obliged to meet the most rigorous procedural standards and management controls. Only those individuals who are personally registered with the regulators as being "fit and proper" are authorised to give investment advice.

Individually Tailored Services - APCIMS members operate on the basis of providing services which are tailored to suit your individual circumstances and requirements.

The main services available are:

Advisory Services - almost all APCIMS members offer an advisory service in which the professional advises on the purchase, sale or retention of individual stocks.

Dealing or "Execution-Only" Service - this service is designed for investors who do not require advice but who do need a stockbroker to buy and sell shares for them.

Discretionary Investment Management Service - to put it simply, this service gives the manager the authority to buy and sell investments for you without obtaining your prior approval on each and every occasion.

Comprehensive Financial Planning - this can include advice on the placing of cash deposits, pensions, mortgages, life assurance, Personal Equity Plans (PEPs), Tax Exempt Special Savings Accounts (TESSAs) and so on.

How To Find Out More

A comprehensive brochure and a directory of APCIMS members detailing the range of services they offer are available free of charge by writing to APCIMS at 112 Middlesex Street, London E1 7HY, quoting reference DT98.

It's not only the bigger fish who benefit from Trusts

Many people ignore trusts either believing they have a "mystique" about them or that they are only for the super-rich. In fact a trust is very user friendly and flexible and can easily be adapted to suit all individual needs. Trusts allow you to keep your options open.

Whether you want to provide for your children's or grandchildren's schooling, provide for your husband or wife on your death or even protect an inheritance against it being frittered away, a trust is the flexible answer.

Nobody knows what tomorrow may bring, or what costs may need to be incurred. Everyone worries when they die if there will be enough money to provide for their husband or wife, whether they will be properly looked after, or whether there will be enough to pay nursing or medical fees. Yet in addition you might want to direct what happens when your husband or wife dies, who will get what and will all grandchildren (including any as yet unborn) be treated as you want. With a trust you can cover all these options.

You may also be worried that your children could be provided with too much money before they are mature enough to deal with it. Some parents worry that their children will marry "golddiggers" and want to ensure that money is only provided for circumstances of which they approve. Again a trust can offer the protection required whilst still giving flexibility.

It is not to be forgotten that trusts can also be tax advantageous. A lot of inheritance tax planning involves giving money away during one's lifetime. Naturally some people are reluctant to do this if it involves a loss of control. A trust can solve this dilemma as it is possible for you to be a trustee of your own trust thereby retaining a degree of control not only over investments, but also over who gets what and when.

There are different types of trust to cover different situations. If you want to provide that someone has a fixed entitlement, for example you want your husband or wife to have a right to all income for the rest of their life, then this is known as an interest in possession trust. The fixed right need not be to all the income, it can be to a half or any other proportion, and can extend to a right to the underlying capital as well. The choice is yours dependent upon your individual circumstances.

Alternatively you may want no-one to have a fixed right, you way wish to keep things very flexible and decide in the future who benefits and to what extent. In fact you may want the ability to vary this from time to time. In such circumstances you would want a discretionary trust - i.e. one where payments are made at the discretion of the trustees. Typically family trusts are structured in this way with potentially a large number of family beneficiaries and trustees making payments on a needs basis.

Where minor children are involved it is usual to use an accumulation and maintenance trust. This is a form of hybrid between the fixed interest and the discretionary trusts. Up to a set age (not later than 25) it operates on a discretionary basis. Broadly the trustees "accumulate" any income which is not distributed for the "maintenance" of the children. After the set age the child becomes entitled to a fixed interest. These trusts can be very tax effective for minor children if they have no other income. A distribution from the trust can be tax free if it is within a child's personal allowance or at least subject to a low rate of tax if it exceeds this threshold.

Another question to be answered is whether you want the trust to be onshore or offshore. Offshore trusts offer confidentiality and may in some circumstances offer tax advantages over onshore trusts. If you choose offshore typically you will appoint a professional trust company. The choice of jurisdiction is also very important. If you live in the UK you will want to ensure that the jurisdiction has developed trust law, speaks English, is easily accessible, is economically sound and has a good banking system. The choice of professional trustee is typically between banks, solicitors, accountants or a private specialist trust company.

A trust can play a vital role in financial planning. If you have a lump sum to invest, then investing it within the framework of a flexible trust can be very beneficial. However it is not a decision to be taken lightly and appropriate legal advice should be taken on the drafting of the trust, advice should be taken on the tax consequences and trustees experienced in trust administration should be appointed.

Andrew Brown can be contacted on 01628 6669166

Bolt Burdon - a very personal private client service

At Bolt Burdon we offer you an independent service that is friendly, value for money and which allows you to be in control of your financial affairs.

If you come to Bolt Burdon with an inheritance, your savings or a windfall to invest this is how our service will work.

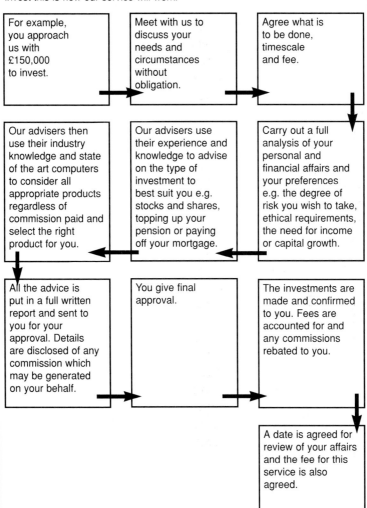

For example, you approach us with £150,000 to invest.

Meet with us to discuss your needs and circumstances without obligation.

Agree what is to be done, timescale and fee.

Our advisers then use their industry knowledge and state of the art computers to consider all appropriate products regardless of commission paid and select the right product for you.

Our advisers use their experience and knowledge to advise on the type of investment to best suit you e.g. stocks and shares, topping up your pension or paying off your mortgage.

Carry out a full analysis of your personal and financial affairs and your preferences e.g. the degree of risk you wish to take, ethical requirements, the need for income or capital growth.

All the advice is put in a full written report and sent to you for your approval. Details are disclosed of any commission which may be generated on your behalf.

You give final approval.

The investments are made and confirmed to you. Fees are accounted for and any commissions rebated to you.

A date is agreed for review of your affairs and the fee for this service is also agreed.

So if you are looking for advice, why not give us a call? We will happily discuss your requirements free of charge at a meeting or on the telephone.

If you would like to know more please phone Paul Willans on 0171 288 4700 or e-mail him at paulwillans@boltburdon.co.uk

1

Introduction

Money makes the world go around, or so the song says, and it is a valid point of view. But from another angle, the world makes money go around, and many of us, in different ways, are playing catch-as-catch-can trying to get a share of it. This book is, in very broad terms, about making the most of that share.

Given the chance, most people like to save money, whether it is for a short-term purpose, such as a holiday, a long-term purpose, such as retirement, or simply for unspecified 'emergencies'. Saving is effectively deferred consumption: you save today to spend tomorrow. This is true even if your savings pass on to a future generation and 'tomorrow' is 50 years hence; sooner or later, the savings will be spent.

While savings could be simply money stuffed under the mattress, investment implies some added value – either actual or potential. Generally, this would take the form of a monetary reward; *Chambers English Dictionary*, for example, defines investment as 'the placing of money to secure income or profit'.

But for some people, the actual rewards may be secondary in importance to the pleasure of going after them. Just as there is enjoyment to be had from horse-racing, so there is in, say, playing the stock market, and there are similar opportunities to study 'form' and look for attractive odds. Of course, it is always good to win, but there can be pleasure in taking part even if some ventures fail.

So before you can decide how to invest, you need first to be clear why you want to. It may be to fulfil a particular need at a specific time, for example to meet expected school fees; it may be a less definite saving for retirement or for the future in general; it may be that you have spare money you feel should be put to good use; or it may be simply for the fun of it.

Having settled the why, you should then have some idea of what you expect to achieve from the investment, which is a first step to deciding the how. Other factors to take into account are:

- the amount of money you have available;
- your attitude to risk;
- your tax position;
- the time you are prepared or able to devote to managing your investments.

As regards the size of investment, there are few limits in either direction. Much of the information in this book could be as well used by someone with just a few hundred pounds to invest as someone right at the other end of the scale, although the majority of readers will perhaps fall into the middle band, with somewhere between a few thousand and a six-figure sum.

Risk and protection

As to risk, again the book aims to cover a wide range. To start with, Chapters 2 and 3 look at various types of investment which provide capital security. Those who prefer rather more spice to life may want to skip these and move straight on to unit trusts or shares. Nevertheless, most people will find some use for this type of investment.

As well as short-term cash-flow management – putting aside money for bills and so on – vehicles such as bank and building society deposits can be useful over the longer term for 'emergency' cash. Most of us like to feel we have some money that is not only safe, but also readily accessible; fixed capital investments can provide this security while also offering some return.

The drawback is that security can become a habit. The amount of safe money that it is sensible to have will differ from person to person: single people with no dependants may need less than families, while those whose only recourse for loans is the bank manager may want to tuck aside rather more than those who have obliging relatives. Deciding when you have enough and can start to move up the risk scale can be like letting go of the side of the swimming pool.

The other important point to remember is that 'safe' investments that guarantee capital security are almost always open to a different kind of danger – inflation. An investment that is not growing in money terms will be shrinking in real terms, as measured by its purchasing power.

To get an idea by how much, you need only look at Table 1.1, which shows how much £1000 would come to be worth, valued in today's terms, given different rates of inflation. Even at the modest rate of 3 per cent, more than a quarter of the value would be eroded over ten years. At 8 per cent, more than half would be lost.

So far, the 1990s have seen reduced inflation and it is tempting to think that it has been controlled, if not wholly overcome. But the long-term record, as shown in Table 1.2, should act as a warning. After the extreme levels seen in the 1970s and at the beginning of the 1980s, inflation reached a low point in 1986 not far above the current level. Yet four years later it had climbed back up to 9.5 per cent, and there is no guarantee the

Table 1.1 *Inflation*

What £1000 would be worth in the future, in today's terms

Years	Annual rate of inflation		
ahead	*3%*	*5%*	*8%*
1	971	952	926
2	943	907	857
3	915	864	794
4	888	823	735
5	863	784	681
6	837	746	630
7	813	711	583
8	789	677	540
9	766	645	500
10	744	614	463
15	642	481	315
20	554	377	215
25	478	295	146

Table 1.2 *Average annual inflation rates*

Year	%
1980	15.1
1981	12.0
1982	5.4
1983	5.3
1984	4.6
1985	5.7
1986	3.6
1987	4.1
1988	4.9
1989	7.8
1990	9.5
1991	5.9
1992	3.7
1993	1.6
1994	2.5
1995	3.4
1996	2.4
1997	3.1

same thing could not happen again. As it is, the rate has crept up from the low of 1993 and both interest rates and inflation have risen in the first year of office of the current government.

It is possible to have an inflation-proofed investment, in the shape of index-linked National Savings Certificates (outlined in Chapter 2) or gilts (outlined in Chapter 4). These will guarantee to give you back your capital uprated by inflation, so in real terms you get back what you started with.

The downside is that this security comes at a price. The current 13th issue of index-linked National Savings Certificates pays tax-free interest equivalent to 2.25 per cent a year compound, for five years, on top of the index-linking. This may currently look better than some building society accounts that lack the inflation proof-ing, but if inflation rises, so will interest rates, so in neutralising the inflation risk you are paying an opportunity cost.

Once you venture beyond the realms of fixed capital invest-ments, you lay yourself open to investment risk. Broadly speaking, this operates on a tit for tat basis – the greater the potential for capital growth, the greater the potential for capital loss. In theory, the upside and downside should be roughly in balance, either in actual amount or when adjusted for likelihood. For example, if an investment is more likely to lose than gain, the possible gain needs to be larger than the possible loss to persuade people into it.

In practice, there are other factors to take into account, not least of which is the investment period. Take, for example, the UK stock market, as measured by the FTSE All-Share Index. Over the long term, the trend is broadly upwards; the 1987 crash, for instance, appears on a long-term graph as only a temporary blip. But for an investor who put money into the market in, say, July 1987 and took it out again at the end of October that year, the loss would have been considerable.

The lesson from this is that the odds improve if you are prepared to commit your money for some time and to be patient. If the market turns down, you may be tempted to cut and run, but if you hold on, the loss is only on paper and may eventually turn round to profit. Conversely, if you have only a short time horizon, the risk becomes much greater and you may be better advised to stick to fixed capital investments. The stock market is not the best home for money that may be needed at short notice.

Another means of controlling risk is to spread your investments around. One of the drawbacks of privatisation issues is that many people who buy them own no other shares. So if the company does badly, they stand to lose a disproportionate amount. At the worst, if you put all your money into a single company that then goes bust, you will lose everything. If, on the other hand, you hold a collection of several different shares, a loss on any one will only be a small part of your investment and may be counteracted by gains elsewhere.

This is the principle behind collective or 'pooled' investments such as unit trusts and investment trusts. Small investors, who lack the resources to achieve a wide spread of direct shareholdings, can instead buy a stake in a large portfolio. A trust will usually have at least 40 different holdings, so the chances of them all failing together are pretty small.

Again, of course, there is a price for safety. If you hold ten shares and one doubles in value, you may wish you had backed it to the hilt and not bothered with the other nine. But if one out of the ten halves in value, you will be grateful for the insurance of the other holdings.

Even with banks and building societies, you should not take safety for granted, bearing in mind the collapse some years ago of the Savings and Investment Bank in the Isle of Man and the more recent crash of the merchant bank Barings. In the UK, and nowadays in several other locations, there is a deposit protection scheme, which guarantees you will get back some, if not all, of your money. But if you are putting money offshore, you should check whether such a scheme applies; if not, only put in as much as you would be prepared to lose, or steer clear altogether.

Tax

Tax is the next factor to consider. A few investments, such as National Savings Certificates and personal equity plans, are tax free; some are subject to income tax, while others are liable to capital gains tax. Depending on your particular tax circumstances, this can influence the net returns you will make and therefore your choice. The main tax rates and allowances are summarised in Table 1.3.

Interest payments and dividends from shares are treated as income and taxed at your highest rate. Interest from bank and building society accounts is normally paid net of basic rate tax, although you can register for gross payments if you are a non-taxpayer, while higher rate taxpayers will have to pay the difference. Share dividends are also paid net and accompanied by a tax credit, with which non-taxpayers can reclaim what has been paid.

In its first Budget of July 1997, the Labour government announced an important change to the tax treatment of dividends from UK shares. From April 1999, the Advance Corporation Tax paid by companies on earnings is to be abolished and the rate of tax credit will be cut to one-tenth. The way tax is calculated will also change, so that the net effect for taxpaying investors will be just the same as at present. However, non-taxpayers will no longer be able to reclaim tax paid on dividends.

The one concession is that shares held in an Individual Savings Account, the new replacement for personal equity plans, will

Table 1.3 *Income and capital gains tax*

Rates of income tax 1998/99		
Taxable income £	*Rate* %	*Cumulative on top of band* £
0–4300	20	860
4301–27,100	23	6104
Over 27,100	40	–

Main tax allowances

Personal allowance	£4,195
Personal allowance (age 65–74)	£5,410
Personal allowance (age 75+)	£5,600
Married couple's allowance	£1,900*
Married couple's allowance (age 65–74)	£3,305*
Married couple's allowance (age 75+)	£3,345*
Single parent allowance	£1,900*
Widow's bereavement allowance	£1,900*
Blind person's allowance	£1,330
Age allowance income limit	£16,200

(Allowance is reduced by £1 for every £2 of additional income above the income limit.)

* Tax relief is restricted to 15 per cent and to 10 per cent from April 1999

Capital gains tax

Annual allowance for individuals	£6,800

(Excess, after taper allowance, is charged at the individual's highest rate of income tax.)

Annual allowance for trusts	£3,400
Chattel exemption	£6,000
Retirement relief (age 55+)	£250,000 plus 50% of gains between £250,000 and £1,000,000

Major exemptions
- Principal private residence
- National Savings Certificates
- Assets gifted to charity
- Life assurance policies, for the original owner
- Betting winnings, including the pools, national lottery and premium bonds

qualify for a 10 per cent tax credit for the first five years of the scheme (see Chapter 9).

The Government's second Budget, in March 1998, brought another substantial tax reform, this time to capital gains tax. This tax is charged, at the same rate as income tax, on the profit made when assets are sold. In the past, very few people have actually paid it because there have been two allowances – an annual exempt allowance and an indexation allowance, designed to cancel out gains that were due purely to inflation.

The annual exempt allowance remains and has been increased, in line with inflation, to £6800 for the 1998/99 tax year. But indexation has been replaced, as of April 1998, by a new system of taper relief. Once an asset has been held for three complete years or more, the proportion of the gain that will be taxable is progressively reduced, down to 60% after 10 years. The scale is shown in Table 1.4.

So, for example, if you sell an investment after five years, only 85 per cent of your gain is potentially taxable. If that amount falls within the annual exempt allowance, you will have no tax to pay; if it is more than the allowance (or you have already used your allowance for other gains), you will have to pay tax on the excess amount.

For assets bought before 5 April 1998, indexation will apply up to that date. That is, the purchase price will be scaled up in line with the Retail Prices Index up to 5 April and then frozen

Table 1.4 *Capital gains tax taper relief (non-business assets)*

Number of complete years of holding asset	Percentage of gain that is taxable
1–2	100
3	95
4	90
5	85
6	80
7	75
8	70
9	65
10	60

DON'T MISS THE BOAT

If you received a tax return this April, don't put it away and forget about it. If you get your tax return to us by 30 September, we'll work out your tax bill for you. Also, the sooner you respond the quicker you will find out if you are due any tax rebate. If you usually get a tax bill, getting your tax return in fast will give you the longest possible notice of next January's payment. And if you're an employee, it means any tax due under £1,000 can usually be collected through your PAYE coding. If you need help, contact your tax office during normal office hours or call the Self Assessment Helpline on 0645 000 444.*

*All calls are charged at local rates. Open evenings and weekends.

Inland
Revenue
Self Assessment - a clearer tax system

9

SELF ASSESSMENT

About nine million taxpayers are sent a Self Assessment tax return each year. You will usually only be asked to complete a tax return if you have additional tax to pay for any year, over and above any tax deducted at source (eg under PAYE or from investment income). You are likely to get a return if you are self employed, a business partner, a company director, or an employee (or a pensioner) with more complex tax affairs.

Your Self Assessment tax return will be sent to you in April 1998 and will cover the 1997-98 tax year which runs from 6 April 1997 - 5 April 1998. Wherever possible the return is tailored to meet your own particular needs. So if you completed a return last year, and your circumstances are unchanged, your return this year will contain just those pages that you need for returning all your income and claiming your reliefs and allowances.

So what is in the tax return pack?

The pack is made up of a basic eight page tax return form together with any supplementary pages the Inland Revenue think you need, a step by step guide on how to fill in each section and a guide on how to work out your tax bill if you want to. (Relax! Providing you send in your return early enough, calculating the tax bill is optional!). Check that you have the right supplementary pages. If not contact the Revenue's Orderline on 0645 000 404.

If you have a tax adviser who, last year, either used computer software to send in your completed return (using the Electronic Lodgement Service) or to print the return form sent in on your behalf, and this has been noted by the Revenue, you will not receive a tax return pack. Instead you will simply receive a notice requiring you to complete a tax return. If you are no longer represented by an agent using return computer software you should ask for a form to be sent to you. But otherwise simply contact your tax adviser so that they can make arrangements to complete your return as they did last year.

What should you do with the new form?

The most important thing to do is to open the pack! Don't put it away behind the clock and forget about it. If you have a tax adviser, show them the tax return straightaway. If you don't have an adviser the first thing you should do is to check that you've got all the pages you need by filling in page two of the return. If you need extra pages call the Orderline on 0645 000 404.

You then need to get all your tax records together, such as bank and building society statements, business earnings, expenses or accounts as appropriate. Having them to hand will save time when you come to filling in the return . In April you may not have all the records you need, but by making an early start you will know what you're waiting for and who you may have to contact for information.

If you have a tax adviser, make sure you send them all the information they will need to fill in your tax return once you have it.

If you are self employed, you should be able to work on your tax return right away.

If you are an employee you may need to wait for some information from your employer before you can fill in your return. Your employer should provide this information to you automatically each year, for example, your P60 which gives details of your pay and tax by 31 May. And if you get benefits from your employment - such as a company car or private medical insurance - you'll get details of the cash equivalents of these benefits by 6 July. These details will need to be entered on your tax return.

If you want the Inland Revenue to calculate your tax, they must receive your completed return by 30 September 1998. You may even be due a tax rebate - the sooner you send off your return, the quicker you will find out.

Whether or not you want to work out your own tax, if you are an employee and your completed return is received by 30 September, the Revenue will arrange to collect any tax you owe, up to £1000, through PAYE in the coming year. If you send back your return after 30 September, the Revenue will still try and collect any tax owed through PAYE but they cannot guarantee to do this.

If you want to calculate your tax, your tax return must be received by the Inland Revenue by 31 January 1999. But you do not have to wait until then - you can send back your return as soon as you like. *However, the 31 January date is critical.* You face a £100 penalty if your return is not received by 31 January and interest on any tax owed after that date. And if payment is not made by 28 February, you will face a five per cent surcharge on top of the tax and interest.

When do you need to pay your tax?

The operation of PAYE and the deduction at source arrangements on things like building society interest continue as before.

But if your Self Assessment shows that additional tax is due after taking into account tax already paid or deducted when you received the income, the additional tax must be paid as a balancing payment by 31 January 1999.

Some taxpayers, mainly the self employed and a few employees, will also have to make payments on account on 31 January and 31 July each year. In simple terms each of the payments on account is one half of the tax (and NIC) bill you paid for the previous year. And the balancing payment (or repayment) due the following 31 January is simply the increase (or decrease) in the tax bill for the current year when compared with the previous year.

What if you need help or advice?

If you need help in filling in your return the first place to look is at the guidance notes in the tax return pack.

If you need extra pages call the **Orderline on 0645 000 404**

If you have a query about Self Assessment or need additional guidance, you can call your tax office, the number is at the top of your tax return, or go to any tax office or tax enquiry centre. If you need help in the evenings or at weekends when the office is closed, you can call the **Helpline on 0645 000 444.**

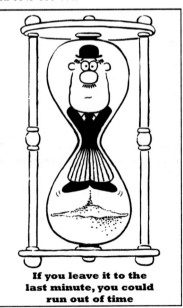

If you leave it to the last minute, you could run out of time

at that value for the purposes of calculating the profit when you sell. From then on, the new taper relief will apply and for this purpose all assets held at 5 April 1998 will be treated as having already been held for one complete year, regardless of when they were actually bought. Assets acquired after 5 April 1998 will qualify only for taper relief, with no indexation.

Whether taper relief is more or less generous than indexation depends partly on inflation – if inflation stays fairly low, most investors should continue to avoid capital gains tax thanks mainly to the annual exempt allowance. But clearly, the longer you hold an asset the more you will benefit from the taper relief and it is just that that the government is aiming to encourage.

The other change relating to capital gains tax was that the Chancellor effectively closed a loophole known as 'bed and breakfasting'. Under this, you would sell shares up to the point that you fully used your exempt allowance and then buy them back the following day. Your portfolio would thus be unchanged but you would have established a new purchase price for the shares you sold, thereby wiping out the gains made to date as far as tax was concerned.

The Chancellor has now introduced a '30-day rule' under which sales and purchases of the same asset within a 30-day period will be identified with each other. In effect, no gain will be realised and the purchase price (for calculating gains in the future) will not change. Some possible ways around the new rule have already been suggested. You could simply delay buying back the shares for more than 30 days, but the price could move against you in the meantime, possibly costing you more than the tax you save. A better possibility for couples is for, say, the husband to sell shares and the wife to buy them back, although this might be caught by future anti-avoidance rules. Thirdly, you could sell one share and buy another of a similar type.

Tax, of course, should not be the only criterion when choosing an investment, nor even necessarily the prime one. But as a broad rule, the higher rate taxpayer will do better from a growth investment, where he can use the capital gains exempt allowance, than from one that produces income on which he will immediately lose 40 per cent.

There are two other factors which may influence choice. First, since 1990, married couples have been taxed independently, whereas before that all investment income was imputed to the husband. They are still entitled to a married couple's allowance but since the start of the 1995/96 tax year this has qualified for tax relief of only 15 per cent.

Meanwhile, each of the couple has his or her own personal allowance, capital gains tax exempt allowance and tax rate. As a result, there may be benefits in transferring investments between you and your spouse – particularly as such transfers are exempt from inheritance tax. For example, income-producing investments could be put in the name of whichever partner has the lower tax rate, while those producing capital growth can be split so as to make the most of the annual CGT allowance. Bear in mind, though, that if you give assets away to your partner, you are not entitled to ask for them back if the marriage breaks down.

The other issue is age allowance. Individuals are entitled to a higher personal tax allowance when they pass the age of 65, with another increase when they reach 75, while a higher married couple's allowance is given where either partner reaches 65 or 75 during the tax year. The trap is that there is an annual income limit (based on the husband's income for the married couple's allowance). If income goes above this level, the allowance is reduced by £1 for every £2 of excess income – a heavy penalty. Hence those who are at or near the limit may do better from growth-oriented investments which they can cash in if they need extra income.

Finally, there is inheritance tax. This does not affect an investor directly, since it only comes into play on death, and gifts between husband and wife are exempt. Nevertheless, with the increase in home ownership, many people may find their total assets go beyond the nil rate band, and it may be worth taking note of the exemptions, particularly if your investment plans extend to your heirs. Details are given in Table 1.5.

Layout of the book

Investments can be categorised in a number of different ways: by product type, by what they achieve in terms of income or growth, or by risk factors. For the most part, this book goes by product type, although Chapters 2 and 3, as mentioned above, lump together investments that offer capital security. Chapter 2 covers high street institutions, such as banks, building societies and National Savings products which are largely available through post offices; Chapter 3 goes further afield into local authority bonds, insurance company guaranteed bonds and off-shore money funds.

Chapter 4 covers gilts, which come halfway between fixed capital and risk investments. If you hold on to a gilt to its maturity date, you will get a fixed return, but meanwhile gilts can be traded, for profit or loss.

Chapters 5 to 9 deal with equity-based investments: shares themselves, unit trusts, offshore funds, investment trusts and personal equity plans, which can be based on individual shares or trusts. While the chapter on equities is largely based on the UK market, a point to bear in mind is that the advantages of spreading your investments can apply equally well on a global scale as on a domestic one.

These days, the major world markets have a tendency to move roughly in line with each other, but there can still be short-term differences, as well as currency factors that will affect the returns. Smaller markets are a law unto themselves, usually displaying significant volatility.

'Smaller', however, is a relative term; the so-called emerging markets currently account for around 5 per cent of total world market capitalisation and the proportion is steadily increasing. While direct investment into these markets – and to some extent, any overseas markets – can be difficult, expensive and risky for the private investor, pooled funds such as unit and investment trusts offer a sensible and accessible route in. A glance at Table 1.6, which shows the capitalisation of the main markets, provides a clear picture of what you are ignoring if you focus on the UK alone.

Moving on, Chapters 10 and 11 cover investments with life assurance companies, which might more immediately be associated with regular savings. This is particularly true of pension plans, covered in Chapter 11; however, retirement planning can be so important, and so few people can expect the maximum

Table 1.5 *Inheritance tax rates*

Amount of transfer	Tax rate
Up to £223,000	Nil
Over £223,000	40%

Relief on transfers made within 7 years of death

Years between gift and death	*% of full tax charge*
0–3	100
3–4	80
4–5	60
5–6	40
6–7	20

Main exemptions
Transfers between husband and wife
Transfers of up to £3000 a year
Gifts to anyone of up to £250 a year
Gifts out of income forming 'normal expenditure'
Gifts on marriage – up to £5000 for parents, £2500 for grandparents, £1000 for anyone else

benefits allowed, that topping-up provision should feature high on the list of priorities for investing windfall cash.

Chapter 12 rounds up so-called alternative investments, including tangibles such as precious metals and diamonds.

The final criterion for choosing investments that was mentioned at the outset of this chapter is the time you have to devote to your portfolio. While some investments take a while to come good, few selections will be right for all time, particularly as your own circumstances and needs will change over time. Constant chopping and changing will generally lose more in costs than it gains; nevertheless, reviews are an important part of the process.

It is not only your own circumstances that will change; the market is also in constant flux. In the past half-dozen years, there have been two major upheavals: Big Bang, which reorganised the operations of the Stock Exchange, and the Financial Services Act, which set up a new system of regulation for the industry.

Neither of these has proved conclusive, in that adjustments are still going on. In March 1993, the Stock Exchange abandoned the development of Taurus, a proposed electronic dealing system, and has now introduced a different and rather less ambitious system called Crest.

The Financial Services Act has undergone a series of alterations since it was introduced. The Act set up a system of self-regulation under the auspices of the Securities and Investments Board (SIB), which in turn delegated authority to self-regulatory organisations. Before 1994, there were four of these: the Financial Intermediaries, Managers and Brokers Regulatory Association (Fimbra), which looked after independent financial advisers; the Life Assurance and Unit Trust Regulatory Organisation (Lautro), which covered insurance companies and unit trust groups; the Investment Management Regulatory Organisation (Imro), which covered fund management groups (including some unit trust groups); and the Securities and Futures Association (SFA), which covered stockbrokers and the like. In addition, the SIB itself regulated a small number of companies.

In July 1994, a new body, the Personal Investment Authority (PIA), came into operation. This is responsible for all retail investment services, encompassing the operations of former Fimbra and Lautro members, plus Imro firms which primarily deal with private, rather than institutional, investors. Since late 1997, the SIB has been replaced by a new 'super-regulator', the Financial Services Authority (FSA). This will eventually take over the responsibilities of the other bodies and it is also intended that there will be a single body to handle complaints. But this is not expected to be finalised for a while and the idea is not universally popular.

While all these initials may be bemusing, they are not without relevance to private investors in general, and the time factor in particular. The less time you are able to devote to looking after your investments, the more you may need to rely on the services of an adviser, and the Financial Services Act aims to ensure that the advice you will receive is honest and competent. It also provides for redress in the case of malpractice.

Details of how the Act and its various creations operate are given in Chapter 13. This also discusses the various types of advice available and how to choose between different services. For example, one of the main planks of the Act is that advisers are 'polarised' into two categories: completely independent, which means offering advice across the full range of the markets in which they operate, or tied to a single company and able to offer only the products it supplies.

At the outset, one of the cardinal rules for independents was that they should offer 'best advice' – the best possible product, in terms of type and supplier, to fit their customers' needs. This has now been adjusted to read 'good advice', in recognition of the fact that no one can be expected to pick in advance the product which will turn in the best performance in some years' time.

While you may be happy to trust your adviser's judgement, you are likely to get more out of the relationship if you understand the basics of the selection process. This book is designed to help in that, and at the end of each chapter there are suggested sources of further information.

One final word of warning. The book only deals with lump-sum investments, hence it does not cover regular savings by way of monthly or annual premiums on life assurance policies or pension plans, or outgoings such as a mortgage. In practice, these may all impinge on your overall financial picture and any part should not be viewed in isolation from the rest.

Having said that, lump-sum investments may arise out of windfall gains such as inheritance and therefore be additional to existing regular, and planned, savings. If you are happy that your basic needs are already catered for, you may be prepared to take a different tack with the lump sum, perhaps involving more risk.

Because the choices are so wide, it is impossible to categorise potential gains. But to whet your appetite, Table 1.7 gives a few key statistics. While there is no guarantee that taking risks will always provide rewards, it does suggest that, over the long term, a little care and imagination can prove fruitful.

Table 1.6   *World stock markets*

Exchange	Capitalisation (US$bn)	% of World Index
Australia	193.4	1.24
Canada	374.4	2.40
France	513.9	3.30
Germany	607.4	3.90
Hong Kong	235.7	1.51
Italy	253.0	1.62
Japan	1812.1	11.63
Malaysia	43.2	0.28
Netherlands	364.2	2.34
South Africa	95.4	0.61
Spain	179.3	1.15
Sweden	208.0	1.33
Switzerland	481.6	3.09
UK	1662.0	10.66
USA	8003.0	51.35

Note: Figures are as at 31 December 1997.

Source: The Financial Times

Table 1.7   *Past performance comparisons*

Value of £100 invested over periods to 30 April 1998

	3 years	5 years	10 years
Building society (30-day account)	108.69	115.85	166.75
Average investment trust (mid to mid)	161.30	216.82	378.80
Average unit trust (offer to offer)	155.29	187.56	330.36
Retail Prices Index	109.02	115.43	154.47
FTSE All-Share Index	194.30	235.47	421.56
MSCI World Index	153.02	178.66	259.13

Source: Reuters Hindsight

2

Fixed Capital Investments (1)

As a starting-point, this chapter will look at the more familiar varieties of investment available through high street outlets. In particular, it will deal with fixed capital products: those which guarantee that the capital you get out will be the same as the capital you put in.

This can be reassuring, but the drawback is that old hidden enemy, inflation, which will progressively erode the value. The rate of inflation is one factor which influences the general level of interest rates; they are rarely substantially above inflation for very long, which means that the real rate of return on the investments discussed here is usually pretty small. Indeed, it can even be negative: in October 1990, for example, the gross return on an instant access deposit of £5000 hit a high of 14 per cent, but inflation was then running at 10.9 per cent – above the net return to a basic rate taxpayer. So these investments are suitable chiefly for short periods, 'emergency' money or the extremely cautious.

Fixed versus variable interest

Most of the investments covered in this chapter pay variable interest, which will move up and down in line with general market rates. But there are a few, including some National Savings products and fixed-term deposits, which pay fixed interest over a predetermined period of time.

Fixed interest rates, like fixed mortgage rates, are something of a gamble: if general rates subsequently go up, you lose; if they go down, you win. As a gambler, you are probably betting on fairly long odds, since the rate offered will ultimately depend on the view of the money market, which has no crystal ball but is generally in a better position to make predictions than the average investor. On the whole, it is better to be guided by your needs and decide whether or not the certainty of a fixed income would outweigh any possible loss.

Variable rates tend to reflect the general economic environment, but different institutions react at varying speeds to underlying changes. It may seem that mortgage rates move up faster than down, while investment rates are sticky in the other direction; in practice the institutions are simply balancing their borrowing and lending against the demand and supply in the market. Broadly, when they are looking to attract investors they will be quicker to raise their interest rates; when they are seeking to increase their lending they will try to hold rates down.

Neither pattern is likely to be consistent for all time, so this should not be a prime factor in deciding where to invest. Of course, it is possible to gain by monitoring all the rates available and switching your investments around accordingly, but this is more valuable if you are locking into a fixed rate; with variable rates, the benefit is likely to be small and short-lived compared with the time and energy you would spend on the research.

The tax position

Until April 1991, bank and building society accounts paid interest net of composite rate tax. This was calculated by the Inland Revenue on the basis of the proportion of savers who were non-taxpayers and therefore worked out at slightly less than basic rate income tax, but the major drawback was that it could not be reclaimed by those not liable for tax.

Nowadays, non-taxpayers can register to have interest paid gross by completing the Inland Revenue Form R85, available at banks and building societies. Otherwise, interest will normally be paid net of lower rate tax, which can be reclaimed by those who are not liable to some or all of it. Lower and basic rate taxpayers will have no further liability, while higher rate taxpayers will have to pay the difference.

National Savings Certificates and tax exempt special savings accounts (TESSAs) are free of both income and capital gains tax (CGT), while the return on gilts is liable only to income tax and will be paid gross if they are held through the National Savings Stock Register (see Chapter 4). A handful of other products pay interest gross, although it will still be liable for tax. These include National Savings accounts, offshore bank and building society accounts (see Chapter 3) and fixed-term bank and building society deposits amounting to £50,000 or more.

Accounts that pay gross have the advantage that you can enjoy the money for a while before the tax falls due, but there is also a potential drawback. In the first year, and the second if you so elect, the tax charged is based on the actual interest received, but thereafter it moves to a 'preceding year' basis. So, for example, in the tax year 1998/99 your tax charge for the account will be based on the interest you actually received in 1997/98. When interest rates are rising, this means you will effectively pay too little tax, but conversely when they are falling you will be overcharged. In this case there is no right of appeal, because the procedure counts as an actual tax charge, rather than a provisional assessment. The only way around it, if interest rates are dropping and you are therefore losing out, is to close the account, as the tax will be calculated on the interest actually paid in the final year. However, the Inland Revenue is then entitled to reassess the previous year's charge and adjust that to the true amount if it is in its own favour to do so (note that it will not offer a rebate if you paid too much!).

In the long run, the overpayments and underpayments should tend to even out. However, when you decide to close the account, you should try to do so in a year when rates have been falling so that any final swing will be in your favour. If you subsequently open another account, this will not affect the tax assessment of the first.

Banks

Current accounts

Time was when a current account was simply a convenient alternative to keeping your money under the mattress. You earned no interest on it, but neither did it cost you anything to run, as long as you kept the account in credit. The high street banks, at least, offered services that were more or less identical to each other, so most people picked the one that was nearest to their home or workplace, or possibly the one their parents used, and then stuck with it for life. This had the advantage, in theory at least, that if you established a track record with your bank you were likely to be looked on more favourably if you needed a loan.

Nowadays, competitive pressures have swept all that aside. There are a host of different accounts offering a variety of facilities and there is more point in shopping around to find one that suits your needs. For instance, there are some that offer, within limits, an interest-free overdraft, particularly on student accounts – students being potentially lucrative customers in the future. Others are linked to a savings account, with an automatic sweep between the two, or provide telephone banking through which you can juggle your money between accounts.

Also, since building societies began to provide cash card and cheque-book facilities, banks have introduced interest payments on current accounts. On the basic accounts, however, the rates are very low, so they should be considered as purely for cash-flow purposes, not as investments.

New players

The changing face of banking has not only pushed the traditional banks into offering new services, but has also prompted a host of new players. Chief among these are the supermarkets: Sainsbury's, Tesco and Safeway have all started offering banking facilities, in conjunction with Bank of Scotland, Royal Bank of Scotland and Abbey National respectively.

Insurance companies have also noted the opportunities – in particular, the potential to retain at least some of a customer's money when a policy matures, instead of seeing it lost to the high street. Standard Life, Prudential, Scottish Widows, Legal & General and Direct Line are all offering savings accounts.

So far, these ventures seem to be proving highly attractive to savers, although Tesco was a victim of its own success at the outset, with the sheer weight of applicants causing administration problems that delayed the opening of accounts. The appeal is in the rates of interest paid, particularly for smaller amounts: at the time of writing, Sainsbury's is offering 6.5 per cent and Standard Bank 6.96 per cent for sums from just £1 upwards, with instant access.

Another innovation is the 'one-stop' bank account, Virgin One, from Virgin Direct. This combines a current account, a credit card facility and a mortgage, all in one. All borrowings are lumped together, secured on the account-holder's home and charged at a single rate. When salary is paid in each month, it immediately reduces the debt, although this will obviously increase again as money is spent during the month. Lump sums can also be paid in at any time to reduce the amount owed. While the account has its attractions, some people may find it harder to keep track of their savings and borrowings when they are all mixed together. Also, while the interest rate is cheap for personal loans and credit, it is relatively expensive for a mortgage, by far the largest part of most people's borrowings. Finally, the account is restricted to minimum mortgage and salary levels.

Higher interest accounts
Just as current accounts have burgeoned, so have deposit-style accounts. These offer better rates of interest but do not normally provide cheque-book or money transmission facilities, though they may have a link to a current account and some offer a cash card.

For instant access accounts there is usually no minimum deposit. Notice accounts, where withdrawals require between one and three months' notice, may require a minimum of £1000 or £2500. Generally, these will allow immediate access with loss of interest equivalent to the notice period, but the penalty may be waived if there is a balance remaining in the account of £5000 or £10,000.

Interest rates generally rise with the amount deposited and the length of notice although there can be anomalies, as the examples in Table 2.1 show.

Money market and high interest cheque accounts
These were once the preserve of merchant banks and licensed

Table 2.1   *Bank account rates*

Amount deposited (£)	Instant access (%)	30 days' notice (%)	90 days' notice (%)
500–999	5.57	5.40	–
1000–2499	5.57	5.40	4.80
2500–4999	5.57	5.40	6.00
5000–9999	5.68	5.80	6.00
10,000–24,999	5.81	5.80	6.20
25,000–49,999	5.81	6.00	6.20
50,000+	5.84	6.20	6.20

Note: Rates net of basic rate tax, applicable as at May 1998. Bank base rate: 7.25 per cent

Source: MoneyFacts, May 1998

deposit-takers, and there are still some that are essentially deposit accounts for large sums of money, with no money transmission facilities. However, most of the major banks now offer some form of high interest cheque account. The services provided are usually more limited than the standard current account; there may be a minimum withdrawal or cheque amount of anything up to £250, or only a limited number of withdrawals free of charge, so for daily purposes you would probably need an ordinary account as well.

But, as in other spheres, competition is leading to improved options and there are a growing number of accounts which have no minimum withdrawal and offer a full range of facilities such as overdrafts, cash card, cheque card, standing orders and direct debits, with free banking as long as you remain in credit. On top of this, the interest rates can be substantially more than the token offerings on basic current accounts.

The one drawback is that they do require a relatively high initial deposit, generally of £1000. There are one or two which offer respectable rates of interest on sums from £1 upwards, but these do not provide the full range of services.

Term deposits

Fixed-term deposits pay a fixed rate of interest for a specified period of time, which may be anything from one month to five years. Some of the smaller banks offer these for as little as £500 but the minimum is usually £2500 or £5000. As a rule, no withdrawals are allowed during the term and the interest rate is fixed at the outset, but rates can vary on a daily basis, so check before you invest.

Very large sums of money, upwards of £50,000, can be placed in money market time deposits through banks. While these may be for a period of some months, it is also possible to place money on overnight deposit with automatic renewal on a daily basis, so that you can leave the money for as long as you like while having instant access to it. Interest rates are set daily or sometimes more frequently and, provided the deposit is at least £50,000, interest can be paid gross.

Building societies

Like the banks, building societies have vastly expanded their range of products in recent years. In terms of the banks versus building societies 'savings war' the societies have largely been the aggressors, moving in on the banks' traditional territory of cheque accounts. They were also granted wider powers by the government, allowing them, for example, to own a domestic bank and to raise more money from wholesale markets. But at the same time, they have faced considerable competitive pressure from each other, with the result that there has been a number of mergers, not only among smaller societies but also between the large ones, a prime example being the recent Halifax-Leeds tie-up. Some societies, such as Abbey National and Halifax, have changed status to become banks.

Banking accounts

Banking accounts come in two types: those which are more or less deposit-style accounts but provide cash card facilities; and those which offer a cheque book and other banking facilities such as standing orders, direct debits and even overdrafts, though this last is rather less common. The services are generally free as long as the account is in credit, but there may be a minimum opening balance – normally not more than £200.

Interest is paid on these accounts and, while it can be rather more generous than bank current accounts, the same caveat applies, that rates are too low for these accounts to be considered as investments proper. For larger deposits, however, the rates offered are comparable to banks' high interest cheque accounts, or similar facilities may be offered through a separate account. The minimum deposit in this case is generally upwards of £2500. Some societies offer postal accounts, which may still provide instant access but carry higher interest rates than the basic cheque account.

Instant access and notice accounts

Despite the vast array of different accounts that come under this heading, there are just three main points to consider in making a choice: the minimum investment, the period of notice required for withdrawals and the interest offered. Table 2.2 shows examples of the better offerings around at the time of writing. As can be seen, the general rule is that interest rates increase with the amount deposited and the length of notice period, though there can occasionally be anomalies where one society's instant access account offers more than another's notice account.

Table 2.2   *Building society variable interest account rates*

Amount deposited (£)	Instant access (%)	30 days' notice (%)	90 days' notice (%)
500–999	4.00	–	5.76
1000–2499	4.00	5.56	5.92
2500–4999	4.40	5.56	6.00
5000–9999	6.04	5.56	6.08
10,000–24,999	6.12	6.24	6.16
25,000–49,999	6.20	6.24	6.24
50,000+	6.28	6.24	6.32

Note: Rates net of basic rate tax, applicable as at May 1998.

Source: MoneyFacts, May 1998

Notice accounts usually allow withdrawals within the notice period subject to an equivalent loss of interest, but the penalty may be waived if, say, £5000 or £10,000 remains in the account. There are also some which offer a bonus if no withdrawals are made during the year. This can be attractive if you do not expect to need access to your money but are not quite prepared to tie it up in a longer term bond.

Deposit accounts are not shown in the table as they are scarcely heard of these days. Although some instant access accounts require a minimum of £500, a number are available for smaller sums, right down to £1, so they have largely superseded the older deposit and paid-up share accounts.

When comparing interest rates you should always go by the Compound Annual Rate (CAR) figure. This takes into account how often interest is credited, whether monthly, half-yearly or annually. If interest is credited more than once a year, the interest paid will itself start to earn interest, so the total return over a year will be that little bit higher.

One other point to watch for is when an account is closed to new business in favour of a new version. Often the old account will carry a lower rate of interest than the new one, although the terms and conditions may be identical. Not all societies inform their investors in this case – the argument being that the postage would prove prohibitive – so you need to keep an eye on developments and be prepared to switch if necessary. Local society branches will have up-to-date information on closed and new accounts.

Fixed-term accounts
Fixed-term accounts fall into two types: those which offer a fixed rate of interest during the term and those on which the interest is variable but guaranteed to be a fixed percentage above the ordinary share account rate. The minimum investment is generally £1000 and terms may run from six months to five years. Withdrawals during the term may be disallowed altogether, or may be subject to a penalty (commonly of 90 days' interest). Examples of fixed rates are shown in Table 2.3.

Like banks, the larger building societies offer money market

Table 2.3 *Building society fixed-term account rates*

Term	Minimum investment (£)	Net rate (%)
6 months	5000	6.04
1 year	5000	6.04
2 years	5000	5.68
3 years	5000	5.48
5 years	5000	5.32

Note: Rates net of basic rate tax, applicable as at May 1998.

Source: MoneyFacts, May 1998

time deposits for sums from £50,000 upwards. Rates change frequently but, once you invest, are fixed for the full term.

Tax exempt special savings accounts

Tax exempt special savings accounts (TESSAs) first appeared in January 1991, having been announced in the previous year's Budget. In a way, they are like a little sister to personal equity plans (PEPs, detailed in Chapter 9); PEPs offer tax-free returns from equity-linked investments, while TESSAs offer tax-free returns from bank and building society deposit accounts.

TESSAs are available to any UK resident over the age of 18 and run for a period of five years. The maximum investment that can be made is £3000 in the first year and up to £1800 in each subsequent year, subject to an overall maximum of £9000. You may have only one TESSA, which must be held individually (ie not in joint names), but if you become dissatisfied with your current provider, you may transfer the account to another, although not all institutions are prepared to accept transfers.

Provided the capital is left intact for the full five years, all the interest earned is tax free. You may make withdrawals equivalent to the interest earned net of basic rate tax, but any larger amount will invalidate the TESSA which will then revert to being an ordinary taxable deposit. However, if you die within the five years, the TESSA will be treated as maturing at that point. All interest earned to date will be free of tax, but from then on it will become taxable as usual.

The first TESSAs matured in January 1996 but the 1994 Budget introduced a follow-on opportunity. Once you have held a TESSA for five years you may use the capital, but not the accumulated interest, to open a 'TESSA 2'. So, if you invested the maximum in your first plan, you can transfer the full £9000 into a new one on which all interest will again be tax free, provided that the capital is left untouched for five years.

You must open the new TESSA within six months of your old plan maturing, but you do not have to put the full £9000 in at once: you can add in the balance up to 12 months later. If you have less than £9000 from your first TESSA, you may invest extra money in the second and subsequent years of the new plan, up to a maximum of £1800 a year and £9000 overall. Finally, you may choose a different bank or building society for your new TESSA, as long as you obtain a certificate from your current provider to show that you are entitled to open the Mark 2 version.

After April 1999, however, it will not be possible to open a new TESSA, as they are being phased out in favour of the new Individual Savings Account (ISA). Existing TESSAs can be continued for the full five-year period, subject to the current investment limits, and when they mature the full capital amount, though not the interest earned, can be transferred into an ISA. The transfer, and ongoing contributions while the TESSA is still running, will not count towards the ISA contribution limits.

While ISAs will be tax-free, the proposed rules allow only £1000 a year to put into a cash element, except for the first year when up to £3000 is allowed. So if you have a maturing TESSA and you like the concept, you should think of opening another while you still can. It does, however, depend very much on your personal circumstances. Some of the returns from the first TESSAs have been rather disappointing; accounts paying a variable rate have been hit by the plunge in interest rates over the past five years. Conversely, fixed-rate plans have turned out unexpectedly well. Over the next five years, however, the opposite could prove true, as interest rates may well rise from their current very low level.

If you are going to hold money in a deposit account anyway,

you may as well hold it in a TESSA, particularly if you pay higher rate tax. Even if you suddenly need access to the money, and therefore lose the tax advantage, you will be no worse off than if you had put it in an ordinary account in the first place.

You may, however, find that the rate of interest does not turn out to be so good. This is because a number of TESSA providers offer a special bonus at the end of the five-year term, at the expense of a lower rate meanwhile. Transferring the account to a new provider may also trigger a penalty, sometimes in addition to a stipulated period of notice, so to get the full benefit, as well as the tax exemption, you have to be prepared to stay the course.

Because of these bonuses, and the various terms attached, it is difficult to compare different TESSAs to determine the best buy. Also, where interest rates are variable, there is no guarantee that today's best offer will still be among the leaders in a year's time. Since you are effectively locked in once you start a plan, providers may be rather more interested in attracting new business than looking after their existing customers; it has been known, for example, for a provider to close an account to new business and then drop the rate paid on it, while offering a more attractive rate on a new product. Although you can transfer in that instance, the penalty charged may mean you lose out anyway.

The choice may be influenced by how much you want to invest. TESSAs may be opened with as little as £1 or £10 a month for those that offer a regular savings option. Some of the best rates, though, apply only if you make the maximum £9000 investment over the term and a number require you to set up a separate 'feeder' account which itself carries a minimum balance, and from which withdrawals are made to fund the TESSA.

You should also bear in mind that, if you are willing to tie your money up for five years, many advisers would consider the stock market was a more natural choice than a deposit account. A couple of TESSA providers have addressed this by creating plans that are linked to stock market performance. These offer a low guaranteed return, of 4 or 5 per cent a year, but with the possibility of a great deal more, depending on how the stock market moves.

The terms of these accounts will vary over time, so check carefully if you are planning to invest. They also carry stiff penalties for withdrawing your money early, so you must be prepared for a full five-year commitment.

National Savings

National Savings products can be divided into three categories: those that pay a return completely free of tax, those that are taxable but pay interest gross, and a couple of one-offs, the First Option Bond and Premium Bonds, which do neither of these things.

Tax-free investments

National Savings Fixed Interest Certificates

National Savings Fixed Interest Certificates can currently be bought for a minimum of £100, with units of £25 thereafter. Recent issues have followed the same pattern: they run for five years with a fixed rate of return in each year. The return increases over the five years, so although you can cash units in at any time, you lose out by doing so. Table 2.4 shows the interest build-up on the current 46th issue.

As Table 2.5 shows, issues are available for varying lengths of time and give different rates of return, depending on the market rates at the time and how anxious the government is to get a slice of the savings market. In 1993, it took a more aggressive stance by doubling the maximum holding in current issue certificates to £10,000 and also doubling the reinvestment limit to £20,000.

Reinvestment is an option at the end of the fixed period, when certificates mature. Instead of taking out your money, you can either continue to hold the certificates or reinvest in the latest issue, for which there is a £20,000 maximum holding on top of the £10,000 for new investment.

Once an issue has reached the end of its fixed period, the interest rate moves to the general extension rate, which is variable and currently 3.51 per cent for the 7th to 40th issues. The 1st to 6th issues come under different rules and are subject to a

Table 2.4 *National Savings Certificates 46th issue*

Years after purchase	Value at end of year (£)	% yield for year	Compound yield % pa
1	103.60	3.60	3.60
2	107.54	3.80	3.70
3	112.27	4.40	3.94
4	118.11	5.20	4.25
5	126.42	7.04	4.80

Note: Value for a £100 certificate; tax-free return.

lower rate of interest. So you will do better to cash in any of these and reinvest in the current issue, rather than retaining them. More recent issues that are still within their fixed period are worth holding on to up to maturity because the guaranteed return is higher than anything you could currently get from a comparable investment.

Table 2.5 *National Savings Certificates, past issues*

Issue number	Dates of issue	Value of £100 certificate after 5 years (£)	Compound annual return over 5 years (%)
33rd	1.5.87–21.7.88	140.26	7.0
34th	22.7.88–16.6.90	143.56	7.5
35th	18.6.90–14.3.91	157.42	9.5
36th	2.4.91–2.5.92	150.37	8.5
37th	13.5.92–5.8.92	146.94	8.0
38th	6.8.92–4.10.92	143.57	7.5
39th	5.10.92–12.11.92	138.63	6.75
40th	13.11.92–16.12.93	132.25	5.75
41st	17.12.93–19.9.94	130.08	5.4
42nd	20.9.94–25.1.96	132.88	5.85
43rd	26.1.96–31.3.97	129.77	5.35
44th	1.4.97–9.1.98	129.77	5.35
45th	9.1.98–26.3.98	127.63	5.0

Index-linked certificates

Like the ordinary savings certificates, the current 13th issue of index-linked certificates has a minimum investment of £100 and a maximum of £10,000, with a further £20,000 allowed for reinvestment from mature certificates. The difference is that here the return is linked to movements in the Retail Price Index over the five-year period. In addition, extra interest is added at a guaranteed rate, which increases for each of the five years. Currently the compound return above inflation is equal to 2.25 per cent a year and is free of tax. All the interest earned is added to the capital value – so that after year 1 you are earning interest on the interest – and repaid in total when you cash in.

As mentioned at the start of this chapter, inflation can be a serious threat to fixed capital investments and the real returns above inflation offered by interest rates can be very small. So in principle, index-linking should be very attractive. In practice, though, it is like any fixed rate: in return for protection against doing worse, you may give up the chance to do better. For example, if inflation remains at the current rate of around 3.5 per cent, the total return on index-linked certificates, including the extra interest, would be 5.75 per cent, above that offered on fixed interest certificates. But if inflation falls again, the cost of the protection may prove too high.

Taxable investments

Income bonds

Income bonds are available from a minimum of £2000 up to a maximum of £250,000 and offer a monthly income, paid on the 5th of each month. The interest rate is variable, but six weeks' notice is given of any change, which will be advertised in newspapers. The current rates are 7 per cent gross for sums up to £25,000 and 7.25 per cent gross for larger amounts, which compares reasonably well with banks and building societies. Income is paid (gross, but liable to tax) direct to a bank, building society or National Savings investment account.

Capital bonds

Capital bonds run for five years and offer a guaranteed rate of return if they are held for the full term. For the current Series L bonds this is 6 per cent gross. You can cash in a bond early, but this would mean you lose out, as the interest rate increases each year, and the amount you get on cashing in is the value at the last anniversary plus a special interest rate since then. No interest is paid on bonds encashed before the first anniversary.

The minimum holding is £100, with a maximum of £250,000. This maximum applies to total holdings of all capital bonds, with the exception of Series A. At the end of the five years bonds are repaid in full, together with all the interest accumulated; no further interest is earned after the fifth anniversary.

National Savings Bank ordinary account

With a basic interest rate of 2 per cent gross, the ordinary account is slightly more lucrative than a bank current account, although the facilities are more limited. Withdrawals are generally restricted to £100 on demand, with written notice required for larger sums, although if you have used the account for at least six months at one particular post office you can apply for a regular customer account, which entitles you to take out up to £250 on demand.

If you keep an account open for a full calendar year, you are then eligible for a higher interest rate for each month that the balance is £500 or more. Even so, this higher rate is only 3 per cent gross. The one feature that does add some attraction for higher rate taxpayers is that the first £70 of interest, or £140 for a joint holding, is free of tax. Otherwise, this is more a home for ready cash than an investment.

National Savings Bank investment account

For smaller sums in particular, this can be an attractive alternative to bank and building society deposits, as the minimum is just £20. There are seven tiers of interest rates which currently start at 4.75 per cent for sums under £500, rising to 6.5 per cent for sums from £50,000 to £100,000, the maximum holding. These are the gross rates; interest is credited gross, so you can enjoy the money for a short while before settling the tax bill. Withdrawals are at one month's notice.

Pensioners Bond

The Pensioners Bond was announced in the 1993 Autumn Budget

and introduced in January 1994. It is available only for people aged 60 or over, although it can be bought by trustees, as long as the beneficiary is over 60. The minimum investment is £500 and the maximum is £50,000 per series, or £100,000 for a joint holding, for which both savers must meet the age requirement.

The interest rate is fixed for the first five years that you hold a bond and for the current 5th series is 6.1 per cent gross. The interest is taxable but paid gross and will be credited on the 19th of each month direct to a bank or building society account or a National Savings investment account.

At the end of five years, National Savings will write to tell you the guaranteed interest rate for the next five years. The money can then be reinvested or withdrawn without penalty. If you want to cash in at any other time, you must give 60 days' notice and no interest will be paid during those 60 days. Partial withdrawals can be made from a minimum of £500 as long as at least £500 remains in your holding.

At the time of writing, the Pensioners Bond has proved popular and the return is reasonably attractive compared with building society accounts. The drawback is that interest rates are now on the increase and if this continues over the next five years it will leave the bond looking uncompetitive. Although you can cash in early, the penalty is quite severe – the loss of interest would amount to about £100 on a £10,000 holding. For some people, the benefits of having a regular fixed income will outweigh the possible loss if interest rates rise. Otherwise, you might do better with the Income Bond, which is currently paying slightly lower interest, but could pay more if rates rise and can be cashed in at three months' notice without any interest penalty.

First Option Bond

The First Option Bond was initially launched in July 1992 and caused something of a furore. The building societies saw it as a serious threat to their own ability to attract savings and Cheltenham & Gloucester took the bold step of raising its mortgage rate – on the grounds that it would have to raise its savings rate to compete with the bond and needed to maintain its margins. The last thing the government wanted, at a time when it was trying to bring down inflation, was to see mortgage costs rise, so it backed off and reduced the interest on the bond.

But governments do not remain intimidated for long and the bond was relaunched in the 1993 Budget. The minimum investment is £1000 and interest is fixed for 12 months at a time. At each anniversary, investors are notified of the new rate for the next year and have the option of continuing the bond or cashing it in. Between anniversaries, the return will be the full value at the last anniversary plus interest at half the fixed rate for the period since then, except that no interest is paid for encashments during the first year. Bonds can also be partially cashed in as long as the value remains above £1000.

Unusually for a National Savings product, interest is credited net of basic rate tax. Higher rate taxpayers will be liable for the difference, while non-taxpayers can apply for a refund. Interest is not paid out automatically, but you can apply for a part repayment equivalent to the amount earned. This should be timed for the anniversary date if possible.

At the time of writing the interest rate is 5.2 per cent net of basic rate tax, which compares reasonably well with building society accounts. There is also a bonus of 0.2 per cent where the value remains at least £20,000 during the year.

Premium Bonds

Premium Bonds are not exactly an investment, as there is no promise of a return – but then again, that could be said to apply to equities and at least with Premium Bonds your capital is always safe. The odds on winning a prize also improve with the size of your holding: at the maximum of £20,000, you should on average win 13 prizes a year, while to win once a year on average you need to hold £1450-worth. Of course, averages do not always work out; although ERNIE is quite impartial, some people seem to be luckier than others.

The minimum investment is £100, with multiples of £10 thereafter. Since 1 May 1996 the monthly prize fund has been calculated as equivalent to one month's interest on each eligible bond at an interest rate of 5 per cent a year. Bonds have to be held for one complete calendar month before they are entered for the draw. There are around 370,000 prizes awarded each month, with 10 per cent of the fund allocated to prizes between £5000 and the £1 million jackpot, 15 per cent to prizes of £500 and £1000 and the remaining 75 per cent providing prizes of £50 and £100. All prizes are free of tax.

For a complete guide to all the National Savings products, mentioned, see Table 2.6.

Where to find out more

Banks and building societies
Information on the types of account offered and current interest rates can be found in local branches. The Building Societies Association (0171 437 0655) can also answer general questions, but will not advise on current rates offered by individual societies. *Money Facts*, a monthly subscription magazine aimed chiefly at professional advisers, gives comprehensive listings of bank and building society accounts, TESSAs, offshore accounts and National Savings products. It is available from Moneyfacts Publications, Moneyfacts House, 66-70 Thorpe Road, Norwich NR1 1BA, telephone 01603 476100.

Money market accounts
Information can be found in newspapers.

National Savings
Booklets on the various products are available at post offices. General information can be obtained by phoning the information helpline on 0645 654000 during normal office hours.

The latest interest rates are also quoted by recorded message on the following numbers:

London: 0171 605 9483/9484
Blackpool: 01253 723714
Glasgow: 0141 632 2766

Table 2.6 *National Savings guide*

Product	Minimum and maximum holdings	Who may buy or invest	Income fixed or variable
National Savings Certificates 46th issue	Minimum £100, maximum £10,000 in addition to previous issues; may reinvest a further £20,000 from mature Savings Certificates	Individuals (also jointly), trustees	Increasing at fixed rate for initial term; variable extension rate thereafter
National Savings Certificates 13th index-linked issue	Minimum £100, maximum £10,000 in addition to previous issues; may reinvest a further £20,000 from mature Savings Certificates	Individuals (also jointly), trustees	Repayment value linked to changes in the RPI plus fixed annual supplement; variable after five years
National Savings income bond	Minimum £2000, maximum £250,000	Individuals (also jointly), trustees	Variable; paid monthly
National Savings capital bond Series L	Minimum £100, maximum £250,000 for holdings in all series, excluding Series A	Individuals (also jointly), trustees	Fixed if held for full five years; no interest paid after five years
Pensioners Bond 5th Series	Minimum £500, maximum £50,000 in addition to Series 1 and 2	Individuals over 60 (also jointly), trustees	Fixed for five years at a time; paid monthly
National Savings First Option Bond	Minimum £1000, maximum £250,000	Individuals (also jointly), trustees	Fixed for 12 months at a time
National Savings Bank ordinary account	Minimum £10, maximum £10,000	Individuals (also jointly), children, trustees	Variable; credited annually
National Savings Bank investment account	Minimum £20, maximum £100,000	Individuals (also jointly), children, trustees	Variable; credited annually
Premium Bonds	Minimum £100, maximum £20,000	Individuals over 16; bonds can be bought for children by parents, guardians or (great) grandparents	No interest

Tax position	Notice of withdrawal	How to buy/sell
Free of income tax and CGT	At least eight working days	Buy: through post offices Sell: repayment form from post offices
Free of income tax and CGT	At least eight working days	Buy: through post offices Sell: repayment form from post offices
Interest is taxable, but paid gross	Three months; in the first year, interest paid at half rate from date of purchase to date of repayment	Buy: application form at post offices, send with cheque to Blackpool Sell: repayment form from post offices
Interest is taxable, but paid gross	At least two weeks; no interest paid if cashed in in first year	Buy: through post offices Sell: repayment form from post offices
Interest is taxable, but paid gross	60 days; no interest paid during notice period	Buy: application form at post offices, send with cheque to Blackpool Sell: repayment form on bond
Interest is taxable; paid net of basic rate tax which non-taxpayers can reclaim	No notice; no penalty if repaid on anniversary date, otherwise interest paid at half the fixed rate since the last anniversary; no interest if cashed in in first year	Buy: application form from post offices to be sent with cheque to National Savings, Glasgow Sell: repayment form on investment certificate
First £70 (£140 joint) of annual interest is free of income tax	Up to £100 on demand; larger amounts require a few days' written notice	Opening and withdrawals at post offices
Interest is taxable, but paid gross	One month	Opening: through post offices Withdrawals: form from post offices to be sent to Glasgow
Prizes free of income tax and CGT	At least eight working days	Buy: through post offices Sell: repayment form from post offices

3

Fixed Capital Investments (2)

The last chapter covered the major institutions that offer fixed capital investments, most of which can be bought through high street outlets. Going a little further afield, there are a number of other products which also offer capital security, but may offer a more attractive rate of income than the standard bank and building society accounts, particularly for smaller investments.

Local authority bonds

Local authority bonds are issued for a fixed term of between one and ten years, over which the capital value remains constant. The minimum investment starts at £500 and the interest rate is fixed throughout the term. The bonds used to be a popular way for local authorities to raise funds, but in the 1980s the administration involved and the availability of cheaper loans from other sources led to a decline in the number of issues. However, there has recently been something of a revival and the bonds that are available are open to any investor – it need not be your own local authority that you buy from.

One drawback is that there is no facility to make withdrawals during the term of the bond, so your money is effectively locked in until the maturity date, although it may be possible to transfer it to a third party on written request. When the fixed term expires, there may be an opportunity to continue the investment for a further period at whatever the going rate of interest is at that time; otherwise you can simply have your original capital returned.

As for the safety aspect, the bonds are backed by the local authority itself, not by central government. Hence they are marginally more risky than a government-issued security such as a gilt and usually offer slightly higher rates of return to reflect this. However, while there is no obligation for the government to help out or provide any compensation in the event of a default, there is a certain presumption that it would act if there was a danger of widespread losses, if only for the sake of political expediency.

Interest is paid out twice a year and will normally be paid net of lower rate tax. If you are a non-taxpayer, you can register to receive interest payments gross by completing Inland Revenue Form R85, in the same way as for bank and building society deposits. Once the bond has been issued, the interest rate will remain fixed for the full term. Hence the longer term bonds are most suitable for investors for whom security of income is a priority – others may find they lose out if interest rates rise in the future. The rates will vary between different authorities and across the different lifespans, and are reset on a regular basis – sometimes daily – so you should check the up-to-date position before investing. Examples of current rates at the time of writing are shown in Table 3.1.

Guaranteed income and growth bonds

Guaranteed income bonds are issued by life assurance companies and are available for terms of between one and ten years, although the widest choice is for periods of four or five years. The minimum investment is generally around £5000 and the interest rate is fixed for the whole term, so these bonds are attractive to investors seeking a regular income, perhaps in retirement, to supplement a pension.

Table 3.1   *Local authority bonds*

Years	1	2–3	4–5	6	7
Typical gross rates (%)	6.25	6.375	6.50	6.50	5.125

Source: MoneyFacts, May 1998

Not all life offices operate in this market and some that do, issue bonds only occasionally. In any case, specific offers will only be available for a limited period, as interest rates will be reviewed at regular intervals. The rates are generally based on the return available on gilts and should give a better deal than a building society deposit, but then again, you may be committing your capital for a longer period.

Interest payments are usually made once a year, though some bonds pay out half-yearly and there may also be a monthly income option on larger investments. Some examples of the rates available at the time of going to press are shown in Table 3.2. These are net rates and apply for investments of £10,000; in some cases higher rates may be available for larger sums.

You might expect that the longer you are prepared to tie up your capital, the higher the return should be, but, as the table shows, this is not always so. The companies have to match the rates that they offer to those they can obtain on their investments, so it depends on the pattern of market interest rates. Remember, too, that the rate is guaranteed throughout the term, so at the longer end you may be sacrificing a small measure of return in exchange for the security of a fixed income.

Once you buy a bond, you are effectively locked into it for the full term. Companies vary in their willingness to provide a surrender value on early encashment, but generally any amount offered will be small. Should the bond holder die, the original capital will be returned, but again, companies have different policies on whether they will add in any income accrued since the last payment. Where payments are annual, this could be a significant amount if the bond holder dies just before a payment is due. For married couples, one way around this problem is to take out a bond on a 'joint life, second death' basis, which means payments would continue to be paid to the surviving spouse for the rest of the term. Should both partners die, the capital sum would be repaid to the estate on the second death. As with annuities, however, this kind of 'extra' may mean the income level is slightly lower.

Another version is the guaranteed growth bond. This operates on a similar principle to the income bond, but the interest earned is accumulated within the bond rather than paid out, so

Table 3.2 *Examples of guaranteed income bond rates*

Term	Income net of basic rate tax (%)	Term	Income net of basic rate tax (%)
1 year	6.25	6 years	5.45
2 years	5.70	7 years	5.25
3 years	5.66	8 years	5.50
4 years	5.55	9 years	5.60
5 years	5.40	10 years	5.50

Applicable for investments of £10,000.

For comparison, these bonds were available when sample interest rates on competing products were as follows:

Product	Term or notice required	Rate net of basic rate tax (%)	Fixed/variable interest
NS Certificates 46th issue	5 years	4.80*	Fixed
NS First Option Bond (£1–20,000)	1 year	5.20	Fixed
Building society instant access (min £5000)	None	5.80	Variable
Building society 30-day account (min £5,000)	30 days	6.08	Variable
TESSA (First issue)	5 years	8.00*	Variable

* Tax free to all investors

Source: MoneyFacts, May 1998

at the end of the term you receive back your capital plus a guaranteed profit.

Tax treatment of guaranteed bonds

The tax position of guaranteed bonds can be complex, partly because they are not all of the same structure. Longer term bonds are sometimes based on a combination of annuities: a temporary annuity, which provides the income payments, and a deferred annuity, which provides the return of capital at maturity. However, a change in the tax treatment of annuities at the beginning of 1992 made this route less attractive and the majority of bonds now issued are based on a single premium endowment policy with guaranteed bonuses.

For a basic rate taxpayer, the composition of the bond is of no concern. Income is paid net of basic rate tax, so you have no further liability. Non-taxpayers, however, cannot reclaim the tax paid from an endowment, so as a rule these bonds are not suitable to those investors.

Higher rate taxpayers are in a different position again. With an endowment, up to 5 per cent of the original sum invested may be withdrawn each year free of tax – it is counted as a return of capital – and any unused part of this allowance can be carried forward to subsequent years. Where a bond pays income annually, the mechanics are such that you will usually be 'in credit' with this allowance for most or all of the term. At maturity, however, tax may be charged on the 'profit', taking into account the money paid out and the amount originally invested. Further details of the taxation of single premium policies are given in Chapter 10.

Older investors who qualify for age allowance may also be affected by the tax rules. For these and higher rate taxpayers, an insurance broker or other professional adviser should be able to offer guidance on the best buy.

Cash unit trusts

Unit trusts are usually associated with equity investments, which are far from capital secure, but cash trusts are a fairly new breed. They invest chiefly in money market instruments and, by virtue of the size of the fund, they can secure top rates of interest. The minimum investment varies between £250 and £5000.

Cash trusts offer complete capital security and in most cases there is no initial charge. There is an annual management charge, which has to be met from the income the trust generates, but it is generally no more than 0.5 per cent. The return varies according to the interest rates available in the market; at the time of writing, gross yields go up to 6.75 per cent.

Income can be paid out or reinvested in the fund. Interest is credited net of lower rate tax, which can be reclaimed by non-taxpayers, while higher rate taxpayers will be liable for the extra amount due. A few trusts provide a cheque-book facility; otherwise, if you want to get your money out, the manager is obliged to issue a cheque within 24 hours of receiving the redemption form.

Further information on cash unit trusts can be found in Chapters 6 and 7.

Offshore deposit accounts

All the major banks and building societies now have offshore branches or subsidiary companies, situated in either the Isle of Man or the Channel Islands. Like their onshore parents, they offer a variety of accounts, depending on how much you want to invest and how quickly you want to be able to access your money. The choices include instant access, 90-day notice accounts, fixed-interest term deposits with periods from a number of months to a number of years, money market accounts and high interest cheque accounts. All of these operate in very much the same way as their onshore equivalents.

As a rule, interest rates are tiered with the size of the deposit and the notice period (see Table 3.3 below). At the bottom end of the scale, minimum deposits start around £1000, while

Table 3.3   *Examples of offshore deposit rates*

Type of account	Gross annual interest rate (%)
Instant access, min £1000	4.60
Instant access, min £5000	6.30
Instant access, min £50,000	7.35
60-day notice, min £10,000	7.75
90-day notice, min £10,000	7.85
Money market account, min £50,000	6.50

Source: MoneyFacts, May 1998

money market accounts start at around £2500 and can go up to more than £100,000.

Offshore deposit accounts enjoyed particular popularity when onshore accounts were subject to composite rate tax, which was deducted at source and could not be reclaimed by a non-taxpayer. Nowadays that advantage no longer exists and for UK residents who are basic rate taxpayers, there is a slight advantage in onshore accounts which deduct only lower rate tax. However, offshore accounts do have the slight advantage that interest is paid gross, so the tax bill is deferred for a while.

The other important consideration is how safe your investment is. 'Offshore' used to be synonymous with shady, or at least dubious, dealing, but the image has been considerably cleaned up in recent years. The Isle of Man, which had a salutary experience with the collapse of the Savings and Investment Bank in 1982, now has a compensation scheme for bank and building society deposits. In addition, building society subsidiaries are covered by their parents for the full amount of their liabilities. The Channel Islands keep a tight rein on financial businesses by having a strict vetting procedure for any institutions applying to set up in the islands.

Offshore money funds

Sterling offshore money funds are similar to the money market funds mentioned in the last chapter, investing in much the same kind of holdings, such as bank deposits and certificates of deposit. In addition, however, there are offshore money funds denominated in a variety of different currencies. These range from major currencies, such as the US dollar, the German D-Mark, the Swiss franc and the Japanese yen, to the less obvious, such as the Belgian franc, the Danish krone and the Swedish krona.

After the UK left the Exchange Rate Mechanism in September 1992, there was increased interest in foreign currency funds which may offer higher rates of interest than their sterling counterparts. However, there is a greater risk involved because of currency fluctuations. This may be reduced if you invest in a managed currency fund, where the manager will switch between various currencies according to their perceived prospects. Even so, while there is the opportunity for gain on the exchange rates, there is equally the chance of capital loss.

Some money funds have no set minimum investment, while others may require £1000 upwards. One point to watch for is that these funds carry an annual management fee. The usual figure is around 1 per cent and anything higher than this should be treated with caution, as it will cut into the returns available.

Taxation of offshore funds

The tax position of offshore funds is a little complex, as they are classified into two types: those with 'accumulator' status, also known as 'roll-up' funds, and those with 'distributor' status.

Prior to 1984, all funds were of the roll-up type, which meant that all interest earned was accumulated within the fund and added to the capital value. As a result, when investors came to sell, they were liable only to capital gains tax on the profits. Since there was the annual exemption allowance to make use of, and the top rate of capital gains tax at that time was only 30 per cent, this provided excellent tax efficiency, for higher rate taxpayers in particular.

Since 1984, however, the Inland Revenue has introduced new tax rules based on the dual classification. Roll-up funds still accumulate all the interest in the old way, but when you come to sell your holding, all the profits – whether they arise from capital gains or interest – are taxed as income.

For investors who are not in need of a regular income, there are still some advantages in roll-up funds, because the tax liability is deferred until you cash in your investment. This means that, meanwhile, you continue to earn interest on the full amount. Also, you will benefit if you wait to sell until your tax rate is lower than it is now, perhaps after retirement. Better still, if you retire or move abroad and cease to be a UK resident, you can escape UK tax altogether by cashing in the holding after you have left the country.

Distributor status was introduced as a special concession. To qualify, funds must distribute at least 85 per cent of their income and this will be taxed in the hands of the investor at normal income tax rates. They must also not engage in 'trading' – primarily, procedures designed to convert income into capital gains and thereby reduce the tax liability. Distributor status is only granted in retrospect, so funds that could be borderline tend to opt for accumulator status rather than risk their investors being faced with an unexpected tax position.

Distributor funds can be useful for non-taxpayers. Even for those who do pay tax, there is a small benefit compared with onshore funds as interest is paid gross, so there will be a short period of grace before you have to give the taxman what is due.

Where to find out more

Information on all the products mentioned in this chapter, with details of current offers and interest rates, can be found in the financial pages of newspapers (advertising and editorial) and in specialist magazines. *Money Facts*, a monthly publication, gives a guide to investment rates, including local authority bonds and offshore deposit accounts. It can be contacted on **01603 476100**. Alternatively, you should consult an insurance broker or other professional adviser.

4

The Gilts Market

In recent years, the government has done a fair amount to encourage saving – with the introduction of personal equity plans and tax exempt special savings accounts. Yet the government itself frequently lives beyond its means by spending more than its revenues, hence the National Debt, which grows rather more often than it is reduced.

National Savings products, outlined in Chapter 2, are one form of borrowing by the government, but by far the biggest chunk is through gilt-edged securities, or gilts for short. These are issued regularly and come in a variety of types. Most have a lifespan of up to 20 years, though some last indefinitely, but although they cannot be cashed in before their maturity date, they can meanwhile be traded on the Stock Exchange.

Gilts are regarded as being one of the safest of all investments. This is not to say that you cannot make a loss on them – the prices fluctuate, so your capital is not guaranteed. But the promises made by the gilt itself – the interest payments and the redemption value – are as secure as you can get; the government has never yet been known to default.

Terminology

One of the off-putting things about gilts is the jargon. If you go along to a building society, the accounts may have fancy names, but the descriptions of 'instant access' or '90 days' notice' are usually pretty clear. In fact, the title of a gilt is descriptive of what it offers, but you need to be able to decipher the code. As an example, let us suppose you are offered £100 nominal of Treasury 9½ per cent 1999.

To start with, 'nominal' refers to the face value of the gilt, which is the amount the government will repay at the date of redemption. This is also called the 'par value'. But between now and the redemption date, the price of the gilt will vary and may be above or below par. So your £100 nominal may cost you more or less than £100, but if you hold it for the rest of its life-span, that is what you will get back. It follows that, at the time you buy, there is an in-built capital gain or loss if the gilt is held to redemption.

The name 'Treasury' can effectively be ignored. Some gilts, like 'War Loan', have names which reflect the original purpose of the borrowing, while most that are around today are called Treasury or Exchequer. Either way, the name has no relevance to the investment characteristics.

The percentage, 9½ per cent in this case, refers to the 'coupon', or the interest rate that will be paid on the gilt. The rate applies to the nominal value of the gilt, so £100 nominal at 9½ per cent will earn £9.50 interest a year. In practice, the true rate of return on your money will depend on the price you pay for the gilt. If you buy below the par value, you will be getting a higher rate than the one quoted. For example, if your £100 nominal costs you £98, the £9.50 interest works out at just under 9.7 per cent. This is known as the 'flat' or 'running' yield of the stock.

Finally, 1999 is the redemption date, when the nominal value will be repaid to whomever holds the gilt at that time. Some stocks are 'double-dated': they carry two redemption dates, for example, 2001–2004. This means that the government can choose to redeem the stock at any time between those dates, but no later than the second one. As a rule, if a stock is standing above its par value as redemption approaches, the earlier date is more likely; if it is below par, the later date.

Types of gilts

Conventional gilts are classified into four types, which are generally shown separately in newspaper price listings. Those with up to five years left to run before redemption are called 'short-dated' or 'shorts'; those with remaining lives of 5 to 15 years are called 'mediums'; 'longs' are those with more than 15 years to run; and half a dozen or so stocks are undated, which means there is no fixed redemption date.

The nearer a gilt is to its redemption date, the closer its price will get to the nominal value, in anticipation of the repayment due. So short-dated stocks should have the least volatile prices. Mediums and longs, on the other hand, may fluctuate substantially in either direction. Because of the difference in coupon, two stocks with the same nominal value and the same redemption date may have quite different prices on the market.

Undated stocks could in theory be redeemed at some point, but it seems very unlikely. The coupons are low, between 2.5 and 4 per cent, so there is no incentive for the government to redeem them, only to have to borrow new money at higher cost.

In addition to these various conventional gilts there is another category, index-linked stocks. With these, both the interest and the capital repayment value are adjusted in line with the Retail Price Index (RPI). In practice, the figure used is the level of the index eight months before payment is due, to ensure that the amount of payment is always known in advance. This is compared with the base index for the stock, which is the level of the RPI eight months before the stock was issued; the base index for each stock is shown in newspaper price listings.

The coupons on these stocks look lower than those for conventional gilts because the figure quoted is the unindexed amount, which is then multiplied up by the inflation factor. Like conventional stock, prices will vary and as the redemption date approaches will move towards the repayment value, but this will be the indexed value, not the £100 nominal.

Gilt prices

The prices of gilt stocks are listed in newspapers alongside other share prices, generally under the heading of 'British Funds'. Prices are quoted in pounds and fractions, which can look a bit bewildering; for example, a figure of $119^3/_{32}$ signals a price of £119.09. As a rule of thumb, $^1/_{32}$ of a pound is roughly 3p.

The prices listed are normally the mid-market prices that applied at the close of trading on the previous day. This will give a reasonable guide, but prices are changing all the time; for an up-to-date figure you would need to consult a broker. You also need to remember that the actual buying and selling prices involve a spread – the buying price will be slightly above the mid-market figure quoted and the selling price slightly below it.

One other factor affecting the quoted price is the accumulated interest. Inevitably there is a time-lag involved in preparing and sending out interest payments and meanwhile stocks could change hands, so the rule is that payments are made to whoever was the registered holder 37 days before the interest payment falls due. At this point the stock becomes 'ex dividend', indicated in price quotations by the letters 'xd'. If you sell a stock that is ex dividend you will still receive the interest payment, but the part of it that relates to the period after you sold will be subtracted from the sale proceeds. Similarly, if you buy a stock ex dividend, this portion of interest will be deducted from the cost, to compensate for you not actually receiving it.

If you buy at other times, you will have to pay for the interest that has accumulated since the last payment date. For example, if you buy two months after the previous payment, your purchase includes two months' worth of interest and the value of this will be added to the price.

Aside from these factors, there are a number of influences on the general level of gilt prices, chief of which is interest rates. In simple terms, if bank interest rates are at 12 per cent, then a gilt with a coupon of 12 per cent should trade around its par value. If bank rates fall to 8 per cent, the gilt looks more attractive and this will drive the price up until the effective yield, based on the purchase price, comes into line with bank rates.

In practice, though, prices will reflect not only current interest rates but the market's expectations of future rates. Once you have bought a gilt, you have locked into a particular rate of return, so if general interest rates fall, you will be doing well. On top of this, a fall in interest rates will tend to mean a rise in gilt prices, so there will be a capital gain if you sell. Conversely, if interest rates are forecast to rise, the prospects are less attractive. Inflation will also affect the true value of both future income and capital value, so, again, prices will be influenced by the market's expectations.

The yield

As mentioned above, the flat yield on a gilt depends on the purchase price as well as the quoted coupon. It can be calculated by dividing the coupon by the price and multiplying by 100. This then represents the interest rate you will get on your investment. But the flat yield is not the whole story. The total return to be made from a gilt also depends on the change in the capital value between when you buy and when you sell or when the stock is redeemed.

If you hold the stock to redemption, you will make a known capital gain or loss depending on the price at which you bought it. Even if you stand to make a loss, this need not mean that the stock is not worth buying. For one thing, if the maturity date is still some way off, the price may rise before then, allowing you to sell at a profit. Alternatively, if you hold on to the stock, the interest payments may be enough to outweigh the capital loss and still represent an attractive return.

This return can be judged from the redemption yield, which takes into account the capital gain or loss as well as the flat yield. The calculation is complicated, but figures are included in newspaper listings and can also be obtained from stockbrokers, who have computer programs designed for the purpose. The figures assume that all interest payments are reinvested in the same stock at the same redemption yield.

A comparison between flat yields and redemption yields is shown in Table 4.1. Here, the high coupon short-dated stocks are standing above their par value and the redemption yield is therefore a lot lower than the flat yield, though still competitive with, say, bank and building society accounts. The low-coupon Funding 3½ per cent stock, on the other hand, offers only a modest running income but a higher redemption yield, as there is a sizeable capital gain to be made.

Table 4.1   *Gross flat and redemption yields on gilts*

Stock	Price (£)	Flat yield (%)	Redemption yield (%)
Exchequer 12.25% 1999	104.72	11.698	6.763
Treasury 9.5% 1999	101.78	9.334	6.927
Treasury 7% 2002	103.31	6.776	6.077
Funding 3.5% 2004	93.06	3.761	4.807
Treasury 8% 2013	121.72	6.573	5.840

Source: MoneyFacts, May 1998

These figures are for gross yields. When tax is taken into account, the picture can change again, as the next section will explain.

Gilts and tax

Interest payments on gilts are made twice a year. If the stock is held on the Bank of England register, interest is paid net of basic rate tax, with the exception of 3½ per cent War Loan which is paid gross. Stocks held on the National Savings Stock Register, accessible through post offices (see 'Buying and selling' on page 74), also have interest paid gross. In either case, taxpayers will be liable for any unpaid amount. Non-taxpayers can reclaim any tax already deducted, but may find the National Savings route more convenient.

Special rules apply to interest that has accrued shortly before you buy or sell. Where accrued interest has been allowed for in the purchase price, that part of the subsequent interest payment will not normally be liable for tax. Conversely, when you sell, you will be charged tax on the amount of interest earned before the sale, calculated on a daily basis. However, these rules do not apply when your holdings of gilts have not recently been worth more than £5000. In this case, tax applies only to interest that has actually been paid; so if the sale price includes an allowance for, say, three months' accrued interest, the profit is treated as a capital gain.

This is an advantage, as all capital gains made on gilts are tax free for private investors. The government caused a scare in

1995 by announcing that in future all gains would be subject to income tax, but eventually decided to exclude private investors from the ruling, although it does apply to companies.

As a result, higher rate taxpayers can continue to use gilts in a tax-planning strategy. By opting for a low-coupon stock and holding it to maturity, they can ensure that most of the return will come in the form of a tax-free capital gain.

The tax change was a prelude to the introduction of a gilts 'strip' market, which finally came into being at the end of 1997. This separates the interest from the capital, with the interest paid out only on maturity, at a guaranteed compound rate. Meanwhile, each part can be traded separately. Strips are likely to appeal primarily to institutions, but could also be useful for investors who have a set liability to meet in the future, such as school or university fees, or even for saving for retirement.

However, the tax position could be a serious drawback. As with ordinary gilts, strips will not be liable for capitals gains tax, but they will be subject to income tax – even though interest is not actually paid until maturity. Tax will be charged yearly at 20 per cent on any increase in the strip's value over the year. So, investors will have to pay tax on an asset that will not actually earn any return until it is sold or matures.

The other potential drawback is that gilt strips, unlike gilts themselves, will not be available through the National Savings Stock Register. To buy strips you will need to go to a stockbroker, which may charge a sizeable commission and may also not accept small deals.

Why buy gilts?

The majority of gilt dealing is done by institutions such as pension funds and insurance companies, but individual investors can also take part. In fact, the Bank of England has made particular overtures to the private investor: it published a free booklet to explain how gilts work; the investment limit for buying gilts through the National Savings Stock Register was raised from £10,000 to £25,000 and the register was expanded to include all existing stocks; the Bank then introduced a simplified application form, published in newspapers, for a new stock issue.

But should you be tempted? When interest rates are low, high-coupon gilts compare very favourably to bank and building society accounts as regards the running yield they offer. If income is your priority, gilts certainly have an appeal, but remember that if high-coupon stocks are at a premium – the price is above the par value – and you hold the stocks to redemption, the high income will be achieved at the expense of a guaranteed capital loss.

This should be viewed in the context of future prospects from alternative investments. Any investment has an opportunity cost – by choosing one, you are giving up the chance of another. Of course, you can never be certain of getting the best, but you can consider probabilities. The lower the rates of interest and inflation, the more likely it is that they will rise in future. This will work against gilts in that the yield will become relatively less attractive, prices will fall, and the ultimate redemption value will be worth less in real terms.

Timing makes all the difference to a gilt investment. Ideally, they should be bought just as interest rates start to fall and sold just as they are about to rise – even though they may appear most attractive when interest rates are at their lowest. But much depends on your investment criteria. On a long-term comparison, gilts have consistently performed less well than equities, but for some investors the fixed income and capital return may carry more weight.

Conventional versus index-linked

If inflation is the enemy of investors, index-linking should be the saviour. The return offered is guaranteed to stay in line with inflation, while the capital value at maturity is also protected from erosion. The redemption value of a conventional gilt, on the other hand, may be worth a lot less by the time it matures.

While current interest rates are influenced by current inflation, index-linked gilts look to the future in that prices will be influenced by expectations about the trend of inflation. Lately, index-linked stocks have tended to outperform conventional gilts; with the economy out of recession, and in the early days of a new government, inflation could start to pick up again. In this scenario, index-linked gilts look more attractive, as the inflation protection will prove rewarding, while if interest rates rise alongside inflation, the prices of conventional gilts are likely to fall, so they have less appeal.

One method used by stockbrokers to judge the relative merits of index-linked and conventional gilts is to calculate the 'break-even inflation rate'. This involves matching the index-linked stock with a conventional issue with the same or similar maturity date. Using a computer, they then work out what rate of inflation between now and redemption would make the (monetary) returns from the two stocks equal. If inflation runs above the break-even rate, the index-linked stock will give a better return.

Of course, it is still a matter of judgement whether inflation is likely to be above or below the break-even rate during the period in question. The further away the redemption date, the harder this is to judge, as inflation is likely to go both up and down more than once meanwhile. But you can at least assess the chances in the light of past experience.

Table 4.2 shows some examples of break-even rates for a basic rate taxpayer. To put these in context, the inflation rate at the time of writing is around 3.5 per cent; the January 1993 figure of 1.7 per cent was the lowest for many years, while in the worst days of 1980, the rate reached 21.9 per cent.

Table 4.2 *Break-even inflation rates*

Stock	Price (£)	Comparison stock	Break-even inflation rate (%)
2.5% 2001	197.06	Treasury 7.% 2001	2.33
4.375% 2004	125.38	Treasury 6.75% 2004	2.55
2% 2006	208.53	Treasury 7.75% 2006	1.91
2.5% 2009	189.25	Treasury 8% 2009	1.95
2.5% 2013	164.53	Treasury 8% 2013	2.04
2.5% 2020	172.75	Treasury 8% 2021	2.01

Note: Break-even rate applies at 20 per cent tax rate on interest.

Source: MoneyFacts, March 1998

Buying and selling

There are three ways of buying gilts: direct from the Bank of England when there is a new issue; through a stockbroker; or through the National Savings Stock Register.

When a new stock is issued, prospectuses are published in newspapers and are also available from the Bank of England. Stocks are auctioned, which means institutions register the price they are prepared to bid and only the highest bidders will receive stock if the issue is over-subscribed. Private investors, however, can register a non-competitive bid and they will then receive stock at the average of the successful bid prices. Usually they are asked to pay the nominal value up-front and the Bank then makes a refund or asks for more money, depending on the average price set.

For recent issues, the Bank has provided shorter application forms as a way of encouraging private investors. The advantage of buying new stock in this way is that there is no commission on the purchase.

For existing stocks, the National Savings Stock Register still offers the cheapest method of buying and selling for small sums although costs were recently increased. The costs are shown in Table 4.3. Aside from costs, there is the advantage that interest

Table 4.3   *The cost of dealing in gilts through the Post Office*

Up to £5000	0.7% subject to a minimum of £12.50 for purchases (no minimum for sales)
Over £5000	£35 plus 0.375% of the amount in excess of £5000

Examples

Purchases		Sales	
Cost of transaction	*Commission*	*Proceeds of sale*	*Commission*
£250	£12.50	£250	£1.75
£1000	£12.50	£1500	£10.50
£5000	£35.00	£2500	£17.50
£10,000	£53.75	£7500	£44.38

is paid gross, which means non-taxpayers avoid the effort of reclaiming tax paid; taxpayers will still have to pay what is due, but benefit from a grace period.

There is a maximum that you can invest in any one stock through the register of £25,000 a day, but there is no limit to the total amount you can hold on the register. New stocks bought through a prospectus can normally be registered with National Savings rather than the Bank of England by ticking a box on the application form, subject to a limit of £25,000 in nominal value. Stocks held on the National Savings Register can only be sold through it, while stocks held on the Bank of England register cannot be sold this way.

The drawback to buying and selling through National Savings is that it has to be done by post. While dealing will normally be carried out on the day instructions are received, you will not know until after the event what price applied.

The alternative is to deal through a stockbroker, which can be done by telephone at a known price. Commissions on gilt dealing are usually lower than for equities, but will still be subject to the broker's minimum, which can be £25 or more in London. Hence this is likely to prove an expensive route for small investments, especially as further commission will be payable when you come to sell.

One other route into the gilt market is through a collective investment such as an insurance company product or a unit trust. This gives you a stake in a portfolio of gilts for a much smaller outlay than buying your own collection, and with professional management as well, but, of course, there is none of the certainty you can get by buying stocks to hold to redemption.

Permanent interest bearing shares

Permanent interest bearing shares (PIBS) are issued by building societies as a means of raising permanent share capital. They are similar to gilts, in that they pay a fixed income, but the majority are irredeemable unless the issuing society is wound up. They can, however, be sold to a third party and are traded on the Stock Exchange.

Interest is paid twice a year and is paid net of basic rate tax, although non-taxpayers can reclaim it. Higher rate taxpayers will be liable for the extra amount. Any profits made on the sale of shares are not liable to tax for private investors, but are taxable for companies under the same rules as for gilts described on page 54.

The interest rates are more attractive than those offered on the standard range of building society accounts, but there is, of course, a capital risk. Share prices move inversely to interest rates and are particularly sensitive to long-term rates. So, for example, if market rates move downwards, prices will rise, which reduces the effective yield as a percentage of the purchase price. This is illustrated in Table 4.4, which shows the prices at the time of writing on a selection of shares and the corresponding yields. All the shares were issued at an original price of 100p, but falling market interest rates since issue have generally driven up the price. Equally, if rates rise again in future, the share prices will fall, so, unlike building society accounts, these are investments you should review regularly.

Currently, there are some 15 PIBS available. As the table shows, the yields vary, reflecting the market's view of the issuing society. Shares can be bought and sold through stockbrokers, who may advise on which appear most attractive. The minimum investment is generally £1000, but most stockbrokers have a minimum commission, which can be around £25, making dealing expensive for small sums. PIBS are not normally liable to stamp duty.

Table 4.4   *Examples of PIBS prices, coupons and yields*

Current price (pence)	Fixed coupon (gross)	Gross yield (%)
132.31	9.375	7.085
155.88	10.75	6.897
159.56	11.625	7.286
182.34	12.625	6.924
190.81	13.375	7.009

Source: MoneyFacts, May 1998

Aside from the capital risk, there are other safety aspects. Interest payments are not guaranteed to be made if the board of the society decides payment would damage business interests or if interest has not been paid on shares and deposits. Also, PIBS are not covered by the building societies' investor compensation scheme, and if the issuing society were to go into liquidation, holders would be last in line for repayment, behind all depositors and ordinary shareholders. On the other hand, if the society is taken over by another, the PIBS will continue as the liability of the society making the take-over.

Last year an investment trust was launched that invests in PIBS in the hope of benefiting from the spate of mergers in the building society world. At the time of writing, the trust has a yield of 5.1 per cent a year, with the prospect of additional cash or shares from bonuses payable if any of the societies whose shares are held undergo a merger or conversion.

Where to find out more

Newspapers such as *The Daily Telegraph* and the *Financial Times* publish the prices of gilts on a daily basis, along with gross interest and redemption yields. Net redemption yields, break-even inflation figures and general advice on buying and selling can be obtained from a stockbroker. Stockbrokers can also provide information and advice on permanent interest bearing shares.

5

Equities

Equities could be said to come somewhere near the top of the investment tree. This is not because they necessarily demand a lot of money – privatisation issues have allowed people to own shares for a down-payment of just £100. But if you had only £100 to invest, the stock market would not normally be considered the ideal place to put it. Most investors come into equities only after they have built up more cautious funds elsewhere.

This chapter focuses mainly on the UK Stock Exchange. In fact, many of the points would apply in a similar way to overseas markets but, despite sophisticated communications technology, dealing in foreign shares tends to be both more expensive and more difficult. Unless you have a very large portfolio, it is more practical to invest abroad through pooled funds such as unit and investment trusts.

The Stock Exchange

The London Stock Exchange has its origins back in the eighteenth century, when people used to meet in coffee houses to exchange shares and arrange deals. It was formally constituted in 1802, in purpose-built premises on the same site as the current building, which was opened in 1973.

The Exchange has two purposes: to act as a market for people wanting to buy and sell existing shares, and to raise money for companies by issuing new share capital. There are also two separate operations involved, jobbing and broking, corresponding to wholesale and retail functions. Jobbers used to be known by the more descriptive name of market-makers – they make a market in shares by acting as primary buyers and sellers and holding stocks on their books – but have now been renamed again, as 'Retail Service Providers' (RSPs). Brokers act as intermediaries between the market-makers and the end-clients, investors; they take orders from their clients and look for the best prices among the market-makers.

Trading used to take place physically on the Stock Exchange floor, but that came to an end with Big Bang, which reorganised the workings of the Exchange. Broking and jobbing firms were allowed to be taken over by companies, where previously they were partnerships, and both functions may now be carried out within a single company. They must, however, be kept separate, by means of a 'Chinese Wall'; this is to guard against any unscrupulous manoeuvring between them at the expense of the investor. If, for example, the broker knew that the market-maker wanted to get rid of some undesirable shares, he could connive at it by advising his clients to buy them.

Another effect of Big Bang was to remove the standard commission levels for buying and selling shares which were previously set by the Stock Exchange. Although some firms still roughly follow the old scales, there can now be wide differences. Much of the competition, though, is at the upper end and, for smaller investors, the general effect has been to increase costs. This is chiefly because brokers set a minimum commission, which can be as high as £40 for a London firm, making small transactions disproportionately expensive. Provincial brokers are generally cheaper, as they have lower overheads, and commission levels also vary according to the type of service provided.

Rolling settlement

The volume of shares traded has increased enormously since Big Bang. While prices are now posted on screens, dealing still involves a mass of paperwork and administrative logjams have not been uncommon, delaying the issue of certificates for shares bought and settlement for shares sold. The Stock Exchange planned to deal with this problem with the introduction of Taurus, a paperless dealing system which would have replaced certificates with electronic accounts, but after years of problems and delays it finally collapsed in March 1993.

Instead, it has introduced a system called Crest. The first step towards this was taken in July 1994 with the introduction of a ten-day 'rolling settlement' period.

Previously, the settlement system was based on two- to three-week periods known as 'accounts'. Settlement of transactions undertaken during any one account would normally take place on a fixed account day, some ten days after the end of the period. Meanwhile, investors could enjoy credit for shares bought, but would be waiting for the proceeds of sales.

Under the new system, settlement for both sales and purchases has to take place within a set period from the transaction date – initially ten working days, reduced to five from June 1995 and expected to shrink to just three days some time in 1998.

Crest helps the process by making all share dealing electronic and essentially paperless. Although you are still entitled to have a paper certificate and your own name on the company register, it will generally be easier and cheaper not to do so. Once settlement is cut to three days, it will be difficult to return a certificate in time for a sale and brokers may also make an extra charge to cover the additional cost of handling paper.

An alternative is to become a sponsored member of Crest, whereby a broker runs a Crest account for you. This will cost £20 a year plus whatever charge the broker makes. The advantage is that you remain on the share register, but the cost could prove too high if you deal only occasionally.

The most common route for private investors is likely to be the use of nominee accounts. These are accounts in the name of a nominee company, which holds shares on the investor's behalf while he remains the beneficial owner. They are already used in a number of situations, such as for discretionary broking services and personal equity plans, and it is forecast that by the end of this year some 12 million shareholdings will be in nominee accounts.

Nominee accounts are certainly convenient, but do have some drawbacks. You may lose out on share perks, since the shares are not registered in your own name, and you will have to make arrangements with your broker if you want to receive copies of annual reports or go to shareholders' meetings. This may involve a cost, on top of any fee charged for running the nominee account.

Another effect is that margin trading may become more popular. This is a facility whereby the stockbroker gives credit to settle share purchases, using existing shares held in a nominee account as security. This is not just a convenient way of making settlements but also allows you to 'gear' your portfolio, by borrowing against it to buy more shares. The disadvantage is that, if the market crashes, the value of shares held as security could end up being worth less than the credit given.

For this reason, stockbrokers are likely to lend only against blue chip shares and will need to monitor portfolios closely. Currently there are no regulations on margin trading but, given the potential risks, rules may be introduced if it becomes widespread.

The Stock Exchange Electronic Trading System

Last October, the Stock Exchange introduced a new dealing system known as SETS – the Stock Exchange Electronic Trading System. Covering deals in FTSE 100 stocks worth a minimum of £4000, this matches buyers and sellers electronically, by computer. A broker, for example, can post a sale order and the system will then come up with the best buy offer currently available.

The expectation, when the system was introduced, was that it would reduce the cost of dealing in shares – the bid/offer spread. This is because it cuts out the market-maker, who usually acts as the middleman between buyer and seller and makes a 'turn' on the transaction. The experience of European stock markets that have moved to similar order-driven trading systems is that spreads have fallen by up to two-thirds.

The early experience here, however, is that spreads have tended to widen, particularly during the first and last hours of a day's trading. The small number of deals done during these times means prices can be erratic and this can be compounded by dealers 'testing the water' or just chancing their arm. As a result, private investors who instruct their brokers to deal 'at best' may get caught out by unrealistic prices at these times. It may be better to specify a price range and also to deal in the middle of the day, when the system is busier and experience shows that spreads have tended to narrow.

Of course, many private investors will be involved in smaller deals that are outside the SETS limit. These will go through retail service providers (RSPs), as the old market-makers are now known. However, they are still likely to be influenced by SETS prices, for better or worse.

The Stock Exchange has been monitoring the early months of SETS and, at the time of writing, is due to announce modifications shortly. It may look to reduce the minimum dealing size and also, in due course, to extend the shares covered beyond those in the FTSE 100 Index. Greater use of the system may well speed the benefits, but meanwhile investors should keep a wary eye on both when and how they deal.

The Alternative Investment Market

The Alternative Investment Market (AIM) was launched in June 1995 as a replacement for the Unlisted Securities Market. As the name implies, it offers an alternative market-place for companies that are too small or not yet ready to seek a main stock market listing.

To join, companies have to supply a prospectus, background details on all directors, details of promoters, names and holdings of major shareholders, a working capital statement and a risk warning.

They also need to have a 'nominated adviser' and a 'nominated broker'. The former must be chosen from a Stock Exchange register and is, in effect, the company's mentor for the market, ensuring it meets the AIM rules. The broker is responsible for providing information to the market and for matching prospective buyers and sellers of the company's shares if there is no market-maker.

For investors, AIM shares generally carry more risks than the main market. This is partly because the companies are mostly smaller and have less of a business track record on which their prospects can be judged, but also because the market itself tends to attract far fewer buyers and sellers – the institutions, which dominate trading, naturally prefer the main market where deals can be much larger. Where there is no market-maker, deals are on a matched basis, which means you could find yourself stuck with shares for which there is no buyer available.

There are, however, tax benefits. Capital gains tax can be deferred on the profit from selling an asset if the proceeds are reinvested in qualifying AIM shares, while any transfer of AIM shares will avoid capital gains tax if it is at cost value rather than market value. Some shares also qualify under the Enterprise Investment Scheme (see Chapter 12), which offers up-front income tax relief and capital gains tax relief on sales. Finally, AIM companies may be eligible investments for venture capital trusts, which offer their investors similar benefits to the Enterprise Investment Scheme, plus tax-free dividends.

Market indices

Movements in the stock market are generally measured with reference to an index. For the UK market, there are two that are principally used: the FTSE All-Share Index and the FTSE 100 Index – known colloquially as 'Footsie'.

The All-Share Index does not in fact cover all shares quoted on the market, but the 900 or so that it does cover account for around 96 per cent of the total market capitalisation. Consequently, it gives the most representative overall picture.

The Footsie, which was begun at the start of 1984, covers the top 100 companies by size. The prices are calculated every minute during the trading day, so it gives immediate feedback to dealers on what is happening.

Although share price movements, and those of unit trusts, investment trusts and so on, are often measured in relation to the All-Share or the Footsie, there are various other indices covering particular sectors, such as smaller companies or individual industries. These can be more relevant for judging the performance of an individual share or specialist trust. For example, smaller companies are unlikely to follow the same pattern as the large companies represented by the Footsie Index; if the smaller companies sector is booming, a share that is performing only in line with the Footsie is probably doing relatively badly.

Private investors

Until quite recently, private investors were very much in decline in terms of their representation in the stock market. Meanwhile, the institutions saw a steady and substantial increase in the funds under their control and took on a heavily dominant position.

While there is still a heavy imbalance in favour of institutions, the private investor has staged a comeback. Currently, about one in four people own shares, a substantial increase on ten years ago. There have been three main reasons for this.

First, there has been an increase in inheritances following on from the growth in home ownership. People who already have a basic portfolio of investments and are then presented with a 'windfall' of, say, £50,000 to £100,000 are quite likely to give some thought to equities. Another factor has been the growth in company share option schemes for employees. The third, and most major, influence has been privatisations.

These have been something of a mixed blessing. They have certainly brought about wider share ownership but, one could argue, of the wrong kind. Few of the new shareholders are active dealers and many simply hang on to the few shares they bought, either for the incentives attached or because they have virtually forgotten they have them.

Perhaps more dangerous was the reputation privatisation issues acquired as 'get rich quick' schemes. Priced to be enticing, the earlier issues in particular gave opportunities to make immediate attractive profits – and many buyers made the most of it, selling the shares as soon as they had the letters of allocation. While there is nothing wrong in making a quick profit, anyone who thought the principle could be extended to other shares, with the same degree – or lack – of risk, is likely to have been severely disappointed.

Another major boost to share ownership has come from the spate of flotations of building societies and insurance companies. Halifax, Woolwich, Alliance & Leicester and Northern Rock have given away £24 billion in cash and shares over the past year and, altogether, some 20 million people have received shares. A number of them no doubt sold almost immediately, but the societies have been encouraging people to keep them – and provide new business – by offering special personal equity plans.

On a positive note, privatisations and flotations have boosted the growth of dealing services aimed at smaller investors. The Stock Exchange is also making overtures to smaller shareholders through a national campaign and a new Private Investors' Committee and stockbrokers have adopted a more user-friendly approach. If privatisations and flotations have helped to dispel some of the fear and mystique that surrounded equities, that is a step in the right direction; the next stage is to learn a little more about the rest of the market.

Ordinary shares

To begin at the beginning, an ordinary share represents a stake in the ownership of a company. In theory, it also confers the right to have a say in how the company is run, at least to the extent of having a vote at the annual general meeting. In practice, of course, most private investors do not have enough shares for their vote to count for much and many do not even bother to go to the meeting; nevertheless, the right exists.

Shareholders are also entitled to a portion of the company's profits, paid out in the form of dividends. As a rule, some of the profits will be kept back to be reinvested in the company itself for future growth. The remainder are distributed at so much per share; the more shares you hold, the larger the total dividend.

In return for these rewards, you take on a risk. Should the worst happen and the company be forced into liquidation, the ordinary shareholder is last in line for getting any of his money back. As a rule, though, you can only lose as much as you put in – you will not be called upon to make good anyone else's losses. This is because companies listed on the Stock Exchange have limited liability – hence the term PLC, or public limited company.

An exception is if the shares have been issued partly paid, as several privatisation issues have. This means that at the time you buy the shares, you pay only part of their price, with subsequent calls being made for the rest of the money. In this case, if the company incurs debts it cannot meet, you could be required to pay over the outstanding balance on the shares you hold. The majority of shares, though, are dealt in on a fully paid basis, so your maximum loss is equal to your investment.

With luck, the worst case will not happen and the company will stay in business, but you still stand to lose a part of your investment if the share price falls. Equally, of course, you will make a profit if it rises. So what factors make a share price move?

The short answer is supply and demand for the shares. Quite simply, if demand outstrips supply – if there are more willing buyers than willing sellers – the price will move up; in the opposite case it will move down. So the next question is, what affects supply and demand?

In the first place, all shares are influenced by what might be termed national events: the general economy and the political situation. Increasingly, these days, they are also affected by international events; one country's exports are another's imports, so a recession in the latter country means they will buy less, restricting export growth in the former.

There are further influences at sector or industry level; again, there are trade factors, and also strikes, which can have a knock-on effect if the striking company or industry is a major supplier to another.

Then you come down to the particular company, and what drives demand here is quite simply the expectation of profit. For individual investors, the anticipated profit may be in the form of capital growth – the expectation that the share price will increase. But what lies behind such an increase is the profit made by the company, translated into rising dividends: it is the income potential that ultimately underpins the share price.

Anticipation also plays an important part in determining share prices. An obvious example is a general election, where the market may react in advance to what people think is the likely outcome. This is referred to as discounting an event – if it happens as expected, there will be little further movement, but if expectations are confounded, it could produce a violent swing.

But while it is perfectly in order to act on guesswork, it is illegal to engage in insider dealing, which amounts to taking advantage of unpublished information that may affect share prices.

Dividends

Dividends are generally paid twice a year, the first payment being the 'interim' dividend and the second the 'final' dividend, paid at the company's year-end. The amount is generally expressed in terms of pence per share, net of lower rate tax; this can be reclaimed by a non-taxpayer, while higher rate taxpayers must pay the difference.

As explained above, dividends underpin the share price and anticipation comes into play. Hence the price will often move ahead of the declaration and, if it fails to live up to expectations, the price can fall back, even though the dividend itself may have increased since the last declaration.

The yield on a share is the gross dividend divided by the share price. The average yield on UK shares is generally around 3 to 4 per cent; as interest rates creep up, this does not look particularly enticing. But what shares also offer is the prospect of growing income and, given inflation, this is a valuable asset.

Yields do, of course, vary, both between companies and between sectors. Broadly speaking, sectors with lower growth prospects will tend to have higher yields. For individual shares, the yield will obviously rise if the share price falls, while the dividend is maintained; the key question then is why the share price has fallen. It may be owing to 'technical' or short-term factors and, indeed, unit trusts in both the Income and Recovery sectors tend to look for just this type of share, which offers capital growth prospects and good income in the meantime. But it may be that profits, and dividends, are expected to fall in the future, so a share cannot be judged by its yield alone.

As mentioned, companies do not usually pay out all their profits as dividends, but retain some for future use. In this case, the dividend is said to be fully 'covered'. Equally, though, they could call upon these reserves to boost dividends in a year when earnings have been low, in which case the payment would be uncovered. Some degree of smoothing from year to year is perfectly acceptable, but a fully covered dividend is always more reassuring.

An alternative to cash dividends is a 'scrip' dividend, where the company offers the option of additional shares instead of money. In some cases, the value can be much higher, and if you are looking for cash, you can simply sell the extra shares. Of course, there will be dealing costs, but you may still come out ahead and companies may also offer a buy-back scheme, which will cut the costs for small investors.

In principle, you cannot lose on this type of offer, but you do need to take care over the capital gains tax implications; if you have already used up the annual exempt allowance, you will be faced with a tax bill, although in the longer term it could reduce the liability on your remaining holdings in the shares. Scrip dividends are also treated by the Inland Revenue as having paid 20 per cent income tax which cannot be reclaimed. If you are in any doubt, you should seek independent advice.

Price/Earnings ratio

Besides the dividend, another means of judging shares is by the price/earnings ratio, or p/e for short. This is calculated as the share price divided by earnings per share and the result shows how many years it would take the company to earn enough to match the share price, if both remained unchanged.

In practice, the p/e ratio is used as a measure of the 'cheapness' of shares – the lower the ratio, the cheaper the share, relative to the company's earnings potential. But it has to be viewed in context. Average ratios vary between sectors and are also affected by the economy in general – high inflation should lead to lower p/e ratios, since future dividends will be worth much less in real terms than the share price you have to pay now.

Also, while a high ratio means a share is relatively expensive and should be viewed with caution, a low ratio is not always a reason to rush in and buy. It could be that the share price is low for good reason, because the market does not rate its prospects.

If you plan to invest overseas, you should bear in mind that p/e ratios may be on a quite different level to those in the UK. In fact, the UK has a relatively low average compared to markets worldwide, while Japan's is notoriously high.

How to buy and sell

It is no longer necessary to have a family stockbroker to gain access to the stock market. As mentioned above, the combination of Big Bang and privatisation issues has boosted the growth of new dealing services, often with low or no minimum investment requirement, while stockbrokers have been opening their doors to newcomers with a more obvious welcome than was once the case. Some larger companies have also become involved in share-dealing services, particularly where they offer corporate personal equity plans that may include the shares of other companies.

Banks have also expanded the range of dealing services they offer. National Westminster, for example, has a computer-based 'Touchscreen' service that offers instant dealing. It was initially developed in response to privatisation issues but, at the time of writing, it can now be used to deal in 500 different shares and is available in around 300 branches across the country, for both customers and non-customers.

Several banks also provide postal and telephone dealing services, the latter generally confined to existing customers, while the former are open to anyone. For the most part, these are purely dealing services, though occasional advice may be given.

If you want more comprehensive advice, a bank may have its own associated stockbroker service, but you may be just as well off choosing a broker for yourself. The Association of Private Client Investment Managers and Stockbrokers (Apcims) produces a brochure that includes a directory of its members, outlining in brief the services they offer.

But there was a setback for private investors on 1 January 1996 when the Stock Exchange decided to abolish the rule that at least 25 per cent of new share issues had to be set aside for retail investors. Floating companies can now decide the proportion for themselves – or place all shares with institutions.

However, a couple of brokers have responded by setting up new services that provide information on forthcoming new issues and a way of participating.

Another way for smaller investors to play a more active role in the stock market is through an investment club, of which there are now more than 1000 in the UK. ProShare, an organisation dedicated to promoting wider share ownership, offers a matching service to put people in touch with existing clubs or with each other if they want to start a new club. It also publishes a manual on setting up and running a club.

Computer software for investment tracking

Advances in computer technology in the last few years have put investment software within the budget of the individual investor. At the same time, the range of products on offer has also expanded so that there is now a wide variety of software available for general portfolio management, charting or both. The increasing popularity of Microsoft Windows has inevitably made its presence felt as well. Though there are still programs that can run without it, they are increasingly in the minority. A Windows program typically provides a better graphic display than one that runs under DOS (Microsoft's Disk Operating System) but it usually also requires a more powerful computer. If your budget is limited, there is nothing wrong with using one of the perfectly competent DOS programs still available on an older machine.

One of the first things to consider is where to obtain the raw material upon which to base your decisions – your data. If you have a small or inactive portfolio, copying information manually from a newspaper into your software is easy enough. This quickly becomes tedious as a portfolio becomes larger, so most investment programs these days allow you to enter data automatically from your modem (if you are getting it from a bulletin board or the Internet) or Teletext (if you have a text card fitted to your computer). The seriously enthusiastic, who like to monitor their investments throughout the day, will probably want a real data feed such as Market Eye or Tenfore.

As one might expect, the middle ground of the investment software market is rather crowded. Apart from a number of

British companies, there is also a significant US presence. Investors looking just for charting software could do worse than look at products from Equis, Omega or Market Arts. They are all visually attractive but are obviously aimed primarily at the American market. In terms of features, they represent excellent value for money, but do have a strong bias towards technical analysis (basing investment decisions on previous price activity rather than company profit performance or yield). In addition, they generally place far less emphasis on portfolio management than their British competitors. The UK software companies offer a pretty broad spread of products, so it is important to be very clear what you are actually looking for. Just asking for 'investment software' is also asking for trouble. If you always base your buy and sell decisions on the quality of company management or gross profits, there is little point paying for a charting program with a large number of irrelevant features.

Of the British companies, Indexia comes the closest to the US approach, with its products focused mainly on technical analysis, although portfolio management is certainly not excluded. The range extends from Intro, which is aimed at the small or novice investor, to Indexia II Plus which incorporates an impressive range of analytical and charting tools. All the products are compatible with each other, so moving up the product range does not involve a new learning process each time. Though the software is not Windows based, it still produces clear charts and is quick in operation.

Updata Softwares takes a slightly different approach with its program Invest. The software has rather less emphasis on technical analysis and more on information management. It has been designed to run in conjunction with a Teletext card, though it will accept information from other sources as well. The program runs under Windows and is therefore able to support DDE (Dynamic Data Exchange). Invest uses this to share information with other Windows programs. This is particularly handy for portfolio management, as you can have your existing holdings (or possible acquisitions) laid out in a spreadsheet for analysis and continually updated by the DDE link. Those who have a Teletext card can also build their own choice of database with Invest using the free information supplied.

Synergy Software aims to provide an integrated solution to investment tracking with its STAR system. This provides the user with charting, analysis and data in one package. Data is retrieved from Synergy's own bulletin board in compressed form (to reduce call costs) and then distributed automatically to the database files. The portfolio management facilities allow the creation of up to 60 separate portfolios and a range of reports to be generated on each. A capital gains tax module is also available which will automatically calculate any chargeable gain (allowing for RPI indexation) on any portfolio.

Pricetrack is an inexpensive program based around a set of spreadsheets that follows a similarly integrated approach on a subscription basis. The subscription covers the data and any software upgrades with customers having the choice of either weekly or monthly updates on floppy disk. The information provided includes not only prices but also fundamental data such as dividends and annual results. The program is split into three modules which cover database manipulation/graphing, reports (such as company results) and portfolio management. The focus of the program is to allow you to monitor the performance of your own portfolio as well as screen the markets for future investment opportunities.

Winfolio DF 4.0 from Mann Made Software offers a similar set of features but also incorporates an automatic long-term investment method. Originally developed for unit trust investment, it has now been extended to cover equities, bonds and PEPs as well and accepts data from Prestel, Teletext or manual entry. It offers simple but visually attractive charting and allows you to simulate buy/sell decisions as well as including basic portfolio management.

Apart from the companies already mentioned, there are now several firms who specialise in distributing a range of investment software from various developers. Market Data Centre is an agent for nine software companies and also stocks an enormous range of books on the subject of investment and analysis. It usually has several of its packages installed on computer so customers have the opportunity to see a range of products in action when trying to decide what to buy. Trendline Systems stocks a range of American software as does Comcare. Both companies can arrange demonstrations of products.

Synergy Software (STAR) Tel: 01582 424282
Indexia (Intro, Indexia II and Indexia II Plus) Tel: 01442 878015
Updata (Invest) Tel: 0181 874 4747
Pricetrack Tel: 01275 472306
Mann Made Software (Winfolio DF 4.0) Tel: 01204 385159
Market Data Centre Tel: 0171 522 0094
Trendline Tel: 01707 644874
Comcare Tel: 0161 902 0330

Finding a broker

When it comes to choosing a broker, the first step is to make sure what type of service you want. As regards share dealing, there are three options, as follows:

1. *Execution-only.* This is essentially for dealing only, with no advice given, although company reports or recommendations may be available. Some brokers may be prepared to accept 'limit' orders, under which you specify a maximum buying or minimum selling price; others may only be prepared to deal 'at best' – the best price that can be readily obtained on the market.
2. *Advisory.* This is offered by the majority of brokers and may cover individual share purchases and sales or provide a comprehensive portfolio service. At the outset, the broker will discuss with you your needs and desires, without obligation; thereafter you will be consulted before any transaction can take place and you can also initiate consultations or deals.
3. *Discretionary.* In this case, you hand over all responsibility to the broker, although there will be an initial discussion to sort out your aims, attitude to risk and so on. You will also be kept informed of all transactions, as well as receiving regular valuations and reviews.

In addition to these dealing services, stockbrokers may also offer a comprehensive financial planning package. This would include, for example, advice on cash management, school fees planning, retirement planning, life assurance and tax planning.

The majority of stockbrokers are regulated by the Securities and Futures Authority, through which they are authorised on an individual basis to give advice. Clients are eligible for the Investors Compensation Scheme in the event of default, and brokers generally also carry professional indemnity insurance against fraud and negligence.

Costs

The stockbroker's charges will usually be in the form of commission on dealing, though where there are additional financial planning services there may be an annual fee. The level of commission charged will vary from firm to firm, but will generally depend on three factors:

1. *The type of service*: execution-only dealing is usually cheaper than advisory or discretionary facilities.
2. *The location of the broker*: provincial brokers are usually somewhat cheaper than their London counterparts by virtue of having lower overheads.
3. *The size of the deal*: the scale of charges reduces for larger transactions and there is usually a minimum charge at the bottom end.

On top of the commission, you will also be liable to stamp duty at 0.5 per cent. Examples of charges are shown in Table 5.1.

You may be able to deal within specified price limits, or at the best available price in the market that day. Once the order has been executed, you will receive a contract note from the broker, showing the price of the shares and the dealing costs. Settlement will follow within three working days of the transaction.

Shares in a portfolio

The minimum portfolio size specified by stockbrokers varies considerably, from firm to firm and depending on what type of service you want. Equally, different brokers will vary in their views on what constitutes a sensible minimum, regardless of

Table 5.1 *The costs of buying shares*

£1000-worth	
Stockbroker's commission	£22.00
Stamp duty at 0.5%	5.00
Total	£27.00
£10,000-worth	
Stockbroker's commission	£133.50
Stamp duty at 0.5%	50.00
Total	£183.50
£25,000-worth	
Stockbroker's commission	£263.50
Stamp duty at 0.5%	125.00
Total	£388.50

what they might be prepared to accept – some will say around £25,000, others anything up to £100,000.

Chiefly, it depends on your circumstances and the amount of risk you are prepared to accept. The points to bear in mind are first, that small deals cost relatively more than larger ones, as Table 5.1 shows, and second, that to achieve a spread of risk you should think in terms of holding 10 to 15 shares. If you were to put £5000 into each of ten holdings, that would mean a portfolio of £50,000; if you then add in 'safety' money in alternative investments, you can begin to see why some advisers think in terms of six figures.

If you are only investing the odd few thousand, you will be restricted to the UK and only a small number of shares at that, whereas a unit trust, for instance, could give you a stake in a worldwide spread of holdings.

Having said that, there is nothing to stop you going directly into equities with any amount to invest. The so-called 'Super Sid' investor would usually be in the £5000 to £20,000 bracket and stockbrokers are generally prepared to accept smaller sums than they used to, particularly as they might now see only the equity portion of a larger portfolio, whereas in the past they tended to be given charge of all a client's investments. The only 'rule' is to appreciate the risks involved and the same is true of speculation; as the saying goes, if you don't know whether you are a speculator or an investor, the stock market is an expensive place to find out.

There are, of course, a host of such sayings, many of them contradictory, and there is no guaranteed formula for investment success. If you plan to be a middle of the road, long-term investor, the best attributes are probably moderation and patience: don't expect to get rich overnight and don't hold out for even bigger profits at the risk of losing what you already have. Few people ever manage to buy at the very bottom of the market and sell at the very top; if you can come somewhere close, you should find ample rewards.

One other point on portfolio organisation is that it is worth considering using a personal equity plan for the first £6000, the maximum investment that is allowed per year in a general plan (a further £3000 can be put into a single company plan). Peps are due to be replaced next year with Individual Savings Accounts (ISAs), which will have a lower annual investment limit, so it is all the more worth while considering PEPs at the moment. The advantage is that all income and capital gains arising from the investment are tax free. Against this have to be set the plan charges; for unit trust-based plans, there are usually no charges other than those on the trusts themselves, so if you are investing in trusts as well as equities, you may do better to use the PEP allowance for the former. PEPs and ISAs are discussed in detail in Chapter 9.

Other ways to play the market

Warrants

Buying shares is not the only means of investing in the equity market. An alternative is to buy warrants, which may be available on the shares of trading companies and investment trusts.

A warrant conveys the right to buy a share in a company at some future time. The price is fixed at the outset and known as the 'exercise price', and the option may be taken up on specified 'exercise dates'. These may be a particular day, or a set of dates, each year up to a final date when the option lapses.

Buying the share would be worthwhile if the exercise price plus the original cost of the warrant add up to less than the current market price of the share, although if you plan to sell the share for a quick profit, you would also have to take your sale costs into account. If there is no opportunity for profit, the right to buy need not be taken up, but the warrant will lapse without value once the final exercise date has passed.

Like shares, warrants are traded on the Stock Exchange so can be bought as investments in their own right with no intention of taking up the exercise rights. The price of a warrant is generally much lower than the price of its related share, but will move in line with it, giving you exposure to the share's fortunes for a lower outlay.

But, by the same token, warrants are much more volatile, and therefore riskier, than the shares themselves. If, for example, the share price rises by 50p, the warrant price will rise by a similar amount, but the lower starting-point means the proportionate rise will be much greater. Equally, the effect of any fall in the share price will be enhanced. This is called the 'gearing' on the warrant, which is measured as the share price divided by the warrant price.

A high level of gearing offers high potential rewards but also greater risk. The other factors involved are the remaining lifespan, up to the final exercise date, and the premium, which is the excess of the exercise price plus the cost of the warrant over the current market price of the share. The longer the lifespan, the higher the premium may be, as there is more time for the share price to rise high enough for the warrant to generate a profit.

Assuming the risk is acceptable, warrants can be suitable for higher rate taxpayers as they do not pay any dividends. Hence there will be no liability to income tax; profits will be taxed as capital gains, which can be offset by the annual £6800 exempt allowance.

Options

Futures and options contracts both come under the generic heading of derivatives – a family of financial instruments that allow a number of techniques, both to increase and decrease risk. But while futures are out of the price range of the ordinary investor, options can be very useful. They are traded through the London International Financial Futures and Options Exchange (Liffe) and there are a number of stockbrokers who will deal in them on behalf of private clients. You can go to one of them for just this service alone, even if your main portfolio is handled by a different firm.

The options used by private investors are based on either individual shares or an index. In the former case, a standard contract covers 1000 shares in a particular company, while index options are based on the value of the FTSE 100 Index. In either case, there are two types of option: 'calls' and 'puts'.

Take the case of an equity option. Here, the buyer of a call option has the right to buy a quantity of shares, at a specified price, at any time between now and the expiry date, which can be up to nine months away. A put option confers a similar right to sell shares. The buyer of the option is not obliged to take it up, but if he chooses to, the seller must honour it; either way, the seller gets to keep the cost of the option, which is known as the 'premium'.

Suppose you expect a share price to rise. Instead of buying the share itself, you can buy a call option, which will cost a lot less. If the price does then rise – above the price specified in the option, plus the premium you paid for it – you have two choices. First, you can exercise the option, then sell the shares for a profit. Alternatively, you can sell the option, for a higher premium than you paid, making a smaller profit but for a much lower outlay than if you had bought the actual shares.

Put options can be used as insurance if you believe that the price of a share you hold will go down. If it does fall, you can exercise the option and thereby limit your losses. If the price rises instead, you can simply let the option lapse and perhaps recoup its cost by selling the shares at a profit.

You can also sell, or write, options, but unless you are prepared to take on a heavy risk you should only do so if you have the shares to sell or the money to buy. Suppose, for example, that you hold shares whose price looks likely to remain rather flat. You can then write a call option against them. If your predictions are correct, the buyer of the option will probably not want to exercise it, so you have gained the premium for no outlay. If the share price rises and the option is exercised, you will lose out on the price rise, but you still keep the premium, so you will be better off than if you had sold the shares at the original market price.

As with equities, dealing services in options can be on an execution-only, discretionary or advisory basis. For the beginner, an advisory service is probably best, as it allows you to build up a knowledge of the market. Commission scales tend to start somewhat higher than those on equities, but again, it will vary from firm to firm, so it is worth shopping around. A list of firms that deal in options can be obtained from Liffe.

One other possibility is to bet on the index, which can be done through a couple of organisations. The effect is similar to using an option, but losses are not automatically limited – you have to decide to close the bet if the index is moving against you. Winnings are also tax free, as the betting tax will be paid by the company and included in the quoted price spreads.

Other types of share

As well as ordinary shares there are other types that investors may consider.

Preference shares carry the entitlement to a fixed dividend each year. Most of them are 'cumulative', which means that if the dividend is missed one year, it would have to be made up later if the company resumes dividends on its ordinary shares. Preference shares also take priority over ordinary shares if the company is wound up. Currently, with interest rates at low levels, the income from preference shares looks attractive but, as with any shares, the capital value is not guaranteed.

Convertible stocks are securities which carry a fixed dividend plus the option to convert them into ordinary stock, at a set price, at some fixed time in the future. They also rank ahead of ordinary shares in the event of liquidation. Again, the yields look attractive when interest rates are low, and there is also the chance of making a profit from the conversion.

Debentures are loans to a company that are secured on a specific asset, such as property. The yield is fixed and there is a stated redemption date when the loan will be repaid.

Stock market terms

Most readers will no doubt have come across stock market jargon, at least to some extent, but this is a reminder of the more common terms.

Bear: someone who believes the market will fall
Blue chip: companies regarded as high quality and the safest – said to be named after the highest value chip in poker
Bull: someone who believes the market will rise
Nominee account: a facility whereby shares are held on behalf of an investor in a company's name
Partly-paid: an issue of shares on which only part of the price is paid up-front
Rights issue: the offer of new shares in a company to existing shareholders at a price below the current market price
Scrip issue: a free issue of shares to existing shareholders
Stag: someone who buys a new issue in the hope of selling immediately for a quick profit

Where to find out more

A directory of private client stockbrokers, listing their services, can be obtained from the Association of Private Client Investment Managers and Stockbrokers, 112 Middlesex Street, London E1 7HY; tel 0171 247 7080.

A free information pack and a list of brokers dealing in traded options can be obtained from Liffe, Cannon Bridge, London EC4R 3XX; tel 0171 623 0444.

Other useful telephone numbers are:

The Stock Exchange: 0171 797 1000
The Securities and Futures Authority: 0171 378 9000
ProShare: 0171 600 0984

6

Unit Trusts and Offshore Funds (1)

Unit trusts, offshore funds, investment trusts and life assurance products all have a common characteristic: they pool investors' money into a large fund, so that smaller investors can participate in a broad spread of assets that they could never achieve by their own means. The concept was set out in the prospectus of the very first investment trust to be launched, in 1868, and it is still quoted by that trust in its literature today: 'We intend to provide the investor of moderate means with the same advantages as large capitalists in diminishing the risks ... by spreading investment over a number of stocks.'

The primary advantage of collective investments, as they are known, is this reduction of risk. If you hold only one share and it crashes, you lose everything, but if you have a stake in a portfolio, one failure will be cushioned by other successes. There are also other plus points which will emerge over the next few chapters, such as professional investment management, ready access to overseas markets and certain tax benefits – particularly through personal equity plans, which are discussed in Chapter 9.

Unit trust investments can start from as little as £500 for a lump sum and there is no set maximum. As mentioned in the last chapter, many people would consider £25,000 to be the working minimum for a direct investment into the stock market, but investors with up to £100,000 available may find that the range and scope of collective investments will amply satisfy their requirements. Larger investors may also find them useful to add an overseas content to their holdings, even where they are investing directly in UK equities.

The growth in the unit trust industry over the last decade has been substantial. In 1984 there were 102 companies, running 687 trusts, which had a total value of £11.7 billion. At the end of 1997, there were 153 companies, operating 1680 trusts, with a total value of funds under management of £163 billion. These trusts span a huge variety of geographical and industrial special-isations, from broad-based UK General funds to Asian Smaller Markets or International Technology. Investment choice is examined in the next chapter.

The size of companies, and the number of trusts they run, vary considerably: the top ten alone account for over £70 billion of funds under management and the top 20 for over £97 billion, as shown in Table 6.1. Most companies are members of the Association of Unit Trusts and Investment Funds, which can supply a range of information and contact details.

Unit trust regulations

A unit trust is subject to a trust deed, which lays down the terms under which it operates, for example, where and how it will invest, the calculation of unit prices and the charges it may levy. The money in the fund is held on behalf of investors by trustees, generally a bank or insurance company, who are responsible for ensuring that the managers conform to the rules laid down in the trust deed.

The regulation and authorisation of unit trusts is in the hands of the Securities and Investments Board, which lays down rules on what investments are available to a unit trust. The bulk of the portfolio will normally be invested in quoted shares or gilts, but up to 10 per cent may be in unquoted securities, including up to 5 per cent in other unit trusts, and up to 5 per cent may be invested in warrants. Trusts may also make use of traded options and futures contracts for the pur-poses of efficient fund management, but these must be cov-ered by holdings of cash or near cash, such as government securities.

Table 6.1 *Top 20 unit trust groups by funds under management*

Group	Funds under management (£m)
Schroder	14,148.6
M&G	9330.7
Mercury	7523.5
Perpetual	7137.9
Fidelity	6666.8
Gartmore	6374.7
Barclays	5773.9
Threadneedle	5385.9
Standard Life	4442.5
Save & Prosper	3702.3
Friends Provident	3697.6
Prudential	3030.8
Hill Samuel	2994.0
Aberdeen Prolific	2767.7
Morgan Grenfell	2611.0
TSB	2595.7
Legal & General	2452.9
Norwich Union	2366.4
Abbey	2041.8
Equitable	2005.5

Source: Association of Unit Trusts and Investment Funds, January 1998

To ensure that a trust preserves an adequate spread of risk – which, after all, is a prime objective – not more than 5 per cent of the portfolio can normally be held in the shares of any one company. However, provided the total of 5 per cent plus holdings does not itself exceed 40 per cent of the portfolio, an individual holding may go up to 10 per cent. This means that if one share suddenly shoots up in value, it will not have to be immediately sold. In practice, a trust would normally have upwards of 40 different holdings, depending on its size, so it is likely to be well within the limits.

The other main rule is that a trust cannot hold more than 10 per cent of any one company's issued share capital. This is to ensure that a trust does not build up a controlling stake in a company, which could undermine its basic objectives.

Charges

There are two types of charge levied by unit trust managers: the initial charge and the annual charge. The level of these will be specified in the trust deed and the managers cannot raise the charges above that level without getting permission from the unit holders. For this reason, the levels stipulated are sometimes higher than the charges that are actually applied; this gives the managers the flexibility to make an increase at a future date without the bother of seeking permission.

In recent years there has been a tendency for charges to rise, so trusts that have been in existence for many years may carry lower charges than those more recently launched, unless the managers have sought permission for an increase. These days, the typical initial charge is between 5 and 6 per cent. Some gilt trusts have a lower charge, around 3 per cent, and cash trusts also have a very small or zero charge, while the specialist over- seas trusts tend to carry the highest fees.

Out of this initial charge, the managers pay commission to intermediaries who sell the trusts for them. The usual amount of commission is 3 per cent, with the rest of the charge going towards the managers' costs, such as advertising. But if you buy direct from the managers rather than through an intermediary, the 3 per cent allowed for commission will still be charged and simply kept by the managers. Sometimes, however, the man- agers may make a special discount offer. Introductory discounts, of 1 per cent or possibly more for large investments, are quite common during the launch period of new trusts.

The annual charge is commonly between 1 and 2 per cent, though again cash trusts generally have a lower charge, around 0.5 per cent, while specialist trusts are likely to be at the top end of the scale.

In most cases, the annual fee is taken out of the trust's income, but some trusts now charge it to the capital account instead. This is done to maximise the income that can be paid out, but investors should bear in mind that it will reduce the capital growth from the trust and may ultimately lead to a lower total return. Opponents of the idea have also argued that it is not tax effective: investors stand to receive relatively higher income and lower capital gains, whereas most will be liable to tax on the former and not the latter.

While it may seem best to go for trusts with the lowest charges, performance can be a more important factor in determining the investment return. Obviously, the higher the charges, the better the performance needs to be for the same result, but over longer periods, differences in performance – as the next chapter will show – can be more than large enough to wipe out the effects of a higher charge.

Normally you should think of holding on to unit trusts for at least a medium-term period, say three to five years. If you buy and sell more frequently, the initial charge on each purchase could start to eat into your returns. However, if you do plan to be an active investor, this effect can be lessened by sticking with one management group.

Most managers offer a discount on switches between their own trusts, as an incentive to investors to keep their money within the group. The amount varies from 1 per cent to as much as 4 per cent, which means switching can be done at very little cost.

Bid and offer

If you look at unit trust prices in the newspaper you will see that there are two quoted, the 'offer' price and the 'bid' price. The offer is what you pay to buy units, while the bid is what you get when you sell. The difference between them is usually greater than the quoted initial charge of 5 to 6 per cent, because the calculations are based on complex rules laid down by the regulatory authorities.

To start with, a trust must have a creation price and a cancellation price. The creation price is based on the value of the shares in the trust's portfolio (valued at their offer price, which is the price at which they could be bought on the market), plus stockbroker's commission and stamp duty. To that is added any cash held by the trust plus accumulated income from dividends and interest payments, and the whole lot is then divided by the total number of units in existence.

The cancellation price is almost a mirror image, being the value of the shares held in the portfolio at their bid price, less the stockbroker's commission, plus cash and accumulated income, again divided by the total number of units.

The full offer price that the managers can charge when selling units then becomes the creation price plus the initial charge. The full bid price, which is the minimum at which the managers can buy back units, is equal to the cancellation price.

The difference between these two is called the full spread and can be as much as 10 or 11 per cent. In practice, of course, few people would be prepared to buy an investment that would immediately drop 11 per cent in value, so the managers normally quote prices somewhere between the two extremes. The 'dealing' spread, which is the difference between the two quoted prices, is typically around 6 or 7 per cent. An illustration of the various prices is shown in Table 6.2.

When a trust is in demand, with new money coming in, the managers are likely to be buying more shares for the portfolio, so the quoted prices will move towards the top end of the range to reflect the costs of this. In this case the trust is said to be on an 'offer basis'.

Correspondingly, when more people are selling the trust than buying it, the managers may need to sell shares to meet the redemptions. The prices will then move towards the bottom end of the range and the trust is said to be on a 'bid basis'.

These price movements within the permitted range stem from the aim to be fair to all investors, particularly those who continue to hold units. For example, if sellers were given too high a price, it would dilute the value of the trust for the remaining unit holders.

As long as you buy and sell on roughly the same basis, it makes little difference where the prices are within the range. But if you buy when the trust is on an offer basis and sell when it is on a bid basis, you will effectively suffer the full spread.

Generally, managers will not move abruptly from one to the other, but will try to anticipate the trend of demand – whether the market is rising or falling – and move gradually over several days. But a very large order can force a sharper movement, so it is possible that the price can move against you quite suddenly.

There have been proposals, not as yet carried through, to allow certain variations in unit trust pricing. One in particular is the

Table 6.2 *Price calculations*

	Price		
Maximum offer price = creation price + initial charge	106.00p		⎫ 9.75% full spread
Minimum offer price = minimum bid price + dealing spread	102.67p	⎱ 6% initial charge / Offer price range	⎱ 6.25% dealing spread
Creation price = offer value of shares + commission + stamp duty + cash + accumulated income, divided by number of units in issue	100.00p		
Maximum bid price = maximum offer price – dealing spread	99.37p	Bid price range	
Minimum bid price/cancellation price = bid value of shares – commission + cash + accumulated income, divided by number of units in issue	96.25p		

option to replace part or all of the initial charge by an 'exit fee' which would be applied if units were sold within a given period from purchase. The argument in favour of this is that more money would be invested up-front, while the trust can still recoup its costs if investors switch in and out quickly. Exit fees are already in use on some personal equity plans (see Chapter 9).

Different types of unit

Unit trusts may offer either or both of two types of unit: accumulation and distribution. Accumulation units are designed to reinvest any income earned by the trust with a corresponding increase in the unit price. Distribution, or income, units instead pay out the income, usually twice a year, although some pay quarterly or annually.

The difference is simply a matter of convenience. Trusts that have the sole aim of producing capital growth, and those that invest in certain overseas markets, have a very low yield – in the case of Japan, it may be virtually zero. To pay out to every unit holder twice a year could cost more than the income itself, so it is easier to accumulate it into the fund. The managers will, however, send out information on the income that has been accumulated as investors will have to declare it for tax.

Distribution units are used by trusts that are designed for income or a combination of income and growth. Payments are made net of lower rate tax. Some trusts offer to reinvest the income in further units, but this will usually mean paying the initial charge each time. If you do not want the income, and there is a choice available, accumulation units should prove more cost effective.

When you buy distribution units in a trust, the price will include an allowance for any income that has accrued since the last payment date. So when you receive the next distribution, part of it will represent the income earned since you invested, while the rest is in effect a return of the extra amount you paid for the units. For tax purposes, this portion – known as an 'equalisation payment' – counts as capital; it is not liable for income tax, but will be deducted from the purchase price in calculating any capital gains tax liability.

Funds of funds

A few years ago, a new type of unit trust was introduced, referred to as a 'fund of funds'. This is a kind of 'super trust' which invests across the range of the group's other trusts and thereby acts as a managed fund.

Initially, the concept attracted a fair degree of scepticism but now a third or so of the management groups offer such a trust. The advantage claimed is that it offers the equivalent of an investment management service for relatively small sums. For smaller investors, highly specialised trusts can be too risky, as performance is very volatile and timing – when to buy and sell – is crucial. Through the fund of funds, the investor can obtain a stake in these specialist trusts at lower risk, because the portfolio is spread over a range of trusts and the manager makes the decisions on his behalf.

One drawback is that the fund of funds is limited by the other trusts run by the group. Obviously, it would not be worth while unless the range of trusts it can invest in is fairly broad. But even then it may not be possible to get the best mix, because the individual trusts have their own objectives which may not fit with the overview of the fund of funds. For example, the investment strategy of the Japan trust, which is focused solely on that market, might not be the best approach for the Japanese portion of the fund of funds, which takes a global view. And, of course, if the Japan trust happens to be performing badly, the fund of funds manager has the difficult choice of whether to invest in a poor fund or not to be in Japan at all.

So far, the performance of the funds of funds does not suggest that they have any particular advantage over ordinary international trusts, which also take a global view and are not limited in their investment choices.

Cash trusts

Cash, or money market, trusts are a more recent innovation, born out of uncertain stock market conditions. Unlike the normal run of unit trusts, cash trusts do not involve any risk to your capital, because they invest in fixed capital instruments. In most cases they carry no initial charge and the annual charge is generally only 0.5 per cent.

One aim is to provide a temporary refuge for investors who want to sell holdings in equity trusts when the stock market is falling. The managers benefit because the money stays with the group, while investors may also benefit because they will qualify for any switching discount the group offers if they later go back into an equity trust.

Cash trusts can also provide a higher income than bank or building society deposit accounts. By pooling investors' money into one large fund, the trust can secure top rates of interest on the money market, while the minimum individual investment is generally only £1000 or less. Cash unit trusts are not eligible for inclusion in a personal equity plan, but the new Individual Savings Accounts (ISAs) that will be introduced in 1999 can include a cash element of up to £1000 a year (£3000 in the first year). This could help to increase the popularity of cash unit trusts, which in turn could make rates even more attractive.

A few cash trusts provide a cheque-book facility for larger investments, so that you can have instant access to your money. Otherwise, if you want to sell, managers are obliged to issue a cheque within 24 hours of receiving the necessary documentation.

Index tracking trusts

While most trusts are actively managed, index-tracking trusts – 'trackers' – take a passive line. The aim is to track the movement in one or another stock market index: there are index trusts based on the UK, the US, Europe, Japan, South East Asia and worldwide. One way of doing this is to buy holdings in every stock that is included in the index, but for the US, for example, this would be impossible, as there are just too many. Instead, the trust will aim for a representative sample in appropriate portions. Generally, trusts do not expect to be spot on every time, but will set a target margin of error.

Not surprisingly, the concept has both its supporters and its critics. On the downside, it does not seem much of an achievement simply to match the index, especially as investors will do slightly worse than that when charges are taken into account. It is also worth remembering that a tracker trust will follow the index downwards as well as upwards, while traditional trusts have the option to go partly into cash to avoid the worst of a fall.

A further point to note is that, among UK funds, some track the All-Share Index and some the FTSE 100. In the last couple of years the latter have performed much better, as it has been large companies, particularly in the banking and pharmaceutical sectors, which have led the market. But in the last few months, smaller companies have done relatively better, so there could be a reversal.

Supporters of trackers point out that many trusts consistently underperform their relevant index; over longer periods, the average performance of funds in any one sector may well be below the index for that market. So while a tracker is never likely to be top of its sector in the performance tables, it is never likely to be bottom either. Trackers can also operate on low charges and have been prominent in recent price competition, particularly with newcomers to the unit trust market.

Trackers now look set to receive a considerable boost from the government's proposed 'CAT' standard for ISAs. CAT stands for cost, access and terms and the standard will be awarded to plans that the government believes are suitable for first-time investors. For equity ISAs, only tracker funds will qualify for the CAT standard.

Again, the idea has its supporters and detractors. On the plus side, simplicity and low cost should help to encourage new and smaller savers. But there is a danger that the CAT standard will be taken as a guarantee of performance, whereas other funds may in fact produce much better returns, particularly in a market downturn. There is also a risk that if too much money goes into index trackers it could ultimately distort the market itself.

A new form of tracker investment has recently made its appearance in the UK, having already proved popular in the US. Known as a Train – from tradable index security – it comprises a single share in the index itself. The advantage of this is that it is easy to get in and out of the market quickly, which is not the case for a standard tracker holding a whole portfolio of shares. Costs should also be lower. The one fund that has so far been launched is registered in Luxembourg because the rules for retail funds in the UK stipulate a minimum of 20 stocks and Trains technically hold only one. But it is expected that ways may soon be found to introduce UK-based funds.

Futures and options trusts

These are a fairly recent development in the unit trust world and there are currently only around 36 available. The use of futures and options contracts had previously been regarded as potentially too risky for unit trusts – some people felt that if high risk trusts were allowed, it would affect the general reputation unit trusts had of being relatively safe and thereby discourage investors altogether.

One type uses futures contracts to match the performance of an index. Buying futures is cheaper than buying each individual share, so most of the trust's money can be kept in cash, earning interest, which is paid out as income distributions. The trust tracks only the capital value of the index, ignoring share dividends, but with the interest, the total return should be roughly equivalent.

These are called 'bull' funds and are designed for investors who think the market will rise. There are also 'bear' funds, designed for those who think it will fall, which produce the exact opposite of the index movement: when it falls, the trust price rises by an equivalent amount.

Geared futures and options trusts involve higher risk with the potential for greater reward. For example, a 'two times geared' trust would give double exposure: if the index rises by 10 per cent, the trust price will rise by 20 per cent, but falls will also be doubled. However, as with any unit trust, your loss is limited to your initial investment.

A third type uses futures and options in a hedging role to reduce risk. The effect is that when the market is falling, the value of the fund should fall by less than the index, so that losses are cut, while in a flat market returns should be enhanced. In rising markets, however, the fund may underperform the index, so some growth potential may be sacrificed in return for the protection against a fall.

The mechanics of futures and options contracts are described more fully in Chapter 5.

Warrant trusts

Spring 1994 saw the launch of the first unit trust to invest in warrants. These may be issued by trading companies, investment trusts and offshore companies and it is intended that the unit trust will hold a mix of all three.

The mechanics of warrants are explained in Chapter 5. The main point to bear in mind is that the price of a warrant is generally much less than that of its related share, but price movements of the two are broadly in line. This means that the proportionate movement in the warrant price will be much greater: if the share price rises, the gain on the warrant can be several times as much, but losses will be similarly magnified.

Because of this volatility, the unit trust should be considered a relatively high risk investment, although the risk is tempered to some extent by the spread of holdings and the facility to switch heavily into cash if the market is unattractive.

Protected trusts

There is no doubt that, historically, the stock market has provided much better returns than either cash or fixed interest securities. But the short-term volatility of equities puts many people off. Protected trusts are an attempt to capture most of the upside of equities while limiting, or even eliminating, any losses. They do this by using part of the fund to buy derivatives – put or call options on the chosen index.

Some funds have a fixed investment period, at the end of which you are guaranteed your original money back plus a proportion of the growth in the relevant index (or indices). You may take money out before then, but in that case the guarantee is lost. Other funds have no fixed term but lock in gains and protect against loss on a rolling quarterly basis. This has the advantage of flexibility, but the returns may be limited. For example, one type uses 'put' options to guarantee that investors will never lose more than 5 per cent of their initial investment over a given period. At outset it sets a minimum selling price for units which depends on whether the stock market has gone up or down. If the unit price has risen by 10 per cent or more over the period, the minimum price will be set at 5 per cent below the current unit value, locking in the gains that have been made. If, on the other hand, the market has fallen, the selling price will be set at 95 per cent of the previous minimum. Unlike other guaranteed funds, investors can sell their holdings at any time and still take advantage of the guaranteed minimum price.

The trouble with all protection is that it comes at a cost: the part of your money that is used to buy the 'insurance' is not earning you a return.

The newest fund, at the time of writing, uses around 14 per cent of the sum invested to buy options, so in a rising market you could lose out on a significant amount of growth. The guarantee is 100 per cent of your money back if you withdraw it after three, five or seven years – but you could lose up to 15 per cent if you withdraw at any other time. With this fund, the guarantee is based only on your original investment, so if the market rises strongly for a few years the guarantee will effectively become worthless – but you would still be paying for it, in terms of not getting the full benefit of the market increase.

If market volatility is likely to give you sleepless nights, then protected trusts could be attractive. But it is important to make sure you understand exactly what is being guaranteed and what you are paying for, as well as any limits on access to your money.

Unit trusts and tax

In the 1993 Budget, the basic rate of income tax on dividends was reduced from 25 per cent to 20 per cent. Dividends from a unit trust are paid or reinvested net of this 20 per cent tax and the investor receives a tax credit for the amount paid. Basic and lower rate taxpayers have no further income tax liability, while higher rate taxpayers must pay an additional 20 per cent and non-taxpayers can reclaim the 20 per cent paid.

From April 1999, however, the tax credit will be halved to 10 per cent. The calculation of tax will change, so that taxpayers will be left in the same position as before: higher rate taxpayers having to pay another 20 per cent and the rest paying nothing more. But non-taxpayers will no longer have any reclaim facility, meaning their income will be reduced.

The new rules for capital gains tax, outlined in Chapter 1, may also affect unit trust investors. Trusts themselves have no liability on their dealings, but investors may be liable on gains made when they sell. These can be offset using the annual exempt allowance, which is £6800 for the 1998/99 tax year. Gains will also be eligible for the new taper relief that has replaced indexation – and this is where a problem could arise.

Taper relief starts to apply when you have held an investment for three complete years, building up to a maximum after 10 years. So the longer you hold your investments, the less likely you are to be liable for tax. But if you reinvest dividends, by buying further units, each new purchase will have its own timescale for taper relief. Over 10 years, in a trust with typical half-yearly distributions of income, you would have effectively made 21 purchases, including your original investment. Sorting out any tax liability could become extremely complicated.

The way round this is to buy accumulation units, which automatically roll up dividends and reflect the value in their price. There are no actual new purchases of units, so taper relief will simply be based on the initial purchase. Unfortunately, accumulation units have rather gone out of fashion and are no longer available on many trusts, so unit trust groups may need to rethink this to avoid a nightmare for their investors.

Special facilities for the investor

Share exchange schemes
Unit trust groups run various schemes designed to encourage investors to buy their units. Most groups offer 'share exchange' schemes for people who want to sell direct holdings in shares to invest in unit trusts instead. This has become increasingly popular for privatisation issues.

There will always be a cost advantage to the investor. Occasionally the managers may want to keep your shares for their own trusts, in which case they may pay you the offer price for the shares, or a mid-market price, rather than the bid price less selling expenses which you would receive if you sold them privately. Otherwise, you will be paid the bid price but the managers will either bear the sale costs themselves or offer a discount.

Regular savings schemes

As well as accepting lump sums, many unit trust groups offer regular savings schemes, starting from a minimum of around £50 a month. As a rule there are no penalties for stopping or taking money out, and lump sums can also be added in at any time. Income would not normally be paid out, as the administration would be too complex, so trusts which offer accumulation units are preferable.

Even if you have a lump sum to invest, it can be better to 'drip feed' it into a trust over a period rather than put it all in at once. This is due to a phenomenon known as pound-cost averaging. The argument is fairly straightforward: if you invest a bit at a time, you will benefit from times when the price falls because the same amount of money will buy more units. With a fluctuating price, the average cost of units over a period will be less than their average price. On the other hand, if you buy all at one go, the price could be at a peak or a trough, so timing becomes all-important – and few people can be confident of getting it right.

Table 6.3 gives an example of the mechanics of pound-cost averaging, using large price swings to clarify the effect.

Schemes for a regular income
Table 6.3 *Pound-cost averaging*

Month of purchase	Unit price	Number of units bought for £50
1	100p	50
2	80p	63
3	125p	40
4	90p	56
5	85p	59
6	110p	45
Average price	98.3p	313 units bought for £300; average price paid: 95.8p

Only a small number of trusts pay a monthly income, but many groups now offer monthly income portfolio schemes. Most trusts pay out dividends two or four times a year, so by packaging together three or six trusts with different distribution dates, a scheme can produce monthly payments.

The trusts in a package may not all pay out on the same day of every month and, more particularly, are not likely to pay the same amount. A refinement is to incorporate a deposit account in the scheme which will collect all the dividends and then pay out level amounts each month.

There are two drawbacks to packaged schemes offered by unit trust groups. First, you are restricted to the trusts of that group, which may not all perform well. Second, the trusts included in the package may not be ideal for your requirements. Several schemes include a gilt or fixed-interest trust, which can boost the income level at the outset but provides little opportunity for capital growth and thereby rising income over time.

The alternative is to put together your own package, choosing the type of trusts you want from different groups. Several professional advisers run schemes of this type or can assemble one to match your particular needs. In some cases you can choose the level of income you want, but you need to remember that if you choose a level higher than the trusts are actually paying out, units would have to be cashed in to make up the difference. Over time this would make progressive inroads into your capital, so you would do better to settle for a lower income to start with and hope capital growth will boost it.

Keeping track of your investment

Generally, managers revalue at least once a day and prices are quoted in both the *Financial Times* and *The Daily Telegraph*. However, most groups now deal on a 'forward pricing' basis, which means that the deal is carried out at the price set by the next valuation. The remainder use 'historic pricing', which means the price used is that of the most recent valuation, but they must deal at a forward price if it is requested and will also move to forward pricing in certain circumstances, for example if there is a large movement in the market.

So the prices published in newspapers are not necessarily what you will be quoted if you sell that day, but unless a very large deal has just gone through, there is unlikely to be a substantial difference from one valuation to the next. The *Financial Times* indicates whether dealing is on a forward or historic basis, and also shows the cancellation price, so you can see whether a trust is on a bid or offer basis.

Another source of information is the manager's report on a trust, which is usually sent out to unit holders twice a year. Among other things, this will list details of the trust's holdings and any changes made since the previous report; it will also give a commentary on performance and how this ties in with the markets in which the trust invests. Although the information will be somewhat out of date by the time you receive it, it does provide a guide to the general strategy being followed.

How to invest

Investments can be made through an intermediary, such as a bank, stockbroker or financial adviser, or you can deal directly with the unit trust group by telephone or post. Advertisements in the national press may also carry a coupon form for buying units.

Initially, you will receive a contract note, which gives details of the amount invested, the price and the number of units bought, and subsequently you will be sent the certificate. To sell, you can simply send the certificate to the group and a cheque will be issued within a few days.

Some professional advisers provide unit trust portfolio management services, usually for a minimum sum of £10,000 or so. These are looked at in Chapter 7.

Offshore funds

'Offshore' is a slightly misleading term, conjuring up visions of exotic islands where the very rich go to escape the rigours of taxation. Offshore funds can, indeed, be based in places such as Bermuda and the Cayman Islands, but the more prosaic definition is simply a location that is outside the UK mainland. The traditional bases for funds that might attract UK investors are Jersey, Guernsey and the Isle of Man, but the development of EU regulations has made Luxembourg a popular choice – the Channel Islands and the Isle of Man are outside the European Union (EU) – and more recently Dublin has established an offshore centre.

Offshore funds are collective investments but can take various forms; they may be open-ended, like unit trusts, or closed-ended, like investment trusts. The exact structure and legal framework will depend on where they are based.

Regulation

Moves to allow cross-border dealing in collective investments within the EU have resulted in an array of rules and jargon. For a start, European funds are often referred to by the French acronyms 'SICAV' and 'SICAF'. The former are open-ended funds, which means the size is unrestricted and will increase or decrease according to demand and supply; the latter are closed-ended, which means they have a fixed amount of capital.

Open-ended funds can apply for the status of UCITS (Undertakings for Collective Investment in Transferable Securities), which is granted by the regulatory authority in the country of origin. The main UCITS rules are drafted by the EU, but stipulations on how and where a fund may invest come under local regulations and may vary from country to country. At the time of writing, cash funds and funds of funds cannot qualify as UCITS, but the EU directive is being amended to encompass them. Once a fund has UCITS status, it can be freely marketed throughout member states, subject to marketing rules laid down by each individual country.

The *Financial Times* lists offshore funds as being one of three types: SIB recognised, Regulated and Other. The first category refers to funds that have been approved by the Securities and Investments Board, which means that they may be freely marketed in the UK, in the same way as unit trusts. Funds with UCITS status get this approval more or less automatically.

Funds based outside the EU can also apply for SIB recognition if their country of origin has 'designated territory' status. This is granted by the SIB to countries where the local regulations and compensation scheme arrangements are deemed to be of similar standard to those applying in the UK. From the investor's point of view, if a fund is SIB recognised, it is not too important where it is based, as it will be subject to much the same level of regulation as UK funds.

Regulated funds are those that are authorised under local regulations but have not obtained SIB recognition. This does not necessarily mean that they are less well regulated; it may simply be that the managers are not looking to attract UK investors or, in the case of European funds, that they wish to invest outside the limits of the UCITS rules. These funds can still be sold to UK investors, but only through private placements; they cannot use direct advertising or mailing.

Some countries allow funds to be set up and operated without coming under regulation. These are listed in the *Financial Times* under the heading of 'Other Offshore Funds' and are often aimed at institutional rather than private investors.

Taxation

For a UK investor, offshore funds are subject to one of two tax regimes. The fund may have 'distributor' status, in which case it must pay out at least 85 per cent of its income, which is paid gross but is subject to tax at the investor's normal rate. Any capital gains made on selling out of the fund will be liable to capital gains tax, subject to the usual annual exempt allowance.

Alternatively, the fund may be of the 'accumulator' type, which means all income is rolled up within the fund. No income tax is payable while you are invested, but when you come to sell, all gains are liable to income tax, whether they derive from income or capital growth.

Which of the two is preferable depends on your circumstances. If you are a higher rate taxpayer now, but expect to drop down to basic rate in future, then with an accumulator fund you can defer the tax bill to that point. Alternatively, if you are looking for capital growth, a distributor fund would mean a small tax bill each year, but the bulk of the return would be in capital gains, against which you have the annual tax-exempt allowance (£6800 for the 1998/99 tax year).

The problem with distributor status is that it is only granted for a year at a time, and in retrospect. Although the income distribution rule is fairly easy to comply with, there is another rule that bans 'trading'; this is designed to prevent funds cheating by turning income into capital gains, but the wording is rather vague and funds have occasionally been caught out. If you cash in your holding and distributor status is then refused, you can face an unexpected income tax bill.

Some years ago, when income tax went up to 60 per cent against a capital gains tax rate of 30 per cent, this was a severe penalty. Now that the two rates have been equalised, it is less drastic, but there is still a disadvantage because of the exempt allowance for capital gains tax.

Pros and cons

With so many onshore unit trusts and other funds available, the obvious question is, why look offshore? Originally these funds were primarily aimed at those who were non-resident for tax purposes and could therefore gain a tax advantage; there were few attractions for the UK investor. But the developments in EU regulations, combined with certain restrictions on UK-based unit trusts, have meant that a number of companies are now finding that an offshore base presents greater opportunities.

The major feature that is driving the UK unit trust companies to set up offshore is the facility to pay dividends gross. This is particularly attractive for funds that focus on producing income, such as bond funds and, in future, cash funds. Although the income is ultimately taxable in the hands of a UK investor, there may be cash flow advantages in gross payments, and for non-taxpayers it saves the trouble of reclaiming tax paid.

Another issue is investment flexibility: offshore funds can invest in areas that are not available to unit trusts, such as currencies and commodities. Even where the investments are of the same type, the restrictions may be fewer or non-existent. For example, a unit trust may invest only up to 10 per cent of its portfolio, in total, in countries that are not on the SIB's list of recognised stock exchanges. A Dublin-based UCITS fund, on the other hand, could put up to 10 per cent in each of these countries, and some may be wholly unrestricted.

A potential drawback is that, even if a fund is SIB recognised, it does not come under the UK compensation scheme. In some cases, the local regulations may in fact offer a higher degree of protection, but some areas do not operate any compensation scheme. You should always check that the fund assets are held by an independent custodian and, for preference, stick to those run by a well-known name.

Offshore funds are often based on a single price, to which the front-end fee is added, rather than having a bid/offer spread like unit trusts, so they may be slightly cheaper to buy into. Annual charges, on the other hand, may be rather higher than for onshore trusts because, in addition to the management charge, the fund may have to meet the fees of the auditor and the custodian or trustee.

Umbrella funds

Umbrella funds, the first of which appeared in 1984, technically consist of a single overall fund which comprises several different sub-funds or share classes. One of the main advantages for some time was that investors could switch their holdings between the different sub-funds without being liable to capital gains tax, which would only arise when they sold out of the whole fund. Unfortunately, this loophole has since been closed and CGT now arises on all switches, just as it would if you moved from one unit trust to another run by the same group.

However, there may still be an advantage in cost terms, as the initial fee will be waived for switches between sub-funds. Some companies also run a parallel portfolio management service, which will look after your investments within the fund and make appropriate switches, but there is an extra charge for this. The main drawback of umbrella funds is that you are committing yourself to just one company, which may not have the best performing funds across the full range.

Another point to watch out for is whether the fund intends to apply for distributor status. This is granted to the umbrella fund as a unit, which means each separate sub-fund must comply with the regulations. If one fails, the fund as a whole fails, which has tax repercussions for the investor as outlined above.

How to invest

As mentioned, funds that have obtained SIB recognition can be freely marketed in the same way as unit trusts, but others can only advertise indirectly, by offering to send out a prospectus. In either case, but particularly the latter, it is probably worth while consulting a professional adviser.

Open-ended investment companies

While unit trusts with UCITS status can theoretically be sold throughout the EU, in practice they are not attractive to Europeans, who prefer the single price and the tax structure of a SICAV. As a result, several UK companies have set up offshore operations, mainly in Luxembourg and Dublin, to run SICAVs. But as SICAVs can be sold in the UK, and the range of funds offered generally parallels the groups' unit trusts, some are questioning whether there is a need to run two separate operations.

Obviously, it would be a considerable loss to the UK investment industry if management groups abandoned unit trusts in favour of offshore SICAVs. As a result, the government introduced the idea of SICAV-style funds, known as Open-Ended Investment Companies (OEICs), that could be operated and sold in the UK. OEICs are something of a cross between unit trusts and investment trusts. Like unit trusts, they are 'open-ended': shares are created and cancelled according to demand, with no set minimum or maximum number. But like investment trusts, they are companies, with quoted shares and a board of one or more directors.

OEICs have no bid/offer spread but a single price, to which an initial or dealing charge can be added. They may also issue more than one class of share, which may be differently priced or denominated in different currencies. In this case, they will be run in much the same way as umbrella funds.

While the Treasury regulations for OEICs came into effect on 6 December 1996, details of their tax treatment were not finalised until last year and it is only recently that the first funds have appeared. However, several investment groups have now announced plans to convert their unit trusts to OEICs.

There are two main advantages to OEICs. First, the single

price structure, with the initial charge added on, should be simpler and clearer – you can see the charge you are paying, whereas, with a unit trust, it is hidden within the bid/offer spread. Second, because OEICs can operate as umbrella funds, several unit trusts can be converted into sub-funds of a single OEIC. This should allow economies of scale and so cut costs.

But there are also drawbacks. Because of the single price, investors can sell out of a fund for a better price than the manager could actually get for selling the underlying shares and if sales are high this will dilute the value of the fund for remaining investors. Hence OEICs can charge a 'dilution levy' in such cases, which effectively brings back the concept of a bid/offer spread.

When unit trusts are converted, there is likely to be some merging, which could mean a change in the asset allocation or investment objective of each trust. It could also bring an increase in charges for some investors; if, for example, a low-cost trust is merged with a higher cost one, the ongoing charge may be pitched in the middle, in which case some investors will benefit while others end up paying more.

Finally, the umbrella structure could raise problems if one of the sub-funds defaults in any way, as the other funds could be obliged to bail it out. Thus you could be invested in a fund which is doing very nicely and then suddenly lose a chunk of your money to shore up an ailing fund elsewhere in the umbrella. Unit trusts, on the other hand, operate individually so are 'ring-fenced' against this possibility.

Where to find out more

The Association of Unit Trusts and Investment Funds produces general performance figures and other statistical data, but does not offer advice or recommendation on individual trusts or management groups. It runs the Unit Trust Information Service, which can provide an introductory booklet, a unit trust user's handbook and a directory of trusts, and can be contacted on 0181 207 1361 or by writing to 65 Kingsway, London WC2B 6TD. The groups themselves also have a range of literature on their own products.

The *Unit Trust Yearbook* is published annually by Financial Times Business Enterprises and contains details of both management groups and all unit trusts available.

Unit trust prices are quoted in daily newspapers such as *The Daily Telegraph* and the *Financial Times;* the *Financial Times* also publishes the prices of offshore funds.

7

Unit Trusts and Offshore Funds (2): The Investment Choice

In recent years there has been a degree of consolidation in the unit trust market, which has slightly reduced the number of companies operating in this field. Nevertheless, the number of trusts has continued to grow steadily, as Table 7.1 shows. With well over 1600

Table 7.1 *Authorised unit trusts*

Year	Number of trusts	Number of companies
1981	529	93
1982	553	99
1983	630	91
1984	687	102
1985	806	110
1986	964	121
1987	1137	139
1988	1255	153
1989	1379	162
1990	1407	154
1991	1400	157
1992	1456	151
1993	1528	156
1994	1559	162
1995	1633	160
1996	1676	159
1997	1680	153

Source: Association of Unit Trusts and Investment Funds

available, it is difficult to know where to start, especially as many have similar aims and specialisations. The best way is probably to decide first what type of trust you are after, and then to choose between the different management groups offering that type.

On the most basic approach, trusts can be divided into four types:

1. trusts whose primary objective is to produce income;
2. trusts whose primary objective is to produce capital growth, either with a general portfolio or specialising in a particular country or sector;
3. trusts that aim to provide a mix between income and growth;
4. cash trusts.

The first three of these groups may invest in the UK or overseas (or, in the case of international trusts, both). The fourth type is in a sense a sub-section of the first, since the aim is income, but cash trusts differ from others in that they do not involve any capital risk.

Unit trust categories

Looking in more detail, the Association of Unit Trusts and Investment Funds sets out 25 separate categories of trust for the purpose of making performance comparisons. These are grouped under seven headings, as follows.

UK funds
All trusts with at least 80 per cent of their investments in the UK.

UK Growth and Income
Trusts with at least 80 per cent of their assets in UK equities, which aim to produce a combination of income and growth. These trusts must also aim to have a yield of between 80 and 110 per cent of the yield of the FTSE All-Share Index.

UK Equity Income
Trusts which invest at least 80 per cent of their assets in UK equities and which aim to have a yield of more than 110 per cent of the yield of the All-Share Index.

Lump-Sum Investment

UK Growth
Trusts which invest at least 80 per cent of their assets in UK equities and have a primary objective of achieving capital growth.

UK Smaller Companies
Trusts which invest at least 80 per cent of their assets in the shares of companies which form part of the Hoare Govett UK Smaller Companies Extended Index.

UK Gilts
Trusts which invest at least 80 per cent of their assets in UK government securities.

Other UK Fixed Interest
Trusts which invest at least 80 per cent of their assets in corporate or public fixed interest securities.

UK Equity & Bond Income
Trusts which invest at least 80 per cent of their assets in the UK, but less than 80 per cent in either UK equities or UK gilt and fixed-interest securities, and which aim to have a yield of 120 per cent or more of the FTSE All-Share Index.

UK Equity & Bond
Trusts which invest at least 80 per cent of their assets in the UK, but less than 80 per cent in either UK equities or UK gilt and fixed-interest securities, and which aim to yield no more than 120 per cent of the FTSE All-Share Index.

Managed
Trusts whose portfolio contains at least three asset classes, with at least 50% denominated in sterling or hedged to sterling; at least 35 per cent must be held in UK equities and at least 10 per cent in non-UK equities. A balance of 10 per cent or more should be held in one or more of the following: UK gilts or bonds, non-UK government or corporate bonds,

cash or property. The property element must not exceed 10 per cent of the portfolio.

International
Trusts with a portfolio that is less than 80 per cent invested in any one geographical area (with the exception of the International Fixed Interest sector).

International Equity Income
Trusts which invest at least 80 per cent of their assets in equities and which aim to achieve a yield of above 110 per cent of the yield of the FT-Actuaries World Index.

International Growth
Trusts which invest at least 80 per cent of their assets in equities and which have a primary objective of capital growth.

International Fixed Interest
Trusts which invest at least 80 per cent of their assets in fixed-interest stocks. This includes all such trusts, regardless of whether they have more than 80 per cent in a particular geographic sector, unless it is the UK, in which case they come under the UK heading.

International Equity & Bond
Trusts which have less than 80 per cent of their assets in either equities or fixed-interest securities.

Japan
Trusts which invest at least 80 per cent of their assets in Japanese securities.

Far East

Including Japan
Trusts which invest at least 80 per cent of their assets in Far Eastern securities including a Japanese content that is less than 80 per cent.

Lump-Sum Investment

Excluding Japan
Trusts which invest at least 80 per cent of their assets in Far Eastern securities but exclude any Japanese content.

North America
Trusts which invest at least 80 per cent of their assets in North American securities.

Europe
Trusts which invest at least 80 per cent of their assets in European securities, including the UK, but not exceeding 80 per cent in the UK.

Global Emerging Markets
Trusts which invest at least 80 per cent of their assets indirectly or directly in emerging markets, as defined by the World Bank, without geographical restriction. Indirect investment, such as China shares listed in Hong Kong, should not exceed 50 per cent of the portfolio.

Specialist
Trusts which invest their assets in a specialist area, regardless of any geographical specialisation they may also have.

Commodity & Energy
Trusts which invest at least 80 per cent of their assets in commodity or energy securities.

Property
Trusts which invest at least 80 per cent of their assets either directly in property itself or indirectly in property company securities.

Investment Trust Units
Trusts which are able to invest only in the shares of investment trust companies.

Fund of Funds
Trusts which are able to invest only in other authorised unit trust schemes.

Money Market
Trusts which invest at least 80 per cent of their assets in money market instruments.

Index Bear Funds
Funds which are designed to inversely track the performance of an index by using derivatives.

In addition, there are exempt trusts and personal pension trusts. Neither are relevant to the ordinary investor; exempt trusts are available only to tax-exempt institutions, such as pension funds and charities, while personal pension trusts are for use only with pension contracts (see Chapter 11).

Table 7.2 shows some past performance results for each of the categories outlined above. These figures, which are compiled on a regular basis by the Association of Unit Trusts and Investment Funds, show the realisation value of £1000 invested over various time periods in the median fund in each sector – the middle one in the performance rankings, rather than the average.

Past performance, as the saying goes, is not necessarily a guide to the future; as the table demonstrates, different sectors may come to the fore over different periods. It is also important, in looking at figures of this type, to check exactly what they purport to show. Unit trusts are usually shown on an 'offer to bid' basis, which reflects the cash-in value if you had bought and sold on the respective dates. Alternatively, figures may be on an 'offer to offer' basis; this takes out the effect of the price spread and the initial charge, but can give an idea of what the manager has achieved. Statistics are also generally quoted with net income reinvested, which compounds the capital growth; if you are investing to earn income to spend, then obviously the capital return will be rather less.

Also shown in the table, for the purposes of comparison, are the results of £1000 invested in a building society higher interest account and the equivalent figures for the FTSE All-Share Index. Index comparisons should be treated with caution, as an index does not include dealing costs or the charges encountered with a trust. In the case of an overseas trust, there are also currency considerations; the return in sterling terms may vary significantly from the market trend shown by the index.

Table 7.2   *Past performance of unit trusts*

| Sector | Average value of £1000 invested | | |
	5 years	10 years	15 years
Commodity & Energy	1185.23	1682.77	2182.29
Europe	2492.37	4640.54	11,241.87
Far East excluding Japan	974.52	2614.68	4940.32
Far East including Japan	887.51	1521.48	4610.74
Fund of Funds	1703.09	2619.35	–
Futures & Options	1582.63	–	–
Global Emerging Markets	1270.23	2768.56	–
Index Bear Funds	574.85	–	–
International Equity Income	1811.59	3149.76	7509.83
International Fixed Interest	1149.86	1871.61	2723.38
International Equity & Bond	1675.35	2896.79	10,396.16
International Growth	1806.42	3200.59	6794.49
Investment Trust Units	1892.78	3379.14	7567.10
Japan	634.76	787.78	3394.19
Managed Funds	1803.18	3276.95	7104.56
Money Market	1230.58	–	–
North America	2252.24	4846.18	6117.56
Property	1678.63	–	–
UK Equity & Bond	2003.71	3371.65	11,559.21
UK Equity & Bond Income	1789.76	2646.67	6961.81
UK Equity Income	2026.05	3175.07	10,064.18
UK Fixed Interest	1493.35	2055.50	3629.04
UK Gilt	1405.70	2102.06	3284.12
UK Growth	2067.47	3132.34	8455.74
UK Growth & Income	2060.06	3292.33	9084.19
UK Smaller Companies	1995.14	2554.47	7435.51

Note: A gap indicates that no trusts have been in existence that long. All figures are on an offer to bid basis, with net income reinvested, as at 30 April 1998.

Source: Reuters Hindsight

Investment aims

The first step in deciding where to put your money is to determine whether you are looking for income or capital growth. The two are not necessarily mutually exclusive; while trusts that go all out for capital growth will not produce any income to speak of, there are others that combine both objectives. Similarly, the strategies pursued by equity income trusts can often produce good growth, even where that is a secondary aim.

Income trusts

If you are looking for income, you need to bear in mind that investing in equities will not provide you with very high income at the outset. Even so-called 'high income' trusts may yield only around 6 per cent gross which, at the time of writing, beats a building society but not by much.

The advantage of investing in equities, however, is that they should produce some capital appreciation and a rising income over time, while a building society deposit will be static in value and the income will rise and fall with interest rates.

The income comparison is illustrated in Table 7.3, which

Table 7.3 *Annual gross income from a UK equity income trust, a UK equity & bond income trust and a building society 30-day notice account*

£1000 invested 30 April 1988

Year	Equity income trust (£)	Equity & bond trust (£)	Building society (£)
1	56.58	62.14	104.18
2	65.18	74.87	126.75
3	69.86	74.60	129.05
4	70.78	74.82	90.34
5	67.73	67.11	63.90
6	61.49	63.82	43.07
7	62.78	71.90	43.39
8	72.61	77.00	40.40
9	77.32	78.87	28.46
10	86.62	80.46	38.71

Note: Figures relate to the annual gross income paid by the average UK equity income unit trust, UK equity & bond income unit trust and a building society 30-day notice account with a minimum balance of £500, 30 April 1988 – 30 April 1998.

Source: Reuters Hindsight

shows the gross annual income paid by an equity income trust and a building society higher rate account over a ten-year period. The building society provided higher income for the first six years, but was then overtaken by the trust, which would also have grown in capital value. The table also shows the gross annual income from a corporate bond trust, which beats the building society after just two years.

It is possible to get a higher initial income from a unit trust by choosing one of the specialist types: those investing in gilts and fixed-interest securities, convertibles or preference shares. These can offer a starting yield of around 6 to 8 per cent gross. But again, with these trusts there is much less potential for capital growth on the assets, hence the income return is less likely to improve over time.

In general, there is a limit to the amount of genuine income that can be produced, and to go above that level will entail some sacrifice of capital or capital growth potential. A couple of trusts launched in 1993 were specifically designed to convert future capital growth into current income, by the use of options. The trusts invest mainly in blue chip shares and special loan securities, which produce a reasonable base yield, and then also write options, on which a premium is earned. The premium boosts the level of income, but the effect of the options is that any capital growth above 4 or 5 per cent is given up.

Options are also used to limit falls in the capital value, but there is no capital guarantee and in certain market conditions there could be a progressive drop. Of course, this is true of any trust, but with these there is less chance of making it up again in future, since the capital growth potential is restricted. There is also no guarantee on the income: one trust reduced its level from 10 per cent net to 9 per cent.

Even with equity trusts the yield can differ. As a rule, the higher the target yield, the greater the constraints on the manager and the more growth prospects may have to be sacrificed. So trusts with a more modest pay-out now may prove more rewarding in the long run.

But the pursuit of income can work to advantage on the growth side. The yield on a share moves broadly in inverse relationship to its price – if the price falls and the dividend remains the same, it will represent a higher yield. So it may then become an attractive holding for an income unit trust. If the share price subsequently recovers, it will bring a boost to the capital growth on the trust. Of course, as the price rises, the yield will fall, so the manager will sooner or later have to sell in favour of another higher yielding stock. But although he may then miss out on further growth prospects, he equally avoids the danger of hanging on too long and seeing the share price fall back again, so it can turn out to be a useful discipline.

To a large extent, then, if a trust has a good track record for its dividend payments, the capital performance should also be satisfactory. Although past results cannot be relied upon, a consistent dividend history is a fair indication of a manager's ability, as these trusts have a fairly broad range of investment possibilities and are therefore less dominated by market movements than a more specialised vehicle such as a commodity trust.

So the starting-point for choosing an income trust is to weigh up your needs for income today as against income in the future. If you are looking for immediate high income over a short time-span, a fixed interest or preference trust may be suitable. If you are prepared to settle for less now to have more in the future, then think about an equity-based trust or one with mixed holdings. In the latter case, check out the proportions held in ordinary shares as against preference shares or fixed-interest securities; again, the higher the content of ordinary equities, the better should be the prospects of a rising income. Another important point is the level of annual management charge. This will normally be paid for out of the trust's income, so the higher the charge, the less will be left to distribute to unit holders.

If the trust is fairly new, you can only go by its portfolio structure and the charges. If it has a track record, you can also check the dividend history; ideally, payments should at least have kept pace with inflation. Finally, check the capital growth; although this may not be your top priority it will underpin the income return.

Overseas income trusts

The bulk of trusts focusing on income are invested in the UK, but there are a growing number based on overseas markets.

Some of these invest in particular geographical areas, such as North America or Europe, while others are international in scope. These latter trusts are classified under two sector headings, equity income and fixed interest, which have the same characteristics as the equivalent UK trusts.

The overseas equity income trusts tend to have lower yields than their UK counterparts because the stock markets themselves have lower yields, and the management charge may also be higher, which will detract from the return. You should also bear in mind the currency factor, which can add to the degree of risk involved.

Special schemes

As mentioned in Chapter 6, there are a number of schemes available that are designed to produce a monthly income by packaging together trusts with different pay-out dates. If you are looking for regular income, a package has the advantage over an individual monthly-paying trust – of which there are around a dozen – that a spread of investments gives a spread of risk. There will, of course, be a higher minimum investment than for a single trust.

Set packages have the drawback that there may be little or no choice of which trusts are included, which means there may be a higher fixed-interest content than you would like, and also commit you to one management group. The alternative is to put together your own package from among all the income trusts available. If you are prepared to manage with uneven payments, so much the better; aiming to get a similar level of payment on the same day each month will restrict the choice and may mean a sacrifice of overall performance.

Generalist trusts

As mentioned, income and growth are not mutually exclusive targets, as there are a number of trusts which offer elements of both, either through a combination of higher and lower yielding equities, or through a mixture of equities with fixed-interest securities.

These generalist trusts are often regarded as the plain vanilla of the industry, worthy but dull. Most groups have one, and some even have more than one, but they are rarely likely to be the subject of eye-catching advertisements. The yield is generally in the region of 3 per cent gross and they are expected to show steady, rather than spectacular, performance.

Equity & Bond funds are those that mix equities with fixed-interest stocks and have less than 80 per cent in either. The yield can be rather higher than on general funds, depending on the mix of holdings; the greater the proportion of fixed-interest securities, the higher the yield but, as mentioned in the last section, this entails lower growth prospects. Most of these trusts, however, steer a middle course between the two in the same way as Growth & Income trusts.

Although they may never top the performance listings, Table 7.4 shows that the returns are not to be scorned. Certain specialist sectors may well do better, but others will do a lot worse, so unless you have confidence in your powers of selection, or sufficient money to put together a range of specialist holdings, a generalist trust can be a good home for a first investment. Equally, if you are building up a portfolio, a general trust can form a stable core, from which you can venture into higher risk holdings.

Table 7.4 *Past performance of generalist funds*

| Sector | Average value of £1000 invested | | |
	5 years	10 years	15 years
UK Growth & Income	2060.66	3292.33	9084.19
UK Equity & Bond	2003.71	3371.65	11,559.21
Managed	1803.18	3276.95	7104.56
International Equity & Bond	1675.35	2896.79	10,396.16

Note: Figures are on an offer to bid basis, with net income reinvested, as at 30 April 1998.

Source: Reuters Hindsight

Growth trusts

By far the majority of unit trusts available are designed to produce capital growth. They comprise a large variety of types, from broadly based international trusts to those specialising in a particular geographical area, such as the UK or Japan, and those concentrating on a particular industry or market sector. Given this huge range, it is impossible to make generalisations and not easy to set about making a choice. At any one time, different markets will be in the ascendancy, and the time-scale you have in mind for your investment will also have a bearing on where the best prospects lie. However, it is possible to narrow down the choice by considering the following alternatives.

UK versus overseas

Many UK investors naturally incline towards the home market, and there are arguments to support this. For one thing, the returns from a unit trust are in sterling, so if you invest in an overseas trust you are exposed to a currency risk on top of the market risk. Some trusts aim to offset this by using 'hedging' techniques, but that in itself can have certain risks as well as costs.

Second, the stock market will respond to and reflect general factors in the economy, which may be appropriate since your other financial arrangements will be subject to similar influences. On the other hand, the major world economies move very much in line with each other anyway.

Also, any investment in a single market, even one the size of the UK, has limitations in terms of choice of stocks and spread of risk. If you are planning to build up a portfolio of any size, or you already have other UK investments, you should think of spreading your investments further afield for better balance.

International versus single country

If you decide to look abroad, you have the choice between single country trusts and those that maintain a global spread. Single country trusts range from those based on large markets, such as the US, to much more specialised types; for example, trusts focused on Switzerland or Thailand.

The same arguments apply to investing in a single overseas market as to investing in the UK: there is less spread of risk. This is particularly true in the smaller markets, where there may be a limited number of stocks available. There may also be problems or delays in buying and selling which can affect performance and add to the risk. For investors seeking to build an international portfolio, perhaps mainly through direct equity holdings, these trusts can offer convenient access to smaller markets; otherwise they give the chance of high rewards if you are prepared to accept high risk. The more cautious investor, on the other hand, will do better with an international trust or a selection of those based on the larger world markets.

General versus specialised

As well as trusts with a geographical specialisation, there are others which focus on a particular industry or market sector. These may operate on a global basis, such as an international technology trust, or within one particular market, such as a Japanese Smaller Companies trust.

Like trusts with a geographical specialisation, these carry a higher degree of risk than a general or international trust. But whereas you could build a collection of holdings in different countries, it would not be feasible to cover every type of industry. Hence the attraction is less to create a market balance among your investments than to inject a higher risk/higher reward element. Smaller companies, for example, are much more volatile than larger ones; they rise faster, but can also fall faster. Similarly, recovery and special situations trusts seek to take advantage of stocks that are under-priced; if the expected improvement occurs, all well and good, but it depends on how well the manager makes his selections. Industry-specific trusts can be even more dramatic; gold trusts, for example, had a phenomenal run in 1980, but subsequently spent a long period in the wilderness.

Management style

Once you have decided where to invest, you then face the choice of management group. Again, there are no easy answers: no one investment strategy is proved to be right or wrong. However, there are certain considerations which may help to sort out what accords with your own views or needs.

Active versus passive

Some managers take a very active approach, turning over the

portfolio regularly in the search for value, while others operate on a longer term view. The former may have greater potential – if the manager gets it right – but the dealing costs will be higher and results may be more volatile.

Top down versus bottom up

This refers to the stock-picking approach of the manager. Some start from the top: country first (in the case of an international trust), then industry, then the specific share. Others build up from the bottom, choosing shares they think are attractive, with perhaps overall proportions for sectors or countries.

House style

Some management groups have an overall 'house style' within which the managers of individual trusts operate; this may be simply a matter of the risk/reward approach they adopt or may go further, in that, for example, if particular industries are favoured at a given time, they are represented across the range of trusts. In other cases, each trust manager operates at a very individual level. A house style may impose constraints, but the individual approach could lead to a change of fortune, or at any rate of philosophy, if one manager leaves and another takes over.

Hedging and liquidity

Where a trust invests overseas, the returns – which are expressed in sterling, of course – will be affected by exchange rate movements as well as market trends. In some cases the manager may 'hedge' part of the portfolio to neutralise the currency effects; this can – if it works – protect against losses, although it also means missing out on favourable movements and there is a cost involved. Others take the view that if you buy the market, you also buy the currency, and that the two should not be artificially separated.

Similar views are taken on liquidity. Some managers will move out into cash if the market is falling, while others believe it is up to the investor to decide by staying in or selling out of the trust. Obviously, switching out and perhaps buying back in later would mean the investor faced a new front-end charge, but if the trust goes into cash and subsequently reinvests there will be dealing costs, and there could be a loss if the timing is not judged accurately.

Size of fund

There is a theory that a small trust will tend to outperform a larger one. This has some logic, in that a small trust is more flexible and can therefore respond more quickly to changes in the market – assuming the manager interprets the trend correctly. Large funds operating in a small market may also be hampered by a limited choice of stocks.

Small trusts will obviously tend to hold fewer stocks, but larger ones also vary in whether they are widespread or concentrated. The fewer the holdings in the portfolio, the higher the risk/reward ratio, as a gain or loss in any one holding will have a greater proportional influence.

Location

Some groups run their overseas trusts entirely from a UK base, while others have local offices in the major markets. Naturally, there is much debate over which is better: the objective view from a distance or the 'feel' gained by being on the spot. In fact, those operating from the UK will normally make regular visits to the country and may also liaise with local brokers for information and – particularly in smaller markets – for dealing. Given the sophistication of global communications, one suspects there is not a great deal of difference, and certainly performance results do not point to either approach being consistently more successful.

New launches

One other theory on the relative merits of different trusts is that new launches will do well. This can depend on the reason for the launch and its timing. Some are 'bandwagon' products, investing in a market that is currently rising, in which case they are likely to look good to start with, particularly as they have new money to spend on the most attractive shares, while older trusts in the same market may be stuck with shares that have gone out of fashion.

The ideal timing, of course, is to launch just before a market goes up, to get the full benefit of the rise, but (aside from the difficulty of correctly predicting market movements) it is harder to attract money into a sector that is currently looking dull.

Are you an active investor?

One important question to consider before choosing a trust is whether you plan to monitor and alter your investment actively or simply want to invest and forget about it. In the latter case, you are likely to do best by sticking to fairly general trusts; the more specialist offerings are more volatile and need to be kept under supervision.

If you expect to be active and switch your holdings around between different trusts, this should influence your choice of management group. Of course, you are not bound to stick with the same group and there are drawbacks to doing so: no one group is going to top the performance tables with every trust it runs. But against that there is the advantage that switches from one trust to another within the same group attract a discount on the front-end charge, which can significantly cut the costs of active investment. So you should look for a group – or perhaps two or three – which have a wide range of funds and offer a good switching discount.

Portfolio management services

If you would like your investments to be actively managed, but lack the time or knowledge to do it yourself, there are a number of advisers who offer portfolio management services. These may be run on a discretionary or an advisory basis. In the first case, you would set out your basic aims, such as income or capital growth and the amount of risk you are prepared to accept, and the adviser would do the rest; you would be kept informed of changes to the portfolio and receive regular valuations, but would not be consulted on each deal.

With an advisory service, the adviser would consult you (and vice versa) before any change was made. The minimum for a discretionary service starts at about £10,000; for an advisory service it is likely to be higher, because of the extra work involved. Charging systems vary; the adviser may operate on the commissions he gets on each trust purchase, but it can be more efficient for both sides to rebate commission and charge an annual management fee.

Broker unit trusts

An alternative to a discretionary management service is a broker unit trust, offered by a number of professional advisers (not necessarily brokers). Often an adviser might be running a large number of individual portfolios on a discretionary basis and making similar investments and changes for each. By setting up a broker unit trust he can consolidate these portfolios into one fund, with a single transaction when he buys or sells, thus considerably reducing the administration.

The trust may invest directly into securities or through a range of unit trusts in a similar way to a fund of funds. In either case, it must have a defined investment objective and strategy and will be governed by the same regulations as an ordinary unit trust. Funds are normally valued daily and the prices are published in national newspapers.

The advantage for the investor is that his money is professionally managed, without the need for him to get involved in each transaction, but he still has access to the fund manager and a degree of personal service that he obviously would not get from the manager of an ordinary unit trust. There is, however, an extra layer of charges, as the adviser will charge a management fee, which needs to be weighed up against the 'added value' in terms of improved performance.

Offshore funds

For the UK investor, the appeal of offshore funds lies largely in the fact that they can offer investment in areas that are not open to onshore unit trusts, in particular, currencies and commodities.

Currency funds can be based on sterling or foreign currencies. Sterling funds can be deposit-based, offering the benefits of wholesale money market rates on short-term deposits, or invested in fixed-interest securities, which gives the prospect of capital gains – or a combination of both. Foreign currency funds operate in a similar way, but have the added dimension of exchange rate movements against sterling, which can generate capital gains or losses.

Some companies offer a range of funds based on different individual currencies, with free switching between them. As a rule, though, single currency funds are high risk; markets move fast and timing is crucial to the end result. Unless you have a particular reason for wanting exposure to a certain currency, or have a large amount to invest that can be spread over several funds, you may be better off with a managed currency fund or a management service linked to a range of funds.

Commodity funds are also not for the faint-hearted. Where onshore unit trusts invest only in the shares of commodity-linked companies, offshore funds may additionally use commodity futures contracts or invest directly into the commodities themselves. The outlay required and the risk involved are rather less than if you undertook the same investments on your own behalf – you can only lose the money you put into the fund, whereas with direct investment you could be committed for further sums – but unless you are an inveterate gambler, this type of investment should only be considered within larger portfolios and then only for a small proportion.

Points to watch for with offshore funds are the level of charges, which may be smaller initially but larger annually than onshore funds, and the tax status. As explained in Chapter 6, offshore funds may have distributor or accumulator status. In the first case, at least 85 per cent of the fund's income must be distributed and will be taxed at the appropriate income tax rate in the hands of the investor, while capital gains will come under the standard CGT rules. In the second case, all income is rolled up within the fund and no tax is due while you remain invested, but when you sell out, all profits will be taxed as income at your highest rate.

With foreign currency funds, for example, most of the benefits come from capital gains, so distributor status is advantageous; when you sell, you can make use of the annual CGT exempt allowance before you need pay any tax. With sterling funds that generate interest, accumulator status allows the tax bill to be deferred, which will be a benefit if your tax rate is likely to fall in the future.

8

Investment Trusts

Investment trusts are not trusts, but companies. Their aim in life is to invest their capital somewhere else – in other company shares, in fixed-interest securities and the like. Investors who buy investment trust shares are, therefore, getting a 'slice of the action' of a whole portfolio of shares for the price of one. In this respect, they are similar to unit trusts (with which they are often compared and contrasted) and certainly their basic reason for existing is identical: to provide the small investor with a spread of risk for a modest outlay.

This spread of risk is legally insisted upon by the fact that, to qualify for the tax treatment described below, investment trusts cannot invest more than 15 per cent of their assets in any one security, meaning a theoretical minimum portfolio of at least seven. In practice, trusts are likely to have anything between 40 and 200 holdings. The exceptions to this rule are the shares of other investment trust companies, which themselves will automatically provide a spread of risk. They must also distribute at least 85 per cent of the income they receive from their investments to their shareholders.

The taxation position

Investment trusts are similar to unit trusts in that liability to tax on any gains they make belongs to the shareholder, rather than the company itself. This means shareholders can realise up to £6800 of gains (in the 1998/99 tax year) before being liable to tax.

On the income side, dividends from other companies in which the trust invests are paid net of basic rate tax to the holders of the investment trust shares. Non-taxpayers can reclaim the tax; higher rate taxpayers will have to pay more.

Do investment trusts have a unique selling point? The answer is yes, they have several, some of which may be attractive to investors, others possibly offputting.

The share price and the discount

The major difference between investment trusts and unit trusts is that the former are 'closed-ended' funds of money while the latter are 'open-ended'. Unit trusts expand and contract according to the demand for them; if demand outstrips supply, new units are created; if supply exceeds demand, units are cancelled. Investment trusts, on the other hand, have a fixed number of shares.

This difference in structure has a practical effect on prices. The price of units in a unit trust is directly related to the value of its underlying investments, while the share price of an investment trust moves up and down according to the demand for it – just like the share prices of other quoted companies.

In fact, if you totted up the value of holdings in an investment trust's portfolio and divided by the number of shares in existence, the result (known as the net asset value) is almost certain to be different from the share price. Occasionally, the share price is higher, in which case it is said to be at a premium. More commonly, it is lower, which is described as a discount. At the time of writing, the average discount for all investment trusts was 11 per cent.

Why should the share price stand at a discount? One reason is technical. As a going concern, the investment trust's portfolio is valued at mid-market prices – halfway between bid and offer; but if it were to be liquidated or taken over, the valuation would move to the lower bid basis and there would also be professional costs involved in winding it up. However, the major part of the discount is explained by supply and demand. If the shares of a trust are in demand, the discount will narrow or the price may even move to a premium; if the trust is out of favour, the discount will widen.

There is some debate over whether the discount is a benefit or a drawback. The argument in its favour is that it means you are buying a stake in more shares than you are paying for. For example, if the discount stands at 10 per cent, then every £90 you invest in the trust effectively represents £100-worth of the shares in its portfolio. On the other hand, if the discount is still the same when you come to sell, you will lose the 10 per cent again.

The discount can be thought of as an extra layer of risk – or reward. At one level you have the opportunity to gain or lose with movements in the value of the underlying portfolio. On top of that, you will gain if the discount narrows between the time you buy and sell, and lose if it widens. Broadly speaking, if the market is rising and the value of the portfolio is going up, the trust is likely to be in greater demand and the discount will narrow, so you gain twice over. Conversely, when the market is falling, demand drops off, the discount widens and you lose twice over.

While you should be cautious about buying a trust that is already on a very low discount – the expectation being that it will widen – it would be wrong to place too much emphasis on the discount. The manager's ability to produce good performance is likely to be a much larger factor in the investment return.

One other point about the discount is that if it gets too large the trust can become vulnerable to a takeover. An institution can offer an attractive price to shareholders while still leaving plenty of scope to make profits for itself. A case a few years ago was the Globe investment trust, which was standing at a 20 per cent discount when it was taken over by Coal Board Pension Funds.

After a spate of new issues in 1995, discounts widened quite a bit and there has recently been some takeover activity and consolidation. Indeed, it was even suggested that the future of investment trusts could be in doubt. But they now seem to be returning to favour. Discounts are starting to narrow and, on a broad view, they are a good deal narrower than 10 or 20 years ago. Savings schemes and personal equity plans have led to higher and more consistent demand from private investors, which has helped to bring discounts down and should continue to do so.

Share buy-backs
Although investment trusts are essentially closed-ended, there is one way in which they can influence the number of shares in

existence: share buy-backs. This means, quite simply, buying back their own shares, which should have two effects. First, reducing the number of shares on the market closes the gap between supply and demand, so the discount should narrow. Second, since shares can be bought at a discount, buy-backs should enhance the net asset value of the trust. Both these effects will benefit continuing shareholders.

The drawback is that, if shares are bought back at more than the issue price, it counts as a distribution and the trust will be liable to pay advance corporation tax. This has been a major deterrent, especially for older trusts where shares are worth a great deal more than the issue price. But from next year advance corporation tax is to be abolished, which should open the way for much greater use of buy-backs as a means of influencing discounts and enhancing value for shareholders.

Gearing

The 'magnifying' effect of the discount is itself a form of gearing. But investment trusts can go one better than that: unlike unit trusts, they can borrow money to invest, alongside the shareholders' funds. If, for example, you can borrow money at 10 per cent, and invest it in something that goes up 50 per cent in a year, then you have magnified the profits. (Needless to say, if the stock you are investing in goes *down*, you will have magnified your losses.) An example of how gearing can work in your favour is shown in Table 8.1. In this case, the borrowing is in the form of a debenture stock.

Charges

Unlike unit trusts, investment trusts do not have an initial charge as such, though there are dealing costs when you buy shares just as there are with the shares of other companies. There is also an annual management charge, which tends to vary across the different categories: general trusts carry a charge of around 0.3 per cent of the asset value, while on specialist trusts it can be as much as 1 per cent. Newer launches have also tended to have higher charges than the older established trusts, but even so, they compare well with unit trusts.

Table 8.1   *Gearing on an investment trust*

Capital structure of trust:

4,000,000 5% debenture stock	£4,000,000
6,000,000 £1 ordinary shares	£6,000,000
	£10,000,000

Assume the portfolio doubles in value over five years and that the debenture stock is repaid at the end of that time. The effect is as follows:

	Year 1	Year 5
Value of portfolio	£10,000,000	£20,000,000
Less debenture stock	£4,000,000	£4,000,000
Assets attributable to 6,000,000 ordinary shares	£6,000,000	£16,000,000
Net asset value per ordinary share	£1	£2.67

Thus, while the portfolio has increased by 100 per cent, the assets attributable to each ordinary share have increased by 167 per cent (from £1 to £2.67).

Investment characteristics

The closed-ended structure of an investment trust, mentioned above, influences the management style as well as the share price.

While the unit trust manager must accommodate new money coming in or demands for units to be redeemed, the investment trust manager is working with a fixed pool of assets, regardless of how shares are being bought or sold.

As with the discount, the closed fund has its supporters and its critics. In a rising market, new money attracted into a unit trust can be used to snap up good opportunities, while the investment trust manager may not be able to move so fast. But in a falling market, a unit trust may have to sell its better holdings to meet redemptions, while the investment trust is insulated.

This insulation allows the investment trust manager to make more speculative decisions. Indeed, investment trusts do not have the same restrictions on their holdings as unit trusts – they can invest in unquoted shares and the smaller stock markets around the world that are not yet approved for

134

Trading shares with IG Index

Buying and selling shares can be an inefficient and expensive way of speculating on price movements. There is stamp duty and commission to pay and a potential tax liability on your capital gains and income. The dense layers of charges dilute the benefits of exploiting a successful market view. IG Index offers a fast and much less expensive alternative.

IG Index provide a betting service on share 'futures' that avoids some of the snags of normal share dealing. Any profits are free of capital gains and income tax; there is no Stamp Duty and IG Index pays the betting duty. You are able to deal on the back of relatively low deposit or on credit (subject to status). When you use a broker, commission can be up to 1.5% of the share price, with IG there is no commission.

There are other advantages too. You can bet that a share price will go down as well as up; this can be difficult for private clients using a normal share dealing service. You do not have to wait to be 'filled'. IG's quotes are given quickly and are normally good in £200/point, the equivalent of 20,000 shares.

IG Index quotes prices in all of the FTSE-100 shares, as well as other shares on request, as long as they are liquid in the underlying market. IG will also quote prices in options on individual equities, where these are quoted on the LIFFE market.

IG Index is Britain's leading financial bookmaker. Account holders have the opportunity to make substantial profits by betting on the financial markets. IG Index takes bets on all the major stock indices, commodities, bonds and currencies, as well as shares. IG was founded over 20 years ago and is regulated by the Securities and Futures Authority (SFA).

Of course, trading financial markets can result in large losses as well as large profits, and it is strongly recommended that you only bet with money you can afford to lose. However, although the rewards are potentially unlimited, your maximum possible loss can be capped using IG's flexible risk management service.

IG Index offers two types of account: standard accounts and credit accounts. With the former you send in a deposit on the day you open a bet, while with the latter you are not usually asked for a deposit and you do not have to pay running losses unless they exceed your credit limit.

FOR MORE INFORMATION CALL IG INDEX ON 0171 663 0896

Example 1

It is may. NatWest is trading at 1198p in the Stock Market and you believe that the share will rise over the next six months. You ask for IG's quote for October NatWest, and we quote you 1192/1204. You 'buy' £50/point at 1204. The deposit is £3000 (£50 (bet size) x 60 (deposit factor)). For every penny the quotation rises above 1024 you make £50 and for every point it falls you lose £50. So if you ignore dividends etc., the bet is equivalent to running 5000 shares.

The market does rise over the summer and, by late August, NatWest is trading in the market at 1270. You decide to take your profits and so you ask for IG's quote for October Natwest, which is 1264/76. You close your bet by selling at 1264. Your profit is calculated as follows:

Closing level:	1264
Opening level:	<u>1204</u>
Difference:	60

Profit on a £50/point 'buy' bet: 60 x £50 = £3000 **free of all tax**

Example 2

It is January. The Lloyds Group is trading in the market at 952p. You believe that it is over-valued and will fall in the next two months, and so you call for IG's quote for March Lloyds. We quote 950/960. You 'sell' £25/point at 950, the betting equivalent of 2500 shares. The deposit required is £1000 (£25 (bet size) x 40 (deposit factor)).

Early in March you decide to close the bet. The Lloyds Group is now trading at 1002 in the market. You decide to cut your loss and so ask IG Index for their quote for March Llyods. We quote 997/1007. You close your bet by 'buying' at 1007. Your loss is calculated as follows:

Closing	1007
Opening level:	<u>950</u>
Difference:	57

Loss on a £25/point 'sell' bet: 57 x £25 = £1425

unit trusts. Obviously these can be more risky, but, with no redemptions to worry about, the manager can afford to take a long-term view.

Investment range

From the start, investment trusts had an international outlook. Many were set up in Scotland, which had a long history of looking abroad for opportunities. This is still reflected in today's trusts, which currently number around 340.

One of the problems in classifying investment trusts is that their investment scope is generally much more loosely defined than is the case with unit trusts. Another difficulty for investors is that the older trusts, in particular, often have names that have little to do with their aims: Scottish Mortgage, for instance, is an international general trust with no particular focus on either Scotland or mortgages.

Some guidance is given by the categorisation used by the Association of Investment Trust Companies (AITC). This divides trusts into 29 different sectors, as shown in Table 8.2. In most cases, the definition is that a trust has at least 80 per cent of its assets in the particular sector, but in the case of Smaller Companies, the minimum is 50 per cent and for Venture and Development Capital, it is simply 'a significant proportion' in unquoted companies. International trusts have the broadest definition, of having less than 80 per cent of assets in any one geographical area, and split capital trusts are the most complicated type, with various different share classes.

The variation in scope between trusts within the same category means that performance comparisons are not necessarily on a like with like basis, but to give a general guide to investment returns, Table 8.2 shows the average for each sector, plus a few key indices, over periods to the end of February 1997.

How to invest

Investment trust shares can be bought through a stockbroker, bank or other authorised dealer. When a new trust is launched,

Table 8.2   *Investment trust categories and average performance*

Comparative return to investor of £1000 invested over various periods

Sector	1 yr	3 yrs	5 yrs	10 yrs
Closed End Funds	1312.43	1607.40	2069.90	3955.42
Commodity & Energy	814.76	995.60	–	–
Emerging Markets (single country)	901.61	1068.71	1187.86	–
Emerging Markets	916.45	1157.96	1246.97	2570.98
Europe	1405.99	2080.41	2737.74	4718.43
Europe (single country)	1412.89	1820.60	2358.06	4872.23
Far East: excluding Japan (general)	546.92	580.42	727.76	1946.41
Far East: excluding Japan (single)	545.85	429.82	577.54	813.96
Far East including Japan	729.13	744.91	891.77	1773.60
High Income	1374.64	1661.30	1963.51	2800.35
International Capital Growth	1224.10	1683.54	2105.59	3937.54
International Income Growth	1300.91	1808.62	1911.83	3921.36
International General	1316.93	1733.55	2168.09	4643.12
Investment Companies	1028.34	1357.32	1454.95	2212.32
Japan	709.20	501.58	491.42	692.39
North America	1275.93	1743.34	2111.67	4091.03
Property	1224.36	1640.57	1890.95	1024.58
Smaller Companies International	1074.51	1455.81	1779.70	3010.57
Smaller Companies UK	1124.93	1483.94	1807.33	1934.02
Split – Capital	2104.96	2691.43	3879.72	5182.60
Split – Capital Indexed	1369.36	2023.66	2498.93	–
Split – Income & Residual Capital	1767.20	2436.61	3070.63	–
Split – Income	1229.27	1528.68	1717.59	2553.58
Split – Stepped Prefs	1083.32	1338.71	1532.79	2777.35
Split – Zero Dividend	1104.47	1374.59	1615.44	3416.25
UK Capital Growth	1187.34	1590.63	1937.91	1892.56
UK General	1352.93	1753.24	2204.43	3649.50
UK Income Growth	1381.78	1750.19	2134.50	4266.35
Venture & Development Capital	1098.91	1530.92	2324.35	3014.39
FTSE All-Share Index	1340.86	1943.03	2354.66	4215.57
MSCI World Index (£)	1227.47	1530.21	1786.56	2591.30
Retail Prices Index	1034.75	1090.17	1154.34	1544.67

Note: Investment trust figures are based on size-weighted average and include net income reinvested, over periods to 30 April 1998.

Source: Reuters Hindsight

Big Bang and the advent of screen based dealing systems were probably the two most significant developments that have affected the Stock Exchange this century and, eleven years on, seems as good a time as any to review the changes which have evolved from these two momentous developments.

Just to refresh the memory, Big Bang was the abolition of the fixed rate commission system which, in turn, triggered off the urge to merge, thus creating the large international broking and investment houses which now dominate the city. The abolition of fixed rate commission, coupled with the introduction of screen based dealing systems, opened the doors to the chill winds of competition which drove the average rate of commission charged to institutions down to the .2% level and below. Of equal significance, particularly for the private investor, was the creation of "execution only" dealing services which enable investors to buy and sell shares (without advice) for as little as .9% and lower, as the bargain size increases. Full marks to Lord Parkinson for forcing these changes upon a then reluctant Stock Exchange council who were forced to capitulate under the threat of a referral to the Monopolies Commission.

Execution only dealing services have, without doubt, also benefited from the extension of the City pages in the serious Press, a development spearheaded by The Daily Telegraph. Gone are the days when the editor of a racing section was expected to write the odd article about the stock market if he had the time. qualified analysts and economists now bring sophisticated research and forecasting within the reach of private investor readers who, with the application of common sense, are becoming increasingly confident of making their own decisions.

The last eleven years, therefore, have brought the Holy Grail of investment success considerably closer to the grasp of the private investor; very competitive commission rates, access via the Press to in-depth analysis and sophisticated economic opinions and near real time prices on television represent huge advances in communications. Accompanying these advances is the growth in investment technology, by which I mean mathematical techniques aimed at achieving investment success. Over the years, an ever increasing number of articles and books have been written on investment theory and during my 41 years enthrallment with the Stock Exchange, I have rarely been able to resist reading any article or book on the fascinating subject of investment. Successful investors are usually voracious reads of the serious financial Press because all the information which is necessary for investment success is there to be gleaned but, having gleaned the information, how does the investor use it?

With all the benefits that modern technology and wider Press coverage has introduced, how can the private investor take advantage and compete, and even beat the professionals? The first thing to realise is that, like anything in life, "one gets out as much as one puts in". There may be the odd "lottery winner" investor but not many and, almost invariably, substantial gains only result from substantial effort and the application of common sense.

It is a fact that it has become more difficult to spot a share where investment characteristics have turned positive without finding an army of analysts already ahead of the game, although it is still possible because the regulatory environment within which professionals (Stockbrokers and Fund Managers) operate, necessitate an increased degree of caution. It is becoming more than ever necessary to anticipate events rather than wait for proof, by which time a share price is likely to have moved to a level which represents a profit missed. Intelligent anticipation is the most important, as is the confidence to make a move before the crowd; always remember, there are many intelligent investors around who only achieve average results because of lack of courage. There are many theories and system techniques such as buying last year's worst Unit Trust performer on January 1st and repeating the exercise one year later. Similar systems exist, such as buying the five highest yielding shares in the Index on January 1st, and repeating the exercise one year later with the proceeds of the last year's selection. I consider these types of investment theory to be illogical and prefer to concentrate on mathematical ratios and human factors. Whilst no two potentially successful opportunities are the same, there are certain principles which, if applied with common sense weighting, can achieve extraordinary success. Space does not allow me to elaborate, other than to say that I have always tried to elate a share price to a character analysis of the directors (which can frequently be obtained by simply attending an AGM, especially where small companies are concerned), the profit margin achieved on sales compared to the industry average, the size of directors' shareholdings (and nowadays options) and to the profile; unknown shares have a better chance of coming into their own than those which are already well publicised.

I hope this brief analysis of recent Stock Exchange history will help all who read this splendid book, produced by The Daily Telegraphy, to make good use of the mine of information contained therein.

Brian Stephen Shepherd

Brian Sheppard is Chairman of Sharemarket, a national execution-only share dealing, which is a division of Gall & Eke Limited, who are Regulated by The Securiuties and Futures Authority and Members of the London Stock Exchange.
Mr Sheppard is also Chairman and controlling shareholder in Manchester * London Investment Trust Plc. £1,000 invested in 1981 would now be worth £140,000.

the company must publish a prospectus in at least one newspaper. In some cases, a full prospectus is published, including a coupon to apply for shares; otherwise there will be a contact address given from which you can obtain the full prospectus and an application form.

If you have only a small amount to invest, the minimum commission charged by stockbrokers would be disproportionately high and a much cheaper route is through a savings scheme, of which there are currently 48 available. The first scheme was launched in 1984 and the concept has proved highly successful at attracting private investors into investment trusts.

Despite the name, savings schemes can be used for lump sums as well as regular investments. The minimum can be as little as £20 a month or £200 for a lump sum. Dealing costs are very small – usually 1 per cent or less – because investors' money is pooled within the scheme to buy shares in bulk. In some cases this means that dealing takes place only once a month, so it is a good idea to find out when the deadline is. This and other information on savings schemes can be obtained from the AITC.

Share exchange schemes

As with unit trusts, several companies offer share exchange schemes through which you can swap holdings of equities for investment trust shares. The company will sell the shares on your behalf and may either bear the selling costs itself or offer a special discounted charge. The charge for buying into the investment trust will normally be at the low savings scheme rate, but may be waived altogether.

Keeping track of prices

Investment trust prices are published daily in newspapers such as *The Daily Telegraph* and the *Financial Times*. The Association of Investment Trust Companies publishes a monthly information service, usually around the third week of the month. This gives two sets of performance figures: the total return on £100 invested as measured by the trust's net asset value – which gives an idea of what the manager has achieved in isolation from share price movements; and the share price total return on

£100. In each case figures are over one, three, five and ten years. It also gives a host of statistical data, including the geographical spread of trusts, the total value of assets, the share price, the net asset value, the discount, the gearing potential, the gross yield and the annual growth in dividends as measured over five years. In addition there is information on savings schemes and personal equity plans and a contact list of names and addresses for the management groups.

Variations on a theme

Limited life trusts

Whatever the so-called 'advantages' of the discount, some companies have seen it as a drawback, and they have decided to get round it by offering 'limited life' trusts. These either have a fixed redemption date, at which point the company will be wound up and its assets realised at full market value, or a series of dates – perhaps once a year – at which shareholders have the option to vote for the winding-up of the company.

Either strategy has the advantage that the discount is unlikely to stray up too far; there can be a drawback, however, in that it means fund managers cannot be as far-sighted in their investment policy as they would with an ordinary investment trust.

Split capital trusts

Split capital trusts started out in the 1960s with the aim of accommodating two types of investor within the one trust: those who were seeking high and growing income, but had little or no interest in capital growth; and those seeking capital growth, with no desire for income. This was achieved by having two classes of share: income and capital. More recently the concept has been expanded and split capital trusts may now also include zero dividend preference shares, stepped preference shares and highly geared ordinary shares. All split capital trusts have a fixed lifespan, although shares can be bought and sold at any time.

The original type of income shares offer high income during the life of the trust and a fixed redemption price when it is wound up. The nearer the trust is to its winding-up date, the nearer the share price is likely to get to its redemption value, but meanwhile it may stand above that, reflecting expectations of future income. So if you hold the shares to redemption there may be a capital loss.

A newer type of income share may get a proportion of the assets at winding-up, on top of the fixed redemption price, but only after other classes of share have taken their entitlements. In contrast, 'annuity income' shares have only a nominal redemption value, perhaps as little as 1p, so there is a built-in capital loss, but meanwhile they receive all the income generated from the trust's portfolio. Finally, highly geared ordinary shares, which are found in 'hybrid' trusts paired with zero preference shares, have no fixed redemption price but receive the surplus assets after the zeros have been paid off, and meanwhile receive all the trust's income.

Income shares are suitable for investors seeking high and rising income, particularly if they are non-taxpayers or can hold the shares tax free within a personal equity plan. The highly geared ordinary shares are better suited to experienced investors who are prepared to accept a capital risk in return for potentially high rewards.

Capital shares normally receive no dividends during the life of the trust, but at winding-up they get all the remaining assets after the prior claims of preference and income shares have been met. There is thus a risk involved, but the chance of very good returns. Zero dividend preference shares, on the other hand, have a fixed redemption value and take top priority at winding-up. The return is not guaranteed, as the trust will have to generate sufficient assets to meet the liability, but the risk is very low.

Stepped preference shares offer a combination of income and capital returns, with a fixed redemption value and a fixed rate of annual dividend growth. As with zeros, the returns are not guaranteed, but the risk is small.

Split capital trusts offer a lot of potential for investors who have specific capital or income needs, or are prepared to take on higher risk for potentially high returns. However, because of their complex structure it is important to be sure exactly what each type of share's entitlement is, and what the likelihood is of its being met – for example, what growth rate the trust will have to achieve between now and the winding-up date to repay the various classes of share.

Warrants

Around 129 trusts now have warrants available and new launches sometimes offer a free warrant for every so many shares you buy. A warrant is not itself a share, but gives you the right to buy a share at a fixed price at some point in the future.

The terms, which are set when the warrant is issued, specify the 'exercise price', at which the future share can be bought, and the 'exercise date', on which the option can be taken up. This may be a particular day, or a period between two dates, each year up to the final exercise date. There is no obligation to buy at any point and obviously it will only be worth while if the exercise price, plus the original price of the warrant, compares favourably with the current price of the share.

Of course, once the final expiry date has passed, the warrant becomes worthless. But during their life warrants can be bought and sold just like the shares themselves, so warrants can be bought as investments in their own right, with the intention of selling at a profit, rather than exercising the right to buy shares.

The warrant price is generally much lower than the share price, but its movements are proportionately greater. This is known as the gearing, the level of which is measured as the share price divided by the warrant price. The higher the gearing, the greater are the potential risks and rewards of the warrant. Two other features to look for in choosing a warrant are the premium – the amount by which the warrant price plus its exercise price exceeds the current price of the underlying share – and its remaining lifespan, up to the final exercise date. The longer the lifespan, the higher the acceptable premium: there will be more time for the share price to increase and represent a profit over the exercise price.

One other point to bear in mind is that warrants do not entitle the holder to any dividends. This means there will be no income tax liability, while capital gains will come within the annual £6500 capital gains tax allowance. The exceptions are subscription shares, which do pay an annual dividend, but currently there are only a couple of trusts which issue these.

Lloyd's trusts

The well-publicised losses of Lloyd's insurance market led, in October 1994, to a new approach to attracting capital: allowing investment by limited liability companies. This engendered the launch of a new family of investment trusts.

Lloyd's trusts invest primarily in equities, gilts, bonds or some mix of these. As with ordinary investment trusts, the shares can be bought and sold on the stock market and some of the trusts qualify as holdings for a personal equity plan. In addition, the trusts will use their portfolios to underwrite Lloyd's syndicates, which they may do to a limit of twice the capital involved.

In theory, then, investors' money will work twice over. The underyling portfolio will generate dividends, and offer the potential for capital appreciation, in the ordinary way. On top of that, a proportion of any underwriting profits will be passed on to the shareholder. However, because Lloyd's accounts take three years to complete, these profits would only come through in dividends in the fourth year from launch, which means this year.

The downside is that there are also two ways of losing money. The underlying portfolio may fall in value, while any underwriting losses that are sustained will have to be met by selling assets. But the risk is mitigated by the fact that there will be a time limit on claims for the contracts underwritten, which is not the case for existing Lloyd's Names, and also because, with limited liability, you can never lose more than you invest.

At the time of writing there are about 15 such trusts. A number are fairly small and not very frequently traded, hence there has been no significant movement in share prices to indicate whether the concept is a successful one or not. Information and analysis have also been scarce, partly because it would involve analysing all the underlying Lloyd's syndicates to which the trusts are exposed, which is a highly specialist and lengthy procedure.

The decision on which syndicates to support is obviously a major factor in the potential investment return. The larger trusts have tended to spread themselves across the market, while some of the smaller ones have taken a more specialist approach. To some extent this selectivity can be an advantage; while a large spread should in theory reduce risk, in practice it also reduces choice and makes monitoring more difficult.

Costs are also a consideration. Fees and commission have to be paid to Lloyd's, Lloyd's members' agents and other advisers to the trust, as well as the trust manager, all of which will reduce the returns for investors.

So even if you are prepared for the risks – which means being prepared to lose your entire investment – picking a trust is not straightforward. One way around this is a 'fund of funds', which invests in a selection of the trusts available. Otherwise, you should certainly consider taking professional advice.

Venture capital trusts

Venture capital trusts (VCTs) were first announced in the 1993 Autumn Budget, but there then followed a year of consultation before details were given in the 1994 Budget. The first trusts were launched in 1995.

There were already a number of investment trusts which specialise in the venture and development capital sector. What is different about the new ones is that, in return for meeting specific investment criteria, they will offer considerable tax concessions.

For investments of up to £150,000 a year, there is front-end income tax relief of 20 per cent if you subscribe at launch, no tax on dividends and no capital gains tax on sale profits. There is also rollover relief – capital gains tax on profits from other assets will be deferred if the proceeds are reinvested in a VCT, although it will have to be paid when the VCT shares are sold, unless the money is further reinvested into another VCT. The criterion for all these concessions is that the VCT shares must be held for at least five years.

For its part, the VCT must, within three years of being set up, have 70 per cent of its holdings in qualifying companies – broadly, unquoted trading companies. Investments may include loans, with a minimum term of five years, but at least half the portfolio must be in ordinary shares.

Venture capital is by its nature a risky area – many new ventures quickly bite the dust. On the other hand, VCTs spread the risk, as they invest in a selection of companies and can invest up to 30 per cent of their portfolios outside the venture capital sector – in blue chip shares, say, which would significantly reduce the overall risk. Moreover, the tax reliefs are attractive, although in exchange you are locked in for five years.

There are three main points to consider if you are thinking of investing in a VCT. First, you should look at where it is investing. There can be considerable differences between seed-corn investment, where money is put into companies at a very early stage of their development, and expansion finance, which covers a later stage. The latter tends to be less 'exciting': the potential returns are smaller, but the risk level is also lower. Second, you should look at the management group's track record in the sector, as experience is even more crucial here than in other investment areas. Finally, there are the charges. These are likely to be higher than for the average investment trust, because of the quantity of research needed into each company the trust invests in, although the US practice of charging performance fees seems unlikely to catch on in the UK.

Housing Investment Trusts

The concept of Housing Investment Trusts was introduced in the 1995 Budget as a way of stimulating investment in private rented housing. By way of encouragement, they will be able to pay corporation tax at the smaller companies rate of 24 per cent and will be exempt from capital gains tax.

Properties must be unlet or let under assured shorthold tenancies at acquisition and thereafter they must be let on assured tenancies. There is a maximum property value of £125,000 in London and £85,000 elsewhere.

When the idea was put forward, it was expected that trusts could produce an income of 5 to 6 per cent a year, based on yields on residential property of 10 to 12 per cent, less the costs of management and maintenance. There would also be prospects for capital growth. However, to date no trusts have been launched. If any fund managers do decide to take the plunge, the trusts are likely to appeal mainly to institutions, but private investors may also be attracted – if only in the hope of avenging past losses in the housing market!

Lifestyle products

Until recently, investment trusts were viewed purely as vehicles for investment or saving as an end in itself. But in practice, as discussed in Chapter 1, many people have a specific reason for saving – perhaps their children's future or their own retirement. Some investment trust groups are now responding to this by designing 'lifestyle' products that serve a particular purpose.

This has been prompted in part by new rules, introduced in January 1995, for the disclosure of charges on financial products. This tends to be a disadvantage to insurance companies, whose products have traditionally involved 'front-end loading' of charges, in contrast to investment trusts and unit trusts, which take a flat charge from each investment. As a result, investment trust companies have seen opportunities to compete in new areas.

Pension plans are one example. The plans are underwritten by insurance companies, as they must be administered by an authorised pension provider, but the underlying investment is into investment trusts. The advantages over insurance companies' own plans are that costs tend to be lower and charges are not front-end loaded, which means contributions are generally more flexible – they can be altered, or stopped and restarted, without incurring penalties.

PEP mortgages, discussed further in the next chapter, are another opportunity that investment trusts have taken up, while a few companies provide children's savings plans that take advantage of the child's own tax allowances. As the effects of charges disclosure work through, and competition throughout the financial services industry increases, more such developments are likely.

Where to find out more

The primary source of information is the Association of Investment Trust Companies (AITC), Durrant House, 8–13

Chiswell Street, London EC1Y 4YY. The Association produces a free information pack which provides a booklet on buying investment trust shares plus details of all trusts, savings schemes, personal equity plans and the addresses of the management groups. In addition, it publishes free fact-sheets on personal equity plans, school fees, investing for income, investing for children, split capital trusts, warrants, pensions, mortgages, savings schemes and risk.

For more comprehensive coverage, the AITC offers a monthly information service, which includes statistical data on the trusts, performance figures and a list of contacts for the management groups. Subscriptions are available on a full monthly basis, at a cost of £35 a year, or quarterly, for £20 a year.

For more details, there is an enquiry line on: 0171 431 5222.

9

Personal Equity Plans and Individual Savings Accounts

Personal equity plans (PEPs) were first announced in the 1986 Budget and came into being at the beginning of 1987. The aim was to encourage wider share ownership through tax advantages: all profits within a PEP were free of capital gains tax and all dividends, so long as they were reinvested in the plan, were free of income tax.

However, in the early days, PEPs had little appeal to ordinary investors. A plan had to be held for a full calendar year to qualify for the tax benefits, but a more significant drawback was that the annual investment limit was only £2400. This meant that in practice the tax advantages were worth very little, particularly as few people pay capital gains tax anyway.

Another problem was that, for people who had no other equity investments, £2400 was too small an amount to get a proper spread of individual holdings and even packaged schemes had to be fairly basic to keep the administration charges at a reasonable level. Unit trusts and investment trusts, which can provide a wide spread for a small sum of money, could be included in plans, but only up to a limit of £420 or 25 per cent of the total investment.

So PEPs initially had little interest except for larger investors as a tax shelter for a small portion of their portfolios. But there was a surge in popularity in 1989, when the investment limit was increased to £4800 and in 1990, when it was raised again to £6000. By this time, the rule on holding a plan for a calendar year had been removed, and half the total limit could be put into qualifying unit and investment trusts. Further improvements followed: in 1991, single company PEPs were introduced, with a separate investment limit of £3000, and the scope of plans was widened from UK shares to those quoted in EU countries; in 1992, the £3000 ceiling was removed from qualifying unit and investment trusts, allowing the full £6000 to be invested in these vehicles; and in 1994, the Chancellor introduced a new brand of PEPs investing in corporate bonds.

But in 1997 the new government announced that PEPs were to be ended in favour of a new savings vehicle, the Individual Savings Account (ISA). Under the original rules, up to £50,000 could be transferred from a PEP to an ISA during a six-month transition period in 1999, but any savings beyond that level would become taxable. There was also to be a £50,000 lifetime investment limit for ISAs, so anyone who already held this much in PEPs would have no further tax-free saving opportunity.

After strong representations from the investment industry, the Chancellor relented in the Budget of March 1998. It will not be possible to make any new contributions to PEPs after 5 April 1999, but existing plans can continue and will not affect contribution limits for ISAs. Hence it is worth considering using this year's PEP allowance while you still can, especially as the contribution limits for ISAs will be lower; albeit the idea of a lifetime limit has been dropped.

PEP rules

The investment limits apply to a tax year, rather than a calendar year, and for 1998/99 they remain at £6000 for a general PEP plus a further £3000 in a single company PEP. Plans can be taken out by anyone over 18, and husbands and wives each have their own investment allowance. All profits made within a plan are free of capital gains tax and dividends can now be paid out to the investor free of income tax as well as accumulated tax free within the plan.

Following the 1993 Budget, the income tax 'rebate' on dividends earned within a PEP dropped from 25 per cent to 20 per cent. This was because the income tax rate charged on dividends was reduced to 20 per cent, so the amount that could be reclaimed fell accordingly. Since April 1996, the same has applied to interest payments on cash held in a plan.

For basic rate taxpayers, this has had the effect of making PEPs a little less worth while than before. If you hold shares or trusts within a PEP, you are saving only 20 per cent in tax on the dividends, compared with holding the same investments directly. So where the PEP involves extra charges, the benefits may be marginal or even completely outweighed.

Conversely, for higher rate taxpayers, the PEP advantage is slightly greater than before. If you hold shares directly, you receive dividends together with a tax credit that can be set against your income tax liability. For basic rate taxpayers, this tax credit exactly matches the liability, but higher rate taxpayers have to pay the difference between the value of the tax credit and their tax rate of 40 per cent. As the tax credit is now worth only 20 per cent instead of 25 per cent, the extra tax due has gone up from 15 per cent to 20 per cent. So there is a greater benefit to be had from holding investments free of tax within a PEP.

From April 1999 the picture will change again, as the value of the tax credit will be reduced to just 10 per cent. For holdings outside a PEP, the tax calculation will change, so that taxpayers will be in the same position as before. Hence investing in a PEP should give the same benefits as now. But in practice PEP investors will see their income fall, as the reclaimed tax will be worth only 10 per cent instead of 20 per cent. For non-taxpayers, PEPs will in principle have an advantage they do not have now, as the reclaim facility is to be abolished outside a PEP or ISA. But investors will have to consider whether the 10 per cent tax gain would outweigh any additional PEP charges.

The traditional equity-based PEPs may invest in authorised shares, unit trusts, investment trusts or any combination of these. Shares must be quoted in an EU country, while to be fully qualifying, unit trusts and investment trusts must be at least 50 per cent invested in EU shares. Trusts which do not qualify under this rule may still be included in PEPs, but only up to a limit of £1500.

The newer corporate bond PEPs may invest in fixed-rate bonds issued in sterling by companies incorporated in the UK, with a minimum term to redemption of five years. They may also include preference shares and convertibles.

PEPs must be run by a registered scheme manager and you are restricted to one scheme manager a year for a general PEP, although if you have a single company PEP as well, that can be with a different manager. There is also nothing to stop you choosing another manager in subsequent years. Plan managers include banks, building societies, unit trust groups, investment trust companies, stockbrokers and independent financial advisers.

There are now around 1250 different PEPs generally available, as well as plans run by some institutions specifically for their own clients. These can be divided into six different categories.

Types of plan

Managed PEPs
Managed PEPs are the largest category and the easiest option, particularly if you are making your first foray into the stock market. Essentially, all you need do is hand over your money and the plan manager will make all the investment decisions on your behalf. Some plans invest only in shares, others only in unit or investment trusts and others again in a combination of these.

The minimum for a lump-sum investment can be as little as £500, though some managers will only accept the full £6000. On the whole, plans that include shares are likely to require a larger investment than those based only on unit or investment trusts.

They may also involve higher charges. Some plans carry an initial charge as well as an annual management fee, and on top of these there are dealing charges for buying and selling shares and investment trusts, plus the standard initial and annual charges on any unit trusts included – though a few managers will rebate part of the initial charge or pass on any discounts they negotiate.

PEPs offered by unit trust groups generally have no plan charges other than those on the trusts themselves. Both these and plans run by investment trust companies normally allow the investor to choose which trusts are included, but, of course, the choice is generally restricted to their own range. Also, now that the investment allowance for trusts is the full £6000, few of these managers offer a facility to include shares, so if you want a plan with a mix of holdings you may find more choice with a stockbroker or independent adviser.

Advisory PEPs

Advisory PEPs are available from stockbrokers, investment managers and independent advisers. They generally offer a completely free choice of investments and the final decision is up to the plan holder, but the manager will offer advice on what to buy and sell and when. This type of plan is best suited to investors who already have a fair knowledge of the market but still prefer to have some guidance.

As with the managed share PEPs, there are likely to be initial and annual plan fees, as well as the charges arising on the investments themselves. If you plan to buy and sell actively, the dealing charge is the most important; this can vary from as little as 0.5 per cent to as much as 1.9 per cent. Several managers also have a minimum charge, which makes it expensive to deal in small amounts.

Obviously, the quality of advice is important, but so is the quantity. If you intend to invest actively, you need to be sure you can get advice when you need it, otherwise good opportunities could slip by. You also need to check who takes the initiative – whether it is up to you to request advice or whether the manager will contact you if he thinks the time is right to buy or sell.

Self-select PEPs

As mentioned, PEPs must always be operated by an authorised plan manager. The nearest you can get to a do-it-yourself PEP, under which the investor takes all the decisions, is a self-select plan. These plans are run mainly by stockbrokers and, while in principle any qualifying investment can be selected, the main emphasis tends to be on shares.

The minimum investment can be as little as £250. But

because you are buying your own individual holdings, rather than a stake in a managed pool of money, these plans are better suited to larger investments, which will enable a reasonable spread of shares to be bought.

The prime advantage of self-select PEPs is, of course, that you are not restricted to any one range of unit or investment trusts, or a manager's selection of shares. However, not all self-select plans offer a completely free choice. A few have restrictions on the shares that may be bought, although the limits are generally quite broad – for instance, shares included in the FTSE 100 Index or the FTSE All-Share Index. More importantly, some exclude unit trusts or investment trusts or both, so you should check before you buy that the plan will meet your particular requirements.

Perhaps surprisingly, self-select PEPs can be more expensive than managed plans. Although you are not paying for any management expertise, there are still set-up and continuing administrative costs which will be met through initial and annual charges. More significantly, there will be dealing charges each time you buy and sell. In a managed plan these are kept to a minimum because the manager is dealing in very large sums on behalf of all the plan holders pooled together; with a self-select plan you have to meet all the costs yourself.

This is another reason why these plans are not suitable for small investments. A number of managers have a minimum dealing charge which can be as much as £50, so it is uneconomic for small sums. Aside from that, dealing charges can vary enormously, from as low as 0.25 per cent up to 1.95 per cent of the transaction value. The more actively you intend to run your plan, the more these dealing charges will mount up and eat into any profits you are making.

Since the investment performance is entirely down to your own efforts, charges are the major factor in choosing a plan, but you should also check the services offered and the quality of administration, in particular the speed of response when you give the manager instructions to buy or sell your holdings. If you spot a good investment opportunity that needs immediate action, it will be no good if the manager takes a week to respond, so you need to be sure you can get ready access to give instructions that they will be carried out without delay.

Because the onus is entirely on the investor, these plans are suitable only for the more experienced, with a fair slice of capital to invest and the time to keep track of market movements. If you are already investing in equities on your own account, then the charges become less important – you would face them anyway – and the plan can be used as a convenient trading service, with the manager taking care of all the paperwork.

Corporate bond PEPs

As mentioned above, corporate bond PEPs may invest in fixed-rate bonds issued in sterling by UK companies with terms of five years or more. Bonds in this context are debt certificates issued by a company which pay a fixed rate of interest and carry guaranteed repayment value on a specified date. Government bonds – gilts – are not allowed, nor are bonds issued by financial institutions.

Other allowable investments are preference shares, which offer fixed dividends, and convertibles, which also carry a fixed dividend, plus the option to convert them to ordinary shares at a fixed price on some future date.

Although the concept was set out in the November 1994 Budget, the introduction of the new plans was delayed to July 1995 by debate over what was acceptable for inclusion. Despite a slow start, it has been estimated that they could attract some £6 billion a year by the end of the century.

The attraction is that they offer a high, fixed income – up to about 8 per cent gross. Thanks to the PEP environment, this is tax free and therefore compares very favourably with the much lower taxed rates offered by building societies, or even with a tax-free TESSA.

There is more risk involved than with a building society account, although generally less than with equities. The price of bonds will fluctuate from day to day, so you should not invest money you may need to get at in a hurry. The guaranteed repayment value is also only as good as the company giving the guarantee and this can vary considerably, from large, well-founded firms to small ventures issuing so-called 'junk' bonds. As a general rule, higher rates of income will indicate higher risk, the first being offered as compensation for the second.

Another potential problem is that high demand for the PEPs, and therefore for the underlying bonds, will push up prices, which will lower the yields. It may also force managers to seek issues from smaller companies, increasing the risk level.

There is also the consideration that high initial income tends to restrict the potential for capital growth. Hence the PEPs are likely to be more suitable for older investors, for whom capital is less important, while younger investors should consider equities for better potential total returns over the longer term.

Corporate PEPs

Corporate PEPs are set up by companies, through an authorised plan manager such as a bank, building society or stockbroker, to allow their shares to be held in the tax-free environment of a PEP. They are usually aimed chiefly at the company's own employees and existing shareholders but are available to anyone. A wide range of corporate PEPs is now available, generally based on large companies such as British Gas, BAA and ICI.

A few plans offer the investor a choice of company or specify a minimum holding in one company, after which the investor can choose any quoted shares for the rest of the portfolio. For the most part, though, shareholdings are confined to the one company, so these plans are pretty inflexible. Under PEP rules, corporate PEPs come under the 'general' category, which means you can invest up to £6000, but you cannot take out another general PEP in the same year, so it is very much a case of having all your eggs in one basket.

Of course, you are not committed for all time, only for the current tax year; thereafter you can take out a more balanced plan, or you may already have one from previous years. So if you hold a large chunk of shares in one company, and you have no other current PEPs, it may be worth putting your holdings into a corporate PEP for the tax advantages.

Shares that you already hold cannot be transferred directly into a PEP except within six weeks of buying a new issue. What you can do, however, is a 'bed and breakfast' operation, which means selling your shares and then buying them back again within the PEP.

Once the shares are inside the PEP, the investment will be free of any income and capital gains tax, but beware that the tax gains are not eaten up in plan charges. Many plans have no, or only a small, initial charge, while the annual charge is usually 0.5 per cent, but can be up to twice that. For a basic rate tax-payer this could outweigh the savings.

Single company PEPs

Single company PEPs are similar to corporate PEPs in that they are based on the shares of a single company. This means that they are usually inflexible, but they have the advantage that they carry their own separate investment allowance, of £3000 a year, and can be held in addition to a general PEP.

There are three types of single company PEP: those that are based on one particular company, those where the choice of share is at the manager's discretion and those offering the investor a choice of share. The first type operate very much like corporate PEPs and are likely to have particular appeal to employees of the company who are participating in a share scheme.

Holding the shares within a PEP will bring the usual income and capital gains tax exemptions. But unlike general and corporate PEPs, shares that are already held can be transferred directly into a PEP providing that they have been acquired through an employee share scheme and that the transfer takes place within 90 days.

Non-employees can also invest in this type of PEP, either directly or, if they already hold shares in the company, by using a bed and breakfast transaction. One advantage is that the charges are generally low, with only a nominal or possibly no initial charge and annual fees of around 0.5 per cent.

'Managed' single company PEPs are almost a contradiction in terms, since there is little management involved in a portfolio that consists of a single company's shares. Of course, the manager may decide to switch from one company to another if it appears to give better prospects; there is also the argument that to pick a single share that will perform well can be a harder task than managing a portfolio where a few wrong choices will be compensated by a few right ones. Even so, the charges on these plans can be quite high – as much as 5 per cent at the outset and up to 1.5 per cent as an annual management fee. In some cases, a discount is offered on the initial charge if you also take out a general PEP with the same manager. Otherwise, there may be better value in the corporate-style plan, if there is one available for the share that interests you, or a self-select plan.

Some self-select plans offer a completely free choice of share, while others provide a list for investors to pick from. Again, it is important to check the charges. These tend to be fairly low – one or two plans have no charges other than the dealing costs on the share – but the initial charge can be as high as 4 per cent, which is a hefty sum when you are making your own share selection. Similarly, annual charges vary from none to as much as 1.5 per cent.

Corporate-style single company PEPs generally offer a monthly savings facility and the minimum for lump sums can be as low as £300. Managed and self-select plans are mainly geared to lump-sum investments, from £500 to the full £3000.

Single company PEPs have most appeal for those who have a large amount of money to invest and want to maximise their tax allowances, or for employees acquiring shares in their own company. For the average investor, putting £3000 into the shares of just one company carries a high level of risk, even with the tax advantages, and a general PEP should certainly be considered first. However, since PEPs are to be closed in 1999 and ISA investment limits will be lower, with no separate single company allowance, it is perhaps worth giving a little more thought to single company PEPs than in the past.

Choosing a PEP

The first step in choosing a PEP is to decide on the type of plan that you want. Broadly speaking, advisory and self-select PEPs are for the more experienced investor, corporate and single company PEPs are for the specialist, while managed PEPs suit a range of types, from the more cautious seeking the safer spread offered by unit and investment trusts to the more adventurous seeking to invest in equities but preferring to leave the decisions to a professional. Once you have decided on the type that suits you best, there are various other considerations which may help to narrow the field.

Growth versus income

This distinction applies chiefly to managed PEPs. With advisory and self-select plans, you can simply pick the investments that match your requirements, and corporate and single company plans can also encompass either strategy, depending on the particular share chosen. However, it is worth checking on the plan's procedure for dealing with dividends. If you are looking for a regular income, you may want to receive the dividends as they are paid, so check that this is possible, without an exorbitant charge being levied. Conversely, if you are looking primarily for growth, you are better off with a plan that will reinvest the dividends automatically without a new set of initial or dealing charges.

Managed PEPs may also offer a choice between income and growth objectives, but some are specifically set up for one or the other. It is sometimes said that smaller investors will get more benefit from an income PEP, primarily for tax reasons: few people pay capital gains tax anyway and, over the shorter term, the income tax benefits will be more visible and immediate.

However, the choice depends very much on your investment aims and any other holdings you have in addition to the PEP. For instance, if you require a measure of income, then it will usually make sense to hold income-producing investments within a PEP, to benefit from the tax shelter, particularly if your other investments are not large enough to make capital gains tax a concern. Beware, however, of simply choosing the PEP showing the highest current yield. Often this will be achieved only at the expense of opportunities for capital growth and increasing income in the future, which can prove much more valuable.

If you are not looking for income, but simply want to accumulate capital for future use, then a growth PEP may be more suitable. Even if capital gains tax is not a problem today, the new regime described in Chapter 1 could affect you in the future and a PEP will protect you against that. Growth PEPs can also be useful to meet specific financial needs in the future, such as paying for school or higher education fees, or boosting retirement income.

Charges and services

Charges on the plan are obviously an important factor as they will eat up a portion of the profits made. As mentioned, unit trust PEPs generally add nothing to the underlying charges on the trusts held but, with share PEPs in particular, there is a danger that the additional running costs of the plan could outweigh the tax gains.

In the past couple of years, a number of unit trust and investment trust plan managers have reduced or abolished the initial charge on their plans. In several cases, this has been combined with the introduction of an 'exit' fee if you take your money out, which applies on a reducing scale for the first three to five years.

If you keep up the plan beyond the exit fee period it can be very attractive, as the initial charge may be only 2 per cent or less, instead of the usual 5–6 per cent. But if you need to take your money out suddenly, you can face a penalty of up to 4.5 per cent. In almost all cases this is based on the current value of the plan, so if it has grown since the outset the total charge will be more than if you had paid a normal up-front fee.

The plan managers argue that PEPs should be viewed as a medium- to long-term investment. With a lower initial fee, more money is invested at the outset, which should lead to higher returns. But over longer periods, the recurring annual management fee can have a greater impact on returns, so you should check that this has not been bumped up to compensate for a lower initial charge.

On top of initial, annual and dealing fees, there are a number of others that can crop up. A few plans make a charge for collecting or paying out dividends. A more common extra is a charge for investors to attend shareholders' meetings, where they are entitled to do so. This can be as much as £100 a time, which is a substantial sum if you hold five or six shares and want to go to all the meetings.

Charges may also reflect the services provided. Commonly, statements and valuations of the plan holdings will be sent out half-yearly, but it may be more frequent and there may also be newsletters and reports. Most important is the quality of administration and this can only be tested by experience. It is now possible to transfer from one PEP manager to another, so you should not be afraid to vote with your feet if you are not satisfied with the service you are getting, but again there may be a charge made to transfer out, in or both.

Past performance

Corporate PEPs, and single company plans where the same holding is maintained, can be judged by the track record of the company concerned but managed PEPs, and particularly those investing in shares, are so diverse that comparisons would not be on a like-with-like basis.

With unit trusts and investment trusts, you can check the track records of individual trusts and of the management group generally. As the saying goes, past performance is not necessarily a guide to the future, and today's league leaders are not always the heroes of tomorrow, but a consistent past record is a reasonable indication of potential. Other points to consider are the overall investment philosophy of the plan manager; whether the attitude to risk broadly accords with your own; how actively the plan will be managed; and the degree of commitment to PEPs – whether they are viewed as an important part of a company's business or just a sideline.

PEP facilities

Share exchange

A number of PEP managers offer share exchange schemes through which you can convert existing holdings of shares into a PEP investment in different shares, unit trusts or investment trusts. This is particularly useful if you have small holdings, such as privatisation issues, that would be expensive to sell through normal channels, as the charges are usually low and in some cases the scheme is free.

PEP mortgages

A number of lenders will now accept a PEP as a repayment vehicle for a mortgage in place of the more standard endowment and pension contracts. They can offer greater flexibility, but, of course, there is no guarantee of the eventual proceeds, so lenders may be quite fussy over the plans they will approve.

As a rule they will expect you to make regular savings into the PEP, rather than occasional lump sums.

ISA Rules

Individual savings accounts (ISAs) can be offered from 6 April 1999 and may include any or all of three elements: equities, cash and insurance. For cash and insurance there are investment limits of £1000 a year each, with an overall plan limit of £5000 a year. For the first year, however, the total limit will be £7000 and up to £3000 may be in cash.

The equity element may include any of the investments currently allowed for PEPs: shares, investment trusts, unit trusts, fixed-rate bonds, preference shares and convertibles. There will no longer be any distinction made between 'qualifying' and 'non-qualifying', so investment trusts and unit trusts can be included up to the full limit regardless of where they invest. Shares from an approved profit-sharing or share option scheme may be transferred into a plan at their market value, but 'windfall' shares from a building society or insurance company conversion may not be put into an ISA.

The cash element will include all types of bank and building society accounts, plus taxable National Savings products and supermarket savings accounts. You may also transfer in the capital, but not the interest, from a maturing TESSA and this will not count towards the annual investment limit. Finally, the insurance element can include any single premium life assurance policies or those on a recurrent single premium basis.

Unlike PEPs, investors may take out more than one plan a year, but only within certain limits. You may have a separate plan for each of the three elements, but in this case there is a set limit of £3000 for the equity component as well as the £1000 limit for each of the others. Alternatively, you may take just one plan a year, which must offer the equity component, although it may or may not offer the other two.

Investors will have no income or capital gains tax liability on ISA investments. A 10 per cent tax credit will be paid on the dividends from UK shares for the first five years of the scheme, up to April 2004. As mentioned before, this is less generous than the current PEP position, where the tax credit is worth 20 per cent. It is also less than the effective tax saving on cash deposits, which will continue to be 20 per cent, making cash a more tax-efficient holding in an ISA than equities for basic and lower rate taxpayers. For higher rate taxpayers there will still be a significant benefit.

There will be no statutory lock-in period – money may be withdrawn from a plan at any time – and no minimum subscription, other than whatever plan managers may impose. Finally, the scheme is guaranteed to run for at least 10 years, with a review after seven years to decide if and how it should continue.

Benchmarking

One of the Government's main aims in introducing ISAs is to encourage more people to save. To give people confidence that an ISA is suitable, it has proposed a 'CAT' mark, to be given to plans which meet certain standards on cost, access and terms. The requirements for the CAT mark are specific to each of the three ISA elements; at the time of writing, details have not been finalised but the broad proposals are as follows.

- Cash ISAs must have a low minimum subscription and allow withdrawals within a set number of days, with no penalties no matter how many withdrawals are made. The interest rate must be no more than a set amount below bank base rate.
- Insurance ISAs must have no initial charge and a low annual charge. Again, minimum contribution levels for both monthly and annual payments should be low and the plan must pay back at least the premiums paid to date if it is surrendered after a set number of years.
- Equity ISAs must be based on a UK index-tracking unit trust. As with insurance plans, there must be no initial charge and a low annual charge – expected to be set at a maximum of 1 per cent. There will also be set standards for minimum monthly and annual investments and plan literature must make clear the risks of an equity investment.

The CAT mark proposals have not been widely welcomed, particularly for equity plans. While tracker funds may seem straightforward, there can be wide differences in performance between, for example, funds that track the All-Share Index and those that track the FTSE 100. There can even be significant differences between funds tracking the same index, due to variations in tracking methods and tracking error, neither of which is a particularly simple concept.

The low charges required mean that there is no scope for commission to be paid, so these plans will generally be sold direct – through newspaper advertisements, for example – with no advice given. There is a danger that the CAT mark may be taken as some kind of guarantee of performance, although in practice tracker funds are never likely to be top performers, particularly in a market downturn. In fact, the funds with the best long-term performance record (and traditionally low charges) – investment trusts – have been excluded from the CAT mark altogether, apparently because their closed-ended structure makes them too complex.

At the time of writing, the CAT mark proposals have only just been issued. No doubt investment groups will be making their representations to the government in the coming months and we may well see some changes before the first plans are launched next year.

Types of plans

As the final details of how ISAs will operate have still to be absorbed, there have been no indications as yet of what types of plan we might see – whether, for instance, providers will generally offer all three elements or specialise in one or two.

It would seem to make sense for traditional equity plan providers, such as investment and unit trust groups, to offer a cash facility, but deposit-takers, such as the new supermarket banks, may not necessarily want to get involved with equities. Otherwise, on the equity side, there are likely to be similar types of plan to those we now have for PEPs: managed, advisory, self-select and perhaps also corporate bond and corporate.

ISA facilities

Again, it is too early to know what might be introduced but we can expect ISAs to follow the PEP pattern, at least initially. For instance, providers of PEP mortgages are already looking at ISA mortgage plans and they would probably operate in much the same way. Although the annual investment limit is lower than for PEPs, this should not be any problem for the typical mortgage. On the plus side, the cash element could provide a temporary safe refuge in times of stock market turbulence.

Keeping track of your investment

Prices of unit trusts, investment trusts and shares are quoted in newspapers such as *The Daily Telegraph* and the *Financial Times*. This can give you a general idea of how your investments are performing, although the actual value of the PEP may be affected by additional charges. More accurate information will be given in the statements and valuations sent out by the plan manager, usually at half-yearly intervals, and they may also provide reports on the companies or trusts included in the plan, plus newsletters or commentaries on the investment strategy.

Where to find out more

Chase de Vere publishes the *PEP Guide*, which currently lists around 1100 plans from some 250 managers. Listings include the investment aim of the plan, the minimum investments accepted, the various charges and facilities such as share exchange. There is also a half-yearly supplement issued in January and July which gives performance figures and annualised growth rates for qualifying and non-qualifying unit and investment trusts and companies that currently make up the FTSE 100 Share Index. The *PEP Guide* costs £12.95 and can be obtained by telephoning 0800 526092.

On the second Saturday of every month, *The Daily Telegraph* publishes a performance table covering all the major unit trust and investment trust PEPs, showing performance over one, three and five years. There are also regular articles on PEPs in the personal finance pages.

10

Life Assurance and Friendly Society Investments

Within the last generation, life assurance companies have become sizeable players in the savings market. This is not to say that they have abandoned their traditional role of supplying straightforward protection products such as term assurance, or the savings-plus-protection vehicles such as endowment plans. In fact, this range has been expanding, with the introduction of the likes of critical illness insurance and long-term care plans.

But the fact remains that insurance is generally sold rather than bought, so to maintain a healthy flow of new business, insurance companies have been broadening their horizons in the investment field. Many have associated unit trust companies, but they are also competing for lump-sum investments with their own products.

This chapter looks at the main types on offer. Single premium bonds are a version of collective investments, like unit and investment trusts, that provide smaller investors with a stake in a large portfolio of assets, thereby spreading risk. Annuities are income-producing vehicles and are also put to use in 'hybrid' plans, which aim to produce a fixed level of income plus the prospect of capital growth. They therefore offer greater opportunities than fixed capital investments such as building society accounts, but with a measure of capital risk.

Second-hand endowments are policies which have been sold by their original holders and provide a lump-sum route into what is traditionally a regular savings product. Fourth, the chapter looks at friendly societies, which have similarities with life assurance companies but certain tax advantages.

Finally, there is a review of health insurance products. While these are obviously not investments as such, they can protect your ability to enjoy the fruits of your investments.

Single premium bonds

Single premium bonds – so-called because they are based on a one-off contribution – offer a broad investment choice and a spread of risk for sums starting at around £1000. Although technically they include an element of life assurance, it is relatively small – often it is simply the current bid value of the bond. This means that the investment potential is maximised rather than money being siphoned off to pay for life cover.

The bonds can be invested in a wide range of underlying funds operated by the company. These are similar to the various categories of unit trusts; for example, there are equity funds covering the UK, North America, Europe, Japan and the Far East, as well as broadly based international funds. There are also types that are not found among unit trusts, such as managed funds, with profits funds, currency funds and, to a large extent, property funds.

Managed funds invest in a mixture of equities, fixed-interest securities and property, thus giving the widest possible spread of assets and risk. For this reason, they are the most popular, appealing both to very conservative investors and to those who prefer to leave all the investment decisions to a professional. There can, however, be considerable differences between one managed fund and the next, depending on the investment strategy adopted.

Essentially, there are two types: those which have a more or less set division between equities, fixed-interest and property, which are sometimes called 'three-way' or balanced funds; and those where the manager takes a more active role in determining the proportions. A fairly recent trend is to offer more than one managed fund with differing degrees of risk; for example, Adventurous, Balanced and Cautious (or Conservative). The Adventurous fund will have a higher proportion in equities, which carry the highest risk/reward prospects, while the Cautious fund will lean more towards fixed interest-securities.

In theory, a more actively managed fund should produce a better return by responding to changes in market conditions, but equally there is more scope for wrong decisions. The three-way fund, on the other hand, is likely to produce steadier, if unexciting, returns. Some examples of the past performance of managed funds are shown in Table 10.1.

In the late 1980s and early 1990s, property funds were in the doldrums, thanks to the sliding fortunes of the property market, and many shrank considerably in size. But from mid-1993 performance started to improve, as demand increased with the upturn in the economy. At the time of writing, expectations are for steady, if not spectacular, growth in both the commercial and residential sectors.

The drawback of property funds is that they are unwieldy – property cannot always be sold readily, so the portfolio cannot easily be adjusted to changing market conditions. Managers also reserve the right to delay making repayments to investors for up to six months, to avoid having to sell at a loss to raise cash quickly. In practice, this has only ever been imposed on funds invested in residential property, while the bulk focus on commercial property. Smaller funds are often invested instead in the shares of property companies, which are more tradable, although the returns are subject to different influences.

With profits funds, like managed funds, are invested in a mix of assets, but instead of the value of your holding depending on the value of investments in the underlying fund, with profits funds work by adding bonuses. The bonus rate is declared

Table 10.1 *Past performance of managed funds*

Percentage increase in fund value over different periods			
	1 year	3 years	5 years
Best	29.66	72.84	101.03
Average	18.09	47.94	70.41
Worst	–5.70	11.06	28.42

Note: Figures to 30 April 1998, on an offer to offer price basis.

Source: Reuters Hindsight

annually and depends on the investment profits made by the fund, but a part of these is usually held in reserve to boost rates in bad years. So there should be a 'smoothing' effect on market fluctuations, which reduces the risk. Some companies set a minimum guaranteed bonus rate and there may also be a terminal bonus, although this is not guaranteed.

Companies also reserve the right to make a 'market value adjustment' when money is paid out or switched to another fund. This would arise if the actual investment performance has not matched up to the value that has been credited, and is designed to protect continuing investors in the fund. Although this is likely to apply only in the early years – and is not normally applied on death – it does detract from the apparent safety of these funds.

Taxation

The taxation of bonds is governed by the rules applying to assurance companies. As regards the underlying fund, this will pay tax on investment income and is also subject to capital gains tax on profits from the disposal of assets, hence the fund will set aside a reserve against future liabilities. The tax paid by the fund cannot be reclaimed, which is a major drawback for non-taxpayers.

Basic rate taxpayers have no tax worries on their own score – their liabilities are covered by what the fund has already paid. For higher rate taxpayers, however, it is a different – and rather complex – story. To start with the good news, up to 5 per cent of the original investment can be withdrawn from the bond, free of tax, each year for 20 years – this counts as being a return of capital. If the allowance is not used every year, it can be carried over, so if, for instance, you take nothing out in the first year, you have 10 per cent to play with in the second, and so on. The bad news comes at the end, when you cash in the investment. Tax is then assessed by a procedure known as 'top-slicing'. First, the total profit made from the bond is calculated, taking into account any withdrawals that have already been made, and the resulting amount is divided by the number of years for which the bond has been held. This figure is then added to your income for the year in which you cash in the bond to determine if you are liable to higher rate tax. If so, the higher rate will be applied to the whole of the profit made, and you will have to pay the difference between that and the basic rate tax which has already been paid.

There are two ways to mitigate the tax bill. If you can, you should put off cashing in the bond until a year when you are a basic rate taxpayer – after retirement, perhaps. Then you will have no further liability. You should also opt for the bond to be split into separate segments, each of which is effectively a policy in its own right; some companies do this automatically, others may do it on demand. The advantage is that, if you want to withdraw more than the 5 per cent allowance, you can cash in all of one segment, which gets more favourable tax treatment than making a partial withdrawal above the limit.

Bonds versus unit trusts

Bonds and unit trusts have certain similar characteristics – both offer low-cost access to pooled funds and charges are comparable. Hence there has long been debate about their respective merits for investors.

One drawback of bonds is that capital gains tax is paid by the life assurance company on profits within the bond. With unit trusts, the capital gains tax liability falls on the investor, which hitherto has generally been an advantage. The new capital gains tax rules, described in Chapter 1, complicate the picture somewhat. Life assurance companies are still subject to the old regime, with indexation, while investors come under the new system, with taper relief. If you have already used your exempt allowance, taper relief may be worth less than indexation, particularly if you have switched your holdings from time to time and so not held any for very long. In this case, bonds may be a better option. However, most investors will be able to make use of the exempt allowance, currently £6800 for the 1998/99 tax year, which tips the scales towards unit trusts.

Against this, the returns from a bond are treated as having had basic rate tax already paid, whereas in practice the charge incurred by the insurance company may be well below 20 per cent. Hence the returns may be higher than could be achieved on unit trusts. There is also the annual 5 per cent tax-free withdrawal allowance, which is useful for higher rate taxpayers. If you can cash in at a time when you are subject only to basic rate, and if you are also already using your capital gains tax allowance on other investments, bonds can be tax efficient.

Currently unit trusts can be held within a personal equity plan, which offers complete exemption from both income and capital gains tax for investments of up to £6000 a year. If you have not already used this allowance, it should be a prime consideration.

However, when individual savings accounts (ISAs) come in next year, it will be possible to put up to £1000 a year into a life assurance policy, provided it is on a single premium, or recurrent single premium, basis. Although the investment limit is much lower than for unit trusts, it could provide a boost for bonds if they meet the requirements.

The other main attraction of bonds is the facility to switch between different underlying funds at low cost and without any tax liability. If you move from one unit trust to another, there may be a capital gains tax liability and you will have to pay a new front-end charge; even with a discount offered for staying with the same management group, this is likely to be at least 2 per cent. Bonds generally offer one or more free switches per year, after which there is a small charge of perhaps 0.5 per cent. Of course, you are restricted by the range of funds offered by the company, and it is unlikely that any single company will top the investment tables across the board.

For different investors' needs and circumstances, one or other product is likely to have the edge, so it is a good idea to seek advice before you commit yourself.

Variations on the bond theme

Guaranteed equity bonds
Guaranteed equity investments are a fairly recent innovation, born out of the disillusion with the stock market of many smaller investors after the 1987 crash. At first sight, they seem to be the perfect investment: they guarantee to return a high percentage of any increase in a given stock market index over the investment period, or your original capital if the index should fall.

171

However, you need to check the small print to be quite sure what you are being promised, as there are a number of variations on the theme. The investment period is commonly five years; if you take your money out before then, you normally forfeit the guarantee and there may be early surrender penalties as well. So if the market starts falling just before the end of the period, you could lose all the gains made up to then. Some products have a periodic 'lock-in' facility, whereby gains to date are consolidated into the guarantee; while others average the index value over the last 6 or 12 months, to protect against a last-minute fall.

In several cases, the guarantee applies only to the capital growth in the index, which means the income from share dividends is sacrificed. Over longer periods, this can be quite a lot to give up.

The message is that guarantees only come at a price, but these bonds can be attractive for short periods if you are nervous of stock market movements. For larger sums, though – say £10,000 upwards – you could put together your own package to offset risk, so it is worth taking independent advice.

High income bonds

These are another fairly recent idea, stemming in this case from the plunge in interest rates during 1993 which was a severe blow to building society investors dependent on income.

The bonds generally run for five years, during which time they offer a guaranteed level of income – recently, this has tended to be around 8 per cent a year. They also offer a guarantee on the capital return at the end of the term; this varies a little from bond to bond, but is commonly such that the total return, including all the income received, will be not less than the original investment.

The bonds use quite sophisticated derivative instruments to provide the guarantees, but in essence what happens is this. Part of the original capital is siphoned off to provide the ongoing income, while the rest is invested with the hope that, over the five years, it will grow enough to replace the full original sum, in addition to the income paid, or perhaps even show a profit.

In other words, capital is being sacrificed up-front to provide income, but there is the potential for it to be replaced through investment growth and in the worst case, if the stock market falls, there is a guarantee that you will get back your original investment less the income you have already been paid.

The bonds have attracted a fair amount of criticism, focusing on the concepts of 'income' and 'guarantee'. First, it is argued that the payments made are not truly income, because they are made from capital. Second, the capital guarantee has been called misleading, as it provides for a return of your initial investment *including* the income already paid, not in addition to it. As a result, the regulatory authorities have laid down strict rules on how the bonds should be described in advertisements and product literature and the warnings that should be given.

Certainly you should make sure you know exactly what you are being promised. If the stock market falls, and you get back only the minimum amount guaranteed, you will effectively have lost out on the interest you could have earned meanwhile from a building society account, which would also have preserved your capital intact.

But if, say, you need a 10 per cent annual return to live on, and a building society account is paying only 5 per cent, you would need to draw on your capital anyway. The advantage of a bond in this case is that there is the opportunity for capital growth to replace what you spend, whereas with a building society your capital would simply dwindle.

What you should check is the required annual rate of return on the bond to get back your original capital in addition to the income paid. This will vary from bond to bond, depending on the exact structure and the economic conditions at the time the derivatives are bought, plus the level of income offered. The greater the income, the higher the rate of growth required to pay back all the capital, so there is a trade-off between the income you receive and the chance of getting back your full investment or showing a profit.

Another point to bear in mind is that the money is generally locked in for the full term: withdrawals may be banned completely or very restricted, possibly invalidating the guarantees.

Distribution bonds

These are bonds designed to pay out the dividends accumulated by the underlying fund, so that investors can receive an income without cashing in holdings. They tend to focus on UK equities and gilts, which offer higher dividends than overseas securities.

The income is free of tax for basic rate taxpayers, and also for higher rate payers as long as it is within the 5 per cent annual allowance. But they share with other bonds the drawback that the fund itself is liable to capital gains tax and income tax, which cannot be reclaimed by those not liable.

Personal portfolio bonds

These are bonds which allow you to have your own choice of investments held within the medium of a bond. They are designed for sizeable investments – around £50,000 upwards – which would normally be managed by a stockbroker or financial adviser. Because the investments are held within a bond, investors can avoid tax until the bond is cashed in. Moreover, many of these bonds are held with offshore life companies that are not themselves liable to UK tax.

But now the Chancellor has cracked down – and severely. From next April, holders of these bonds will be liable to a tax charge on 'deemed gains' of 15 per cent of the premiums paid into the bond in any year plus the total deemed gains from previous years. As a result, some insurance companies have stopped selling the bonds and, unless the Inland Revenue relents, they may become a thing of the past.

Broker bonds

Broker bonds are offered by a number of independent financial advisers, not necessarily insurance brokers as the name suggests. They had their origin in the early 1980s, when advisers who managed bond funds on behalf of clients used the power of proxy to make block switches instead of making the same move individually for each client.

Broker bonds have moved on a long way since then. The concept is that clients' money is pooled into one fund, which the adviser will manage, moving it between underlying funds to make the most of current market conditions. These funds can be 'fettered', meaning they are invested with just one life company, or 'unfettered', which means they can be invested across a number of companies, depending on where the adviser sees the best prospects. The latter are more common and offer greater scope for the adviser to give added value, compared with an individual bond.

The advantages of a broker bond are that you have your investment professionally managed, without being required to approve every move, but still have access to the person doing the managing, which would not be the case if, say, you simply put your money into a life company's managed fund. In return, you will be faced with an extra layer of charges levied by the adviser.

So will performance justify the extra cost? Anyone offering a broker bond must be authorised to do so, and life companies are responsible both for vetting the advisers in the first place and for monitoring their performance. However, the Personal Investment Authority has recently strengthened its rules on broker funds. Advisers who offer them must have passed the appropriate exam; must inform clients of a possible conflict of interest in recommending their own funds; must give clients a suitable benchmark for measuring performance and send a letter of explanation if the bond fails to match up to the benchmark at the end of each year; and must reconfirm the fund's suitability for the investor on a yearly basis.

Annuities

Annuities are a means of transforming capital into income. The basic concept is simple: you pay a lump sum to a life assurance company and in return you get an income, at a predetermined level, for the rest of your life. A basic annuity is irrevocable; once you have given up your capital, you cannot have it back.

Annuities operate rather like a mirror image of life assurance. Instead of paying out a lump sum when you die, they pay an income until you die. So the older you are, the fewer payments are anticipated and the higher the rate will be. For this reason, annuities are not normally suitable for anyone under about 65; the income offered would be too low to justify giving up the capital for good.

The income from an annuity is taxable, but only in part. A portion of it is treated as being a return of your original capital, and is

A NNUITY
direct

Maximise your retirement income
Excellent value despite lower rates

If you or your partner are not in good health
or if you smoke, higher pensions are now available.
Bridge any retirement income gap now or in the future.

**We are the largest specialist provider of
retirement income services.
We can help you as we have 25,000 others**

☎ **0500 50-65-75**

---

annuity update **BBC2 CEEFAX 260-267**

Annuity Direct is a trading name of Financial Strategy Ltd, an independent financial adviser
regulated in the conduct of investment business by the Personal Investment Authority.

To: Annuity Direct, FREEPOST, KE 8610, 32 Scrutton Street, London EC2B 2JL ☎ 0500 50-65-75

Fax 0171 684 5001

Please send information on the following...

☐ Retirement income planning

☐ Health insurance and Long term care

☐ Investment and inheritance planning

☐ Guaranteed income

Name (Mr/Mrs/Miss/Ms)

- -

Address - - - - - - - - - - - - - - - - - -

- -

- -

Postcode - - - - - - - - - - - - - - - - - -

☎ -

Annuities in 1998

For those of retirement age or above an annuity is a lump sum investment which provides income for the rest of your life. Normally this income is guaranteed on a basis agreed at the outset - a guaranteed annuity. Investment-linked annuities are available but come with the risk of a variable income.

An annuity is a very simple product and the best purchase for a guaranteed annuity is almost always from the company providing the highest rate of return. But the returns vary greatly from company to company and are sensitive to the investment returns of the underlying investment - for guaranteed annuities, long-term gilt yields.

Annuities can be purchased either with the capital from both personal and employed insured pension funds or with private capital - a purchase life annuity.

Purchase life annuities offer particularly attractive returns for those with a high income need who are 75 years plus and in relatively good health. Pension annuities can be bought by the retiree from the best annuity company, This is called the Open Market Option. All retirees should exercise their Open Market Option even if this subsequently proves that their current company is offering the best rate. You will only know if you have got the best if you have exercised your option to research the market.

New options in annuities

Over the past couple of years extra income has become more widely available for people suffering ill health. This is in two forms -

● Enhanced annuities - for smokers, or those who have undergone operations or are overweight, but individual medical assessment does not take place.

● Impaired life annuities - where individual medical underwriting assessment helps to determine the income level - these are particularly helpful in more severe cases. Income can be increased by anything up to three or four times the "normal" annuity level.

On an annuity for a couple, the increased annuity may be available even if only one of them is ill and it does not have to be the main policy or pension holder who is sick.

Low rates, poor value?

Low inflation and low interest rates have led to lower annuity rates in recent years. This is as a result of lower investment returns from gilts. However, these investment returns are only one part of the total return from an annuity.

An annuity rate consists of the investment return and the mortality return, the mortality return being determined by how many years the life company expects to have to pay your income. You further benefit from taking a pension annuity around normal retirement age as a result of a cross-subsidy from your fellow annuitants who die earlier than anticipated. This cross-subsidy gets smaller if you buy later.

The mortality return now forms a much greater proportion of the total return from an annuity than it did when annuity rates were at their peak in 1990. That it is a greater proportion of the total return is one of the reasons why the true value of an annuity relative to other investments is much greater than a cursory glance at comparative rates would imply.

If you are considering making an investment in stocks and shares the only indication you have of the likely future return is what has happened in the past. By contrast, the investment return within an annuity indicates what the market believes is the correct return for the next 15 years or more for someone lending the Government money. Therefore a crude comparison between these two returns is an attempt to compare apples with oranges.

However, over the long term - and the rest of your life is generally a long term - it has been proved that equity returns have a relationship with gilt yields. This relationship would imply that equity returns will fall over the next decade as long as inflation is kept under control, which seems likely.

Therefore, you can conclude that annuity rates may be low but they may also represent good value for money. They are also unlikely to increase significantly over the next three to four years as UK interest rates are constrained by European rates during the early years of EMU. Therefore, delaying purchase for a year in hope of higher rates is an uncertain option which has the certain cost of your annuity being paid for one year less.

An annuity is a very simple concept and simple insurance policy. However, ensuring that you purchase the one most suited to your need and providing the highest income is complicated and requires expert advice, particularly as many annuity providers deal only through independent financial advisers.

Some help is available in your living room via BBC2 Ceefax, page 260. These rates, provided by Annuity Direct, allow you to track what is happening to annuity returns in the weeks leading up to your purchase.

Stuart Bayliss, Director, Annuity Direct - The Retirement Income Specialists

For a free guide to retirement planning
please phone or use the coupon on our advertisement

PRUDENTIAL

The primrose path to retirement

When you finally reach retirement, you face the prospect of substantial changes in your lifestyle. It requires a full evaluation of both the way in which you spend your time and the financial implications of no longer being able to rely upon a regular salary being paid into your bank account each month.

Changes in working patterns, with most people now having worked for at least three companies by the time they retire, mean that it is likely you will receive several pensions from different sources. Depending upon the type of pension scheme it is possible to have some control over the way in which your pension is paid and the amount of pension. Whilst each pension han its own rules the table below shows to what extent it's normally possible to control who pays the pension, the amount of pension and the way in which benefits are structured.

Type of Pension	Control
State Pensions (e.g. SERPS)	✗
Company - Final salary schemes	✗
Company- Money Purchase schemes	✗
Personal Pensions	✓
Retirement annuity Contracts (i.e. Section 226 plans)	✓
Additional voluntary contributions(AVCs)	✓
Freestanding additional voluntary contributions	✓
Executive Pensions	✓
Small Self Administered Schemes	✓
Buyout bonds (Section 32 plans)	✓

The common characteristic of those pension schemes that can be controlled at retirement is that they are money purchase schemes. That is to say that their value depends wholly upon how much has been invested and the return on the investment. Their value is normally expressed as the size of the pension fund. Whereas the benefits from the state pension and final salary pension schemes are expressed as the amount of annual pension you will receive.

Because of generous tax breaks granted to pensions savings, the Government imposes strict and complex system of controls over the way in which benefits can be paid. These are primarily designed to ensure that pension funds are used to provide benefits in retirement to you as a member of the scheme and your spouse or dependants.

Converting your pension into a regular income

Until only a few years ago there was only one way in which your pension fund could be used to provide an income and that was to use it to buy an annuity. This continues to be the most popular method of providing an income in retirement because it is the safest option. A more recent development has been the introduction of Income Drawdown. This is a

temporary arrangement whereby a regular income can by drawn directly from the pension fund before an annuity is bought. A third option is a facility called Phased Retirement. This enables people to forgo their tax free lump sum and instead receive it as part of their lifetime income.

What's available ?

Type of pension plan	Annuity	Phased Retirement	Income Drawdown
Personal Pension	✓	✓	✓
Retirement Annuity Contract (S226)	✓	✓*	✗
Additional Voluntary Contribution	✓	✗	✗
Freestanding Additional Voluntary Contribution (FSAVC)	✓	✗	✗
Money purchase occupational pension scheme	✓	✗	✗
Buyout bond(Section 32	✓	✗	✗
Executive Pension	✓	✗	✓
Small Self Administered Scheme (SSAS)	✓	✗	✓

* Not all retirement annuity contracts include this facility

However, this article is concerned primarily with options open to you when you come to buy an annuity.

Annuity purchase

It is normally possible to buy an annuity with the proceeds from all types of approved money purchase pension scheme. **An annuity provides the safest, easiest and cheapest way of converting a pension fund into income**. The main benefit of annuities is that they are guaranteed for life. That is why Archy, the cockroach philosopher invented by American Poet Don Marquis said, " Live so you can stick your tongue out at the [insurers]". For the longer you live the more you "profit" from the annuity company. With the advancement of medical science which has led to increased lifespans an annuity provides insurance against the risk of living too long and out living your means.

So what exactly is a pension annuity?

It is an agreement you make with an annuity provider, normally a large insurance company, to pay you an income, normally of a pre-agreed amount for the rest of your life. Most people opt to buy an annuity that is paid monthly as this matches their outgoings and they are used to monthly budgeting. However you could also choose to receive your annuity quarterly, half-yearly or annually.

PRUDENTIAL

How are pension annuities paid?

If you live in the UK your pension will normally be paid by automatic transfer into your bank account. Prudential is also able to pay pensions into building society and National Giro accounts.

If you live in the European community you can have your UK pension paid to you by a UK insurance company. They will provide you with an annuity in sterling and will make payments into a foreign bank account. The amount of pension you receive in the local currency will depend upon prevailing exchange rates. It is not currently possible to buy a Euro annuity, although if the UK joins the single European currency and sterling is withdrawn, all annuities are likely to be paid in Euros.

How are annuities taxed?

All contributions made by you or your previous employer to your pension scheme will have received tax relief. If you are a basic rate taxpayer, for each £100 you invest, the tax man will currently add a further £31. Similarly your employer will have received Corporation tax relief on their contributions to the pension scheme. For this reason, the resulting benefits paid out as an annuity are treated as earned income and income tax is due at your marginal rate.

The annuity provider will handle the payment of income tax for you, usually in the same manner as your employer did under the PAYE system. This means that your annuity will be paid to you net of tax. You will receive a P60 each year that shows the amount of pension annuity that has been paid and the tax deducted.

Remember too, in addition to receiving a pension you will normally be entitled to a lump sum when you retire, paid tax free.

Is the income paid by an annuity fixed?

On retirement, many retired people do opt for a level income, which pays out a fixed gross income each year. This is often because their pension fund is too small for them to afford to build in an element of protection from the effects of future inflation. The risk of buying a level annuity is that inflation could erode the future purchasing power of the annuity. As women age 60 can expect to live for a further 26 years and men a further 24 year it is advisable to build in some protection from the effects of inflation. **Even with inflation running at quite modest levels, the buying power of a fixed annuity is likely to be reduced by between a third and a half during retirement.**

If you can rely on other types of pension for the majority of your retirement income then choosing a level annuity may be appropriate. Many company pension schemes guarantee to provide increases each year in line with inflation, subject to certain limits. Whilst the state pension schemes are currently guaranteed to increase each year in line with inflation.

You can build a number of different forms of inflation protecting into your annuity. The simplest of these is to arrange for your annuity to increase each year by a set percentage, typically by 3% or 5%.

An alternative to this is a with profits annuity. With this type of annuity your pension fund is invested in a with profits fund. In this way you can benefit from annual increases to your pension, as these may be added each year as with profits bonuses are declared. As with profits funds tend to invest in equities the investment returns are likely to be larger than from other types of investment. They are therefore able to provide good long term protection from the effects of inflation. It is also possible to decide how much pension you will receive and hence influence the likely future increases in pension that you will receive. It is therefore an ideal option for someone who needs a rising income, for instance, if you are slowly withdrawing from your business and need to gradually replace your salary.

Alternatively you can provide full inflation protection by buying an index linked annuity. The annuity guarantees to increase each year fully in line with inflation, however high.

Are index linked annuities a good idea?

Currently inflation seems to be under control and many commentators are predicting that the terrible days of double digit inflation are permanently behind us. However, it would be a very brave man who was prepared to say that inflation was dead never to reappear over the next 20 to 30 years. An Index linked annuity provides an invaluable level of protection from the unknown, no one can predict with any certainty whether or when inflation will be back.

Historically, when future inflation was less predictable, the cost of buying an index linked annuity was very high. However, as inflation has come under control, the cost has fallen. Prudential can currently provide an index linked annuity for about the same price as buying an annuity increasing each year by 3.1%. This will change from time to time.

How can I provide for my spouse if I die first?

If you have an occupational pension and are married, a spouse's pension is normally automatically included. Whereas if you have a personal pension or retirement annuity contract you can decide whether or not to include provision for the annuity to continue to be paid to your spouse once you have died.

This is commonly known as a joint life annuity and you can decide what level of annuity your spouse will receive if you predecease them. Many people choose to include a 2/3rds spouse's pension. This means that when they die their spouse will receive an annuity of 2/3rds of the amount they were receiving. Such an annuity would first be paid to you and then to your spouse, after your death.

A less expensive option is to include a "guaranteed" period within the annuity. This guarantees to pay out for a minimum fixed period after you buy it - say for 5 or 10 years- even if you have died meanwhile.

Are there good and bad times to buy an annuity?

The annuity you receive will depend upon the value of your pension fund when you retire and annuity rates available at that time. If you invested, in UK equities for instance, the value of your pension fund may fluctuate daily depending upon the level of the stockmarket. So,

regardless of annuity rates, the amount of pension you could receive from one day to the next can vary quite significantly..

As well as being determined by the value of the underlying investment, the amount of annuity you will receive will depend upon annuity rates in force at the time. These are broadly determined by the yield (income) available from government long dated fixed interest securities (i.e. Gilts). When Gilt yields are low the amount of annuity that can be bought is correspondingly low.

If you don't immediately need the income from your pension fund and feel that either annuity rates are too low or your pension fund has fallen as a result of a temporary blip in the stockmarket, you may wish to defer buying an annuity. The difficulty associated with this decision is that there is a risk that annuity rates may continue to fall and /or the value of your pension fund may fall further. Annuity purchase offer the only cast iron guarantees available.

Can I shop around for my annuity?

When you retire, the provider of your pension plan will give you details of the value of your pension fund and the annuity that they will pay. You have a facility, known as the Open Market Option, to buy an annuity on the open market from any authorised annuity provider. These offer a wide range of annuity rates, with the best value companies providing an income that can be as much as 30% better than the worse company (Source: Carrington Consultants). With such a wide difference between the best and the worse it does pay to shop around.

Prudential are the UK's largest provider of Pension Annuities (Source: ABI February 1998) and we aim to provide consistently competitive annuity rates. We have become the market leader by providing competitive annuity rates both to people with Prudential pensions and to the clients of both specialist and general independent financial advisers.

Prudential can't guarantee to always provide the best annuity rates and so we suggest that you contact a financial adviser who can search the market on your behalf and provide you with the best annuity rates.

You can get an idea of current annuity rates from looking in the Daily Telegraph each Saturday as they normally provide details of current rates.

Please note that the value of the current tax privaleges of pension schemes varies according to each individual's financial circumstances and, if in an occupational pension, those of the employer.

Past performance is not necessarily a guide to the future. The rates of future bonuses in the With Profits Fund cannot be guaranteed. A with profits annuity can go down as well as up.

"Prudential" is a trading name of Prudential Annuities Limited (which is also used by other companies within the Prudential marketing group of companies.) The Prudential Annuities Limited is registered in England and Wales. Registered office at 142 Holborn Bars London EC1N 2NH. Registered number 2554213.Regulated by the Personal Investment Authority for investment business.

therefore tax free, while the rest will be taxed as income at your normal rate. The capital element is determined by scales laid down by the Inland Revenue, based on your age; the older you are, the shorter the likely payment period, so a higher proportion of the return will be treated as capital. However, new scales were brought in at the beginning of 1992 – previously they were based on mortality tables that were around 40 years old, when life expectancy was lower than it is today. The new scales reduced the capital element for any given age, making the after-tax return rather less attractive than before. Examples of current rates are shown in Table 10.2. One exception to this tax rule is an annuity bought with money from a pension fund. This is known as a 'compulsory purchase annuity', because you are obliged to buy it (though you may still have a choice of companies to buy it from), and it is wholly taxable as income. Ordinary annuities that you buy voluntarily are called 'purchased life annuities'.

Variations of annuities

The main failing of a basic annuity is that it dies with you. To take an extreme example, if you handed over £100,000 and died the very next day, your estate would be £100,000 the poorer and the insurance company equally the richer. For insur-

Table 10.2 *Annuity rates*

Purchase price £10,000	Level no guarantee	Level guaranteed 5 years	Escalating 5 per cent, per annum, no guarantee
Male 65, single life	£957.00	£936.00	£640.00
Female 65, single life	£817.00	£810.00	£510.00
Male 75, single life	£1396.00	£1292.00	£1075.00
Female 75, single life	£1154.00	£1108.00	£842.00
Male 65, female 60, joint life	£676.00	£675.00	£381.00
Male 75, female 70, joint life	£873.00	£870.00	£584.00

Note: The table shows gross annual rates assuming payment is monthly in arrears, without proportion.

Source: MoneyFacts, May 1998

ance companies, premature deaths make up for clients who live unexpectedly long, but for your heirs it could be a serious blow.

There are several ways of overcoming this problem. First, the annuity can be guaranteed for a certain period, such as five or ten years. Payments will then be continued for that time, regardless of whether you die sooner. In practice, if the annuity-holder dies, the insurance company may offer his heirs the option of commuting remaining payments to a lump sum.

Second, if you are married but have no other dependants, you could opt for a joint life, second death annuity. As the name implies, this will continue paying income until the death of the second partner.

Third, you can ensure that you (or your estate) at least get back the original outlay through a capital protected annuity. If at your death the income payments so far are less than the purchase price, the insurance company will pay over the difference. All of these options cost money, in that the rate will be reduced, as can be seen in Table 10.2. Rates for women will be lower again, as they have a longer life expectancy.

Annuity rates are also affected by how often the income is paid, whether it is paid in advance or in arrears, and with or without proportion. The latter refers to the position if you die between payment dates – whether or not a proportion of the next payment is made. Obviously, it hardly matters if payments are monthly, but for annual income it could be useful. If you have no heirs and are in no immediate hurry for money, an annuity payable yearly in arrears, without proportion and with no guarantees would give the best possible rate.

Another drawback of the basic annuity is that the income is fixed for life and therefore vulnerable to inflation. It is possible instead to have an increasing annuity, under which payments rise each year, either by a fixed percentage or in line with, say, the Retail Price Index. Two further, much less common, options are with profits and unit-linked annuities, where the income is linked to an investment fund. This means it is dependent on the fortunes of the stock market, so while the long-term trend should be upwards, it can fluctuate from year to year. Both this and the increasing annuity will give a lower income at the outset than the plain level type.

Hybrid plans

One variety not mentioned above is the temporary annuity, which pays out for a fixed period of time rather than for life. These have little application by themselves, but are often used in packaged schemes offered by life companies. Sometimes called 'hybrid' or 'back to back' plans, these combine different products with the aim of providing a reasonable level of income plus the prospect of capital growth.

Plans fall into two types. With one, the lump-sum investment is used to buy a ten-year annuity; payments from this are used to fund the premiums for a ten-year endowment policy, while the surplus provides a running income. At the end of the ten years, the maturing endowment should provide a return of the original capital. With the second type, part of the original lump sum buys a temporary annuity to provide income, while the rest is put into an investment such as a bond, unit trust or personal equity plan, again designed to return at least the original capital at the end of the term.

Some of the packages around now are quite sophisticated. With the second type, for example, you may be able to choose the level of income you want, either by adjusting the amount put into the annuity or by taking additional income from the second investment. But there are two important questions to ask. First, what return would there be if you die during the term? The annuity will normally die with you, so the return may be less than you invested. Second, what rate of growth is needed from the investment to return the original sum, and how realistic is this? Remember that the higher the income you take, the less money will be left to build up capital.

One other point is that the package will usually combine products from the same company, which may not be good for both annuities and investments. You might get a better deal by putting together your own combination from different companies.

Second-hand endowments

These are with profits endowment policies which have been sold by their original holder before maturity owing to a change of circumstances. They can be bought either through auctions or through 'market-makers' – firms which buy up policies to sell on to investors. When you buy a policy the details stay the same – it is still based on the life of the original owner – but you take over responsibility for paying the remaining premiums due. These can usually be commuted to a lump-sum payment, but this is not always beneficial; the discount offered may be negligible and the policy will become non-qualifying in status, which means there may be a tax liability on the maturity proceeds.

While policy auctions have been around for decades, market-makers are a fairly new phenomenon. The market, however, is expanding fast, as selling a policy can give a much better return than the surrender value. For the investor, a second-hand policy can be attractive if you need a lump sum at a specific time in the future; for example, to meet school fees or for retirement.

Policies will normally have run for around two-thirds or more of their total term, so in addition to the basic sum assured, they will have built up bonuses which, once they have been allocated, are guaranteed to be paid at maturity. In some cases, the value of the sum assured plus bonuses can be as much as the purchase price, so your profit then depends on the level of bonuses allocated during the remainder of the term and the amount of the remaining premiums.

The price is determined by the current value of the policy, its original term and the period remaining, the future premiums and the seller's mark-up. Sellers usually quote an anticipated rate of return at maturity, but whether this will be achieved or not depends on the future pattern of bonus rates. The recent trend has been downward, and since most policies bought have fairly short terms to run – between three and ten years – it is not likely that they will pick up again significantly.

Unless you already have some experience in this area, you would be wise not to buy at auction. Like car auctions, they can offer bargains, but you could equally end up paying over the odds if you lack the specialised knowledge. Similarly, policies issued by 'top name' insurance companies offer the safest prospects though they may not be the cheapest. It is usually worth taking some professional advice.

Friendly societies

Friendly societies have been around for a couple of centuries. In some respects their operations resemble those of insurance companies, but on a smaller scale, as they have been subject to tight restrictions on their activities. However, the Friendly Societies Act 1992 has opened the way for expansion and most societies incorporated in 1993. This means that they may own assets directly instead of through trustees and may set up subsidiary companies that can manage unit trust schemes and personal equity plans or do insurance broking. They are also due to be brought under the Policyholders' Protection Act, which has not previously applied to friendly societies.

The societies' chief advantage over insurance companies is that they can issue tax-exempt policies, which invest in funds that are free of income and capital gains tax and pay the proceeds tax free to the investor. These are ten-year plans designed for regular savings, but many offer a lump-sum version, using an annuity from which payments are drip-fed into the plan over its term.

The bad news is that there is a limit on the premiums that may be paid into these plans and this in turn has meant that charges have tended to be relatively high. Since 1994, this limit has been £25 a month or £270 a year. The tax concession will also be underlined by the changed rules for tax credits on the dividends from UK shares, although the 1998 Budget confirmed that friendly society policies would receive the same 10% credit as PEPs and ISAs until 2004.

Investors may take out only one plan each, but children are also entitled to have plans, so a family of four are able to invest up to £1200 a year through monthly savings. Plans do not always have to cease at the end of ten years: some offer the choice to continue paying premiums or to take an 'income' by making regular withdrawals.

Private health care

What would be the use of the highest return on a lump sum investment if you were not healthy enough to enjoy it – or worse, not around at all?

According to research commissioned by PPP healthcare group, 51 per cent of those polled rated health as their most important priority, ahead of personal relationships and financial security. There is a strong argument for using some of your spare funds to pay for private health care in one form or another to ensure a reasonable quality of life. However, as there are several different types of health insurance, it is important to sort out which one is relevant to your needs.

Private medical insurance (PMI)

Currently, some 12 per cent of the population has some form of private medical insurance. Sales have been fairly static during the 1990s, although moderate growth is expected in the future. Certainly the number of providers has grown; there are now 25, offering a wide range of products.

These fall into three broad ranges: low-cost, middle-range and up-market policies. The more you pay, the more coverage you buy. At the top end of the spectrum are plans which include fully comprehensive dental treatment, childbirth, full refund for specialist's fees and outpatient treatment.

Their annual costs vary from about £600 a year to as much as £6000 for a comprehensive family plan. Scales of charges generally depend on your age, where you live and what level of benefits you choose. At the lower end, for example, some types of treatment may be excluded from cover, while for others there is a cash limit. On the most expensive plans, a full refund will be given for most expenses including, for example, the cost of a parent accompanying a young child. Plans may also pay a daily allowance if you have treatment under the National Health Service.

The choice can be somewhat baffling at first glance as the industry players seek to differentiate themselves and establish competitive advantage. There are also derivative products which have a minimal level of cover or may be intended only to meet the cost of major surgery, dental care, hospital costs or accidental cover. As with all insurance there is the question of whether certain types of cover are really necessary to which the counter argument is: 'You won't know whether you need the cover until it's too late.'

One of the problems in picking out just how much cover you need to take out in money terms is knowing the cost of the care itself. As examples, a consultation with a doctor could cost £100, an X-ray £120, having your tonsils out could come to £1000 to £1500 and major heart surgery might run to well in excess of £5000. Charges can vary significantly between different types of hospital and different parts of the country, so it may be worth while checking out your local facilities.

How to choose
It is important to research the market. At the end of this section (page 223) is a list of the major players and their telephone numbers. They will all be pleased to send details of the plans they offer and premium rates. You can also find surveys of plans in financial magazines such as *Planned Savings* and *Money Management*.

A useful reference book is *Laing's Review of Private Health Care*, for which details are given below. This lists a range of useful information about the PMI market and also the names of specialist brokers.

Brokers who really understand the market and the differences between the products and who keep up to date with what is going on can be a real help in cutting through the information undergrowth to find the most appropriate policy.

Permanent Health Insurance (PHI)
If you are employed, your employer may provide sick pay for a period of time if you should suffer a long-term illness that prevents you from working. Thereafter, however, you might have to fall back on state benefits, which are fairly limited. It is therefore worth considering PHI – and even more so if you are self-employed.

PHI provides replacement income after a set 'deferment' period which can be as little as four weeks, but is typically six months – the period for which Statutory Sick Pay is provided. There are special versions designed specifically to cover mortgage payments, but a standard PHI plan will pay up to 75 per cent of your gross earnings (or 90 per cent of net earnings). The shortfall is deliberate; if a plan were to provide as much as you normally earn, so the argument goes, there would be no incentive for you to return to work.

The cost of a plan depends on factors such as your age, occupation, medical history and the length of the deferment period you choose, as well as how much cover you want. It may also depend on the way the plan defines 'inability to work'. The best is that you are unable to do your own normal job, but some policies stipulate that you must be unable to do your own job or any other to which you are suited – meaning that you may be obliged to go back to work in a different, and perhaps less well paid, position.

As long as you qualify for payments, they will generally continue until you are able to go back to work or up to your normal retirement age. A good plan will also pay a proportionate amount if you return to work in a lesser capacity or part time.

Critical Illness Insurance

Whereas life assurance will pay out a lump sum if you die, critical illness insurance will pay out if you suffer a serious illness. The range of illnesses covered can vary between policies, but the core ones – and those most often claimed for – are heart attack, cancer and stroke.

As a stand-alone policy, critical illness insurance has been fairly little taken up since the first plan was launched in this country in December 1986. However, it is becoming increasingly common as an option on a mortgage plan and in this context it seems to have struck more of a chord.

With today's pace of development in medicine, there is much more likelihood of suffering a critical illness than of dying during one's working life. It is also an insurance that is particularly relevant to those without dependants since, unlike life assurance, the person taking out the policy stands to benefit personally. For both these reasons, it should become more popular as it becomes better known.

Long-term care

Long-term care insurance is an even newer development than critical illness cover. The idea is to take out cover in early or middle life that will pay for nursing home care in old age, should it be needed. Under the current rules for state benefits, the local authority will pay nursing home costs only if your total assets, including your home, are less than £8000. Between £8000 and £16,000 there is a sliding scale and over £16,000 you are entitled to no help at all.

Despite this, long-term care insurance has yet to take off. One problem lies in the design of plans: since the need for care could continue indefinitely, and the cost is therefore open-ended, plans are either very expensive or have restrictions on the benefits. Another problem is that people are reluctant to buy insurance for something they may never need, especially when any potential benefits may be 20 or 30 years away.

Mixing and matching

One way in which insurers have tried to add to the attractions of healthcare plans is to combine more than one benefit. Critical illness insurance, for example, is often sold in combination with life assurance and there is at least one plan available that also includes long-term care insurance and a measure of private health insurance. The advantage of this is that it may help to cut the costs, but the drawback is that the benefits will only be paid once. So if you make a claim for a critical illness, you will no longer have any life assurance, whereas with two separate plans you could have both.

Contacts for the main providers

Abbey Life 01202 292373	BCWA 0117 9293742	BUPA 0800 289577	Clinicare 01438 747733	Cornhill 01483 552975
Halifax 0800 142142	MFIA 01162 362420	Norwich Union 0800 142142	Provincial 01539 723415	Exeter Friendly Society 01392 75361
Healthcare Agencies 01753 532092	Nationwide 0800 335555	Permanent Direct 01923 770000	Saga 01483 553553	Guardian Direct 0800 282820
Johnson Fry Healthsave 0171 4511000	NPS 01536 713713	PPP healthcare 0800 335555	Staffordshire 01902 317407	Guardian Health 01303 853400
Lloyds 0800 750750	Northern Bank 01232 333361	Prime Health 01483 553553	Sun Alliance 0800 374351	WPA 0500 414243

Further reading

- *Laing's Review of Private Healthcare*, 1996, Laing & Buisson (London).
- *Money Management* magazine. Last survey December 1996.
- *Planned Savings* magazine. Last survey September 1996.

11

Retirement Planning

Pension planning can be as complex as any other investment described in this book and twice as important. Once you retire, your income will very largely depend on the investments you have built up during your working life and a pension can be the core element. It may seem out of place in a book devoted to lump-sum investment, as pension planning is (or should be) chiefly a matter of regular saving. But there are three good reasons why it should have a prominent place in any investment strategy.

1. Very few people have the maximum possible pension provision. In fact, it is estimated that fewer than 2 per cent of members of company-run pension schemes will retire on the maximum two-thirds of final salary that is allowed by the Inland Revenue. This can arise because the company scheme is not geared to producing maximum benefits, or because the employee does not put in a sufficient number of years of service. Most people, indeed, are likely to end up with a far lower pension than they expect or imagine.

2. Pensions are extremely tax efficient as an investment. All contributions, to whatever type of plan, qualify for tax relief at the highest rate of income tax you pay and the funds in which they are invested are themselves free of all income and capital gains tax. In addition, when you retire, you can take part of the proceeds as a cash lump sum, tax free; the exact proportion depends on the type of pension you have and when it dates from.

3. There has been a host of developments in pensions legislation in recent years, aimed at improving private provision and, alongside that, reducing the burden on the State. As a result, there are now greater opportunities to make your own pension arrangements, through lump-sum investments as well as regular savings.

Personal pensions

Personal pensions, which came on the scene in July 1988, are arguably the most important development of recent times. They are open to anyone who has earnings that are not already covered by a company pension scheme. That includes not only the self-employed, but also those who have freelance earnings in addition to a main job – or, indeed, in addition to a current pension. Moreover, employees have the choice of opting out of a company scheme and taking a personal pension instead.

On the face of it, this is not an attractive choice. For a start, if you take a personal pension, all the costs fall on you – both the charges of the plan and the payments into it. Your employer may make a contribution to it, but there is no obligation for him to do so.

Then there are the benefits to consider. Many large company schemes operate on a 'final salary' basis; this means that the pension is equivalent to a proportion of your salary at the time of leaving the company, typically one-sixtieth per year of service. Should runaway inflation suddenly double your salary, or investment performance not measure up to expectations, that is the company's problem. With a personal pension, all the risk is on your head: you will only get what you put in and the investment growth it achieves.

On top of this, a company scheme will normally offer additional benefits: life assurance, should you die before retirement, which can be up to four times your annual salary; a widow's or widower's pension, of up to two-thirds of your own prospective pension; and guaranteed or discretionary increases in your pension once it is being paid. In fact, from April 1997, it has been compulsory for final salary schemes to provide increases in line with the Retail Price Index up to 5 per cent.

Under the rules, employees who opt for a personal pension are still eligible to have life assurance through a company scheme, but again, there is no obligation on the employer to provide this. If you decide to go it alone, you will have to think in terms of paying for all these benefits yourself.

So why consider a personal pension? The most important reason is job mobility. If you leave a company, your pension entitlement is based on your years of service to that point and your final salary at the time of leaving. Since the beginning of 1985, companies have had to revalue these preserved rights by the lesser of the inflation rate and 5 per cent, which means so-called 'frozen' pensions have been somewhat thawed. But higher rates of inflation, or promotional salary increases, can still make this entitlement look pretty feeble.

Alternatively, you can take a transfer value out of the scheme to put into a new company scheme or a private arrangement. However, transfer values are usually conservatively assessed, so each time you move you are likely to lose out. In contrast, a personal pension can be continued intact across any number of job changes, so, for younger people in particular, it can be a much more stable means of building up benefits.

Smaller companies are also turning increasingly from final salary to 'money purchase' schemes, which are less of a financial commitment. Instead of promising a pension based on salary, these schemes build up a fund of money for each employee which is then used to buy a pension at retirement. This is similar to the way a personal pension operates so, if your employer is prepared to contribute to a personal pension in place of the company scheme, you could be no worse off.

There are limits on the contributions you are allowed to make to a personal pension, which start at 17.5 per cent of annual earnings for those under 35 and increase with age to a maximum of 40 per cent. There is also an overall earnings cap on the calculation, which for the 1998/99 tax year stands at £87,600. However, if you do not use the full contribution allowance in one year, the rest can be carried forward for up to six years. So if you find yourself with windfall cash, you may be able to tuck away a sizeable lump sum by picking up unused allowance from past years.

Types of plan

Personal pensions are available from insurance companies, banks, investment trust groups and unit trust groups and offer a variety of investment choices: with profits, unit-linked, deposit-style and investment and unit trusts. Deposit-type plans offer maximum security with the lowest growth prospects and are suitable mainly for those very close to retirement who need to know their capital is safe. With profits plans invest in a mix of assets and aim to smooth out fluctuations, thereby offering a balance between risk and reward. Unit-linked, investment trust and unit trust plans provide direct exposure to the equity market through a range of funds, which themselves offer different levels of risk and growth prospects. Broadly speaking, the further you are from retirement, the more risk you can afford to take, in return for the likelihood of higher growth.

One other type of plan, which first appeared in 1990, is the self-invested personal pension. This is a 'do-it-yourself' option that gives you a free choice of all allowable investments, which include equities, unit trusts and investment trusts, insurance company funds, deposit accounts and commercial property. These plans are geared towards larger investors, and would not normally be cost effective for lump sums of less than about £50,000. The attractions are that you are not tied to the investment fortunes of one company and there is generally a fixed fee structure which is economical for very sizeable sums.

Contracting out of SERPS

If you are a member of a company pension arrangement, you cannot normally have a personal pension as well. The one exception to this rule is that you can have a 'rebate-only' plan for the purpose of contracting out of the State Earnings Related Pension Scheme (SERPS). In return for giving up your rights under SERPS, you receive a rebate of part of your, and your employer's, National Insurance contributions and this money can be invested in a special personal pension.

Since April 1997, this rebate has been based on your age, varying from 3.4 per cent up to 9 per cent. Previously, the rebate was a flat rate, except that an extra 1 per cent was given to those over 30 contracting out through a personal pension. With a flat rate, contracting out ceases to be worth while after a certain age, around 50 for men and early forties for women. If everyone were to opt back into SERPS at these ages, the State would not be able to afford the scheme, hence age-related rebates are being introduced in the hope of encouraging people to stay contracted-out.

Under the new system, contracting out should be attractive for men up to their mid-fifties and women up to their mid-forties or so. At younger ages, however, it will have less appeal, as the age-related rebate will be lower than the current flat rate. Income is also an important factor: for those earning less than about £11,000, the charges on a personal pension may outweigh the gains on the rebate. It is also important to remember that a plan based only on the National Insurance rebates is not going to produce an adequate pension. So if you are not also in a company pension scheme, you should be making further contributions of your own.

Additional contributions

As mentioned, you cannot make contributions to a personal pension if you are a member of a company scheme. You can, however, make extra payments through an Additional Voluntary Contributions (AVC) scheme. This can be an in-house scheme provided by your employer or a free-standing plan operated by an insurance company.

Why should you do this? The answer is that a company scheme can fall short of the ideal for a number of reasons: it may offer less than the standard one-sixtieth per year of service; the final salary assessment may not include extras such as bonuses and overtime payments; it may not provide the maximum possible death benefits or spouse's pension. Most of all, if you change jobs, you will not clock up the necessary number of years of service and benefits from previous employment may be partly or wholly frozen.

The choice between in-house and free-standing schemes depends on your circumstances. Briefly, an in-house scheme is convenient, as payments are usually deducted directly from salary and the employer will bear the plan charges; but a free-standing scheme can offer a wider investment choice and is yours to take from job to job.

Members of company pension schemes can put in up to 15 per cent of earnings a year, tax free. Compulsory contributions are normally around 5 to 6 per cent, so there is plenty of scope for making AVCs. However, while it is possible to have a single premium plan – to which you can make one-off payments as and when you can afford it – the allowance cannot be carried forward from year to year, so there is less scope for large lump-sum payments than there is with a personal pension.

An alternative route to building up savings for retirement is a personal equity plan. Unlike a pension, there is no tax relief on the money going in, but there is greater flexibility: the investment limits are generally higher; you can get the money out whenever you like; and all the proceeds can be taken as cash, whereas an AVC can only be used to provide income. The two are not mutually exclusive: to maximise savings, you can have a PEP in addition to an AVC.

How much to save

The chief drawback of pensions is that you cannot draw on the money until you reach a minimum age – 50 for personal pensions and normally 60 for company schemes. Other investments may be difficult to convert into cash, but a pension is by nature non-negotiable. Hence most of us contribute only grudgingly – on average, around 4–5 per cent of earnings.

A glance at Table 11.1 shows how inadequate this can be. Even contributing at 10 per cent a year, starting at age 30, will not produce the maximum allowance of two-thirds' final salary at 65. This is based on a fairly conservative assumption for investment growth, but the truth is that the danger of over-funding is pretty remote, while under-provision is extremely common.

On top of that, you may not want to soldier on to the age of 65. If you retire early, not only will you have accumulated fewer rights from a company scheme, say $^{35}/_{60}$ths instead of $^{40}/_{60}$ths, but most schemes also levy a penalty, often up to 6 per cent a

Table 11.1 *How much should you put into a pension plan?*

The columns show what level of pension (expressed as a percentage of final salary) can be expected, assuming that contributions of 10 per cent of salary are made each year.

Age now	Pension[a] at age 65	
	Male	**Female[b]**
	%	%
30	58.9	53.4
35	47.6	43.2
40	39.5	35.8
45	28.7	26.0
50	20.6	18.7
55	14.7	13.3

[a] These figures assume a 2 per cent 'real' growth rate on the pension fund, and that pension contributions keep pace with salary increases, ie they are always 10 per cent of salary. They also assume that all of the fund is taken as a pension, rather than a proportion as a lump sum.
[b] The figures for women are lower at all ages because pension rates are lower for women (they live longer).

Source: Allied Dunbar

year. Hence there is all the more reason to plan now for your future leisure.

The good news is that pension plans are becoming much more flexible. Many insurance company products will allow you to switch without penalty from, say, a free-standing AVC to a personal pension if your employment circumstances change, and contributions can be made in the form of occasional lump sums instead of, or in addition to, regular savings. So there is no excuse for not acting!

Stakeholder pensions

In its manifesto, Labour said it would retain both the basic state pension and SERPS, but would top them up with 'stakeholder' pensions. Details of these are still to come, but the intention seems to be that all but the lowest paid and the unemployed will have to make compulsory pension contributions.

Although plans will be provided by the private sector, the intention is to keep costs down and ensure value for money. Contributions would come directly from wages or salaries and schemes would be flexible to allow easy transfer from one to another. They would also extend beyond retirement needs to include, for example, long-term care and low-cost life assurance. Schemes may be provided by employers and unions, as well as by friendly societies and life assurance companies.

Where to find out more

The financial pages of newspapers run frequent articles on pension issues, as do specialist magazines. For specific suggestions on your own circumstances, you should think of consulting a financial adviser.

There are also a number of bodies which can offer certain types of information and help. The Occupational Pensions Advisory Service can advise on the rights of members of company schemes and can be contacted on 0171 233 8080. To track down pension entitlements you may have from past employment, contact the Pensions Register on 0191 225 6393. If you have any disputes that you cannot resolve with your pension provider, there is the Pensions Ombudsman's Bureau on 0171 834 9144, or, for aspects of personal pensions, the Insurance Ombudsman's Bureau on 0171 928 7600.

12

Tangibles and Other Investments

This chapter looks at alternative investments which do not fit into any of the categories covered so far. Chief among these are 'tangibles' which, as the name implies, are physical objects rather than financial instruments. They can be highly specialised – rarity is often a key factor in their value – and may therefore require a high degree of expertise. Hence investors should be prepared either to do considerable research on their own part, or to put their trust in an expert. Tangibles also tend to be less liquid than financial investments, partly because there is not always a ready market, and partly because of indivisibility – you can sell a small parcel of shares, but you cannot sell one arm of an antique chair.

Tangibles

Tangibles are extremely wide-ranging and can be categorised in a number of ways, but a broad breakdown can be made as follows.

Objects of intrinsic value
This would include items such as precious metals and gem-stones whose value is determined more or less by objective cri-teria rather than any artistic or cultural merit. For this reason, they can be easier to get to grips with, though an understand-ing of the market is still useful.

Arts and crafts
This group covers items such as paintings and antiques, ranging from furniture to silver or porcelain. Specialist knowledge is

more or less essential and some objects may need particular storage conditions. Security and insurance are also important considerations; it is worth checking out specialist art insurers, who can offer better rates with fewer specifications on security measures than the big general companies.

Collections

Collectable items range from those with recognised markets and dealers, such as stamps and coins, to the more esoteric, such as matchboxes and beer mats. The latter, of course, are usually collected for pleasure rather than financial gain, but even in the former case, enthusiasm for the subject is often the key to financial success; the essence of a good collection is that the items have been hand-picked, rather than simply thrown together, so that the sum is greater than the parts.

Other items

Tangibles that do not come into the above categories include, for example, jewellery, exotic rugs and classic cars. Like collectables, these are often bought for pleasure rather than investment gain; for the latter purpose, specialist knowledge or advice is desirable, as the most aesthetic objects are not necessarily the most financially rewarding.

Although there is such a wide variation in types, tangibles do have some common characteristics, which should be borne in mind if you are buying primarily for investment purposes.

1. They produce no income, which can be an advantage to higher rate taxpayers, but meanwhile they involve running costs for storage and insurance. Hence the prospects for capital gain should be enough to finance this ongoing 'deficit' as well as producing a profit.

2. While some tangibles such as gold and precious stones have intrinsic worth, in many cases the price depends on current supply and demand rather than 'face' value. This in turn may be influenced by fashion as much as market trends, as well as economic factors such as inflation which detract from financial alternatives.

3. Some items, especially collectables, may not be freely marketable, so money invested should be truly 'spare' capital that you will not need access to in an emergency.

4. Because the markets are often limited, with little competition, dealing costs or mark-ups may be high, so you need to invest over a longer term before there is an appreciable profit.

Precious metals

As alternative investments go, precious metals have a certain glamour, but investors should not get too carried away with the glitter. Investment value and beauty are two very different characteristics; jewellery, for example, may have increasing value but should not be considered purely for investment purposes, because the retail mark-ups are high and the cost of the workmanship involved can outweigh the intrinsic value of the metal.

Both gold and platinum can be bought in the form of bars and coins. Gold is the more popular choice with investors; while platinum is much rarer, and is underpinned to some extent by industrial demand, it does not have the same history as gold of being seen as the ultimate store of value and haven in troubled times.

In the UK, the one-ounce gold Britannia coin is minted for investment purposes. Other options are the South African Krugerrand and the Canadian Maple Leaf; there are also sovereigns, which are smaller, but these are not always available singly – a minimum purchase might be 20 coins.

An important point to bear in mind is that if you buy coins in this country they will be subject to VAT at (currently) 17.5 per cent. This can be avoided by buying offshore, usually in the Channel Islands, and this can be arranged through a high street bank. On top of the price of the coin, you will also have to pay a dealing charge and transportation costs, including insurance while the coins are in transit.

To continue to avoid VAT, the coins will need to be held offshore, which the bank will do for you. This is also convenient in terms of security, but it does of course mean further charges, for both storage and insurance. Together these would currently come to around £100 a year upwards, depending on the number of coins and their value. Furthermore, any urge to see your treasure should be resisted, as this can incur yet another charge, on top of your own travelling costs.

Given that there are these various running costs, and no income being generated, gold is only attractive if there are good prospects of capital growth. The increasing sophistication of 'hedging' instruments such as futures and options has meant that gold is no longer the prime refuge from inflation that it once was, and after the 'gold rush' of 1980 the metal spent many years in the doldrums. Last year it hit a 12-year low. However, plans have been mooted for a millennium gold coin. The demand this could create would soak up the excess supply in the market and could set the price rising again.

An alternative way of investing in gold is to buy shares in gold mining companies, either directly or through a unit trust. These tend to move ahead of the price of the gold itself and are even more volatile: over 1995, the gold price went up 7 per cent, while share prices rose by a massive 44 per cent. Offshore funds are another possibility; these may invest in shares, physical gold or gold futures, so will respond to different market factors.

There are also both onshore and offshore commodity funds, the former investing only in shares of associated companies, while the latter can include direct investment; these may include some exposure to gold, but within a spread of holdings which can reduce the risk. Finally, you can buy gold options, but these are not currently traded in London, so the dealing cost is relatively high.

Diamonds

Diamonds share some of the characteristics of gold: a hard-headed approach is needed, and jewellery should be ruled out for purely investment purposes, because too much of the cost relates to the settings and there is also the fashion element which can affect the value. Again, it is best to buy and store the stones offshore, which a dealer can arrange for you, but there will be storage and insurance costs.

Diamonds offer rather more scope than gold to pick and choose what you want, because there are a wide range of grades. Stones are categorised by the 'four Cs': cut, colour, clarity and carat (in other words, weight). Each of these may be good, bad or somewhere in between, so there are various possible permutations which will influence the current price and the future prospects.

The conventional rule is that investment stones should be at the upper end of the scale in each category, as quality stones are more likely to hold their value, but you need to take expert advice in the light of how much you want to invest and how long for. It may be, for instance, that several lesser stones will suit you better than a single one of very high quality, as it would give you greater flexibility in selling; but depending on supply and demand in the market, lower quality stones may be less readily marketable.

Tastes can also change. For example, colourless stones used to be preferred to coloured ones, but it is now the latter that fetch the highest prices. In all cases, it is essential to have a certificate from an independent assessor on the quality of the stone.

Like gold, diamonds used to prosper in times of high inflation, but have been less talked of in recent years. As well as market influences, they are subject to investment fads, so can experience sudden booms when prices reach unrealistic levels, as happened in the late 1970s, but can equally undergo long periods of disinterest.

Wine

Wine drinking has enjoyed increasing popularity in this country in recent years, leading to a growing interest in fine wines and corresponding opportunities for investment. Getting it right, though, can be tricky, as there are fashions in types, as well as acknowledged good and bad vintages.

The most popular wines among investors are claret and port. As these take some years to mature, prices and prospects will depend on the time-scale on which you are prepared to invest. If you are willing to tie up your capital for ten years, say, you can go for a fairly young wine and wait for it to reach its prime;

if you are taking only a five-year view, you may need to look at something older, which will be more expensive. You can even make your investment before the wine is bottled, through the wine futures market, in the hope that it will mature successfully to command a high price in years to come. Generally speaking, you should expect to hold claret for at least five years before it becomes profitable, while port should be laid down for at least 20 years.

The minimum investment could be just a few hundred pounds, depending on what you choose, but around £5000 might be a more sensible starting-point. You should aim to buy in cases (12 bottles) rather than single bottles, as the latter tend to be traded only if they are particularly rare. Remember, too, that you will need proper storage conditions, which may require a certain outlay. In addition, you should consider specialised insurance, as a standard household policy may cover you only against theft and not, for example, accidental damage. Alternatively, some wine merchants offer storage facilities, including insurance.

An alternative is a wine investment fund, launched in 1995. Specialising in Bordeaux, this gives you the opportunity to invest in 25 wines picked by the fund manager, for a minimum investment of £2500. There is a charge of 1.5 per cent to 2 per cent to cover insurance and storage costs, plus an exit charge of up to 2.5 per cent. Profits are not taxable, as wine is considered to be a depreciating asset, but the scheme is also not covered by the Financial Services Act, so you do not have the protection of the Investors Compensation Scheme should things go wrong.

There are numerous books available on wine, as well as occasional press articles, and Christie's and Sotheby's both hold regular auctions.

Forestry

One of the main attractions of an investment in forestry is that it attracts substantial tax concessions. For a start, commercial timber that is growing is free from both income and capital gains tax. The 1992 Budget also doubled the business property relief from inheritance tax, from 50 per cent to a full

100 per cent, on commercial woodland. This applies after the first two years of ownership and means that, on the investor's subsequent death, there will be no liability to inheritance tax. With the tax rate currently at 40 per cent for assets outside the nil rate band of £223,000 (except property inherited by a spouse, which is exempt from tax), this represents a considerable saving.

The condition is that the woodland must be run as a commercial enterprise, which may mean you have to employ a qualified manager. The other drawback is that you can no longer claim tax relief on plantation expenses under Schedule D, as this has been phased out. This has removed the attraction of the traditional route into forestry, which was to buy bare land and plant it, offsetting the costs against other income for tax purposes, and then passing on the forest to your heirs as a long-term investment.

During the first 25 years of its life, a plantation incurs a good deal of expense in management and tending, while producing no return, as the trees are too young to be felled. Although the tax relief has been replaced by the Woodland Grant Scheme, this does not offer the same degree of financial support during the maturing phase, hence investors are turning away from new or young plantations towards those that are already mature enough to offer some felling opportunities and thus produce an income from the start. As a result, good quality woodlands of an appropriate age are moving into short supply.

The current outlook for forestry as an investment is good, with timber prices on the increase. But while it is possible to buy part shares through a management company, it has to be remembered that this is essentially a large-scale, long-term investment rather than one of quick returns and in many cases, the tax advantages are a significant part of the appeal.

An alternative route is an investment fund. One launched recently will run for ten years and expects an initial tax-free return of 7 per cent a year, rising by up to 2 per cent each year. The minimum investment was £5000. The fund was open for a limited period only, so if you are interested in this type of investment you should be prepared to take up opportunities quickly as they arise.

Theatre productions

You do not have to be rich to become an 'angel' – a sponsor of a theatre production – but you do have to be sanguine about losing money. There have been some notable successes but, for many productions, even commercial viability is a stiff target. By the time the initial cost and the running expenses have been met, ticket sales have to be very good for you to make a return – many shows fail to make enough even to recoup the original investment.

As well as being philosophical about losses, you need to be hard-headed in your choice of show or producer. Worthy causes are generally not the money-spinners; what matters is not what the critics say, but what the audiences think. The recommended approach is to back a successful producer, rather than choosing an individual production.

The Society of London Theatre operates a scheme on behalf of its members to put investors in touch with producers looking for backers. The minimum investment required is usually £1000 or £2000. An alternative to backing individual productions is a collective fund. The Gabriel Fund was launched some two years ago and units cost up to £5000 each. However, you pay only £1000 up-front and the balance will be called for only if the fund runs out of money and still has losses to meet.

You can also invest in films, through a company called Cromwell Productions, which was set up to provide a novel form of film finance. For as little as £500, you get not only a share of half the net profits and the full return of your money within a fixed time, but also the chance to be in the film yourself as an extra. Four such films have been released so far.

Because of the length of time it takes for a film to get from shooting to screening, you may have quite a wait to get your money back – you can expect it to be about two years before you see your first returns. But you will get a ticket to the première to see a glimpse of yourself and your name in the film's credits.

In the July 1997 Budget, the Chancellor gave the British film industry and its investors a highly attractive tax-break by allowing 100 per cent of production and acquisition costs to be written off for the purposes of income tax. This applies to low-budget British films and will run to July 2000. Neill Clerk Capital has launched a scheme designed to take advantage of this tax allowance. The Take One Partnership will focus on television documentaries and has a minimum investment of £1000.

Information can be obtained from:

The Society of London Theatre
0171 836 0971
Cromwell Productions
01789 415187
The Gabriel Fund
0171 734 7184

Enterprise Investment Scheme

Just as there are theatre angels, so there are 'business angels' – private investors who provide finance for entrepreneurs. They help to fill a gap at the bottom end of the market, backing very small companies for which bank financing may be unsuitable or even impossible to arrange. In many cases, they will also contribute management expertise as well as cash.

The British Venture Capital Association produces an annual directory which can help you find a suitable venture to invest in. Another organisation which provides introductory services is the Local Investment Networking Company (Linc). It produces a monthly bulletin listing businesses which have undergone an initial screening for suitability. The subscription fee is £150 a year.

However, this is a highly risky area, because the companies are small and are likely to have no track record and no security for the funding. Two alternative routes into the venture capital arena are offered by recent government initiatives, which also carry tax advantages: venture capital trusts (VCTs), which are described in Chapter 8, and the Enterprise Investment Scheme (EIS).

The Enterprise Investment Scheme was announced in the

1993 Autumn Budget as the successor to the Business Expansion Scheme, which was phased out at the end of 1993. Dubbed 'Son of BES', it has the same aim of encouraging investment in small, unquoted companies.

The scheme differs from its predecessor in certain respects. The maximum you can invest each year is £150,000, as against £40,000 for the BES, but income tax relief on the investment is limited to 20 per cent. This makes the scheme less attractive for higher rate taxpayers, who could get a full 40 per cent relief from BES investments.

In fact, the scheme as originally announced found few takers; during 1994, the total raised was only about £5 million and no scheme reached its maximum subscription level. This was addressed in the 1994 Budget, which improved the scheme with further tax concessions, while the 1998 budget raised the maximum investment from £100,000 to £150,000.

Investors may get 'rollover' relief on capital gains made from the sale of other assets if they reinvest the proceeds into an EIS. Although this only defers the tax – it will have to be paid eventually when the EIS shares are sold – it does mean that the up-front relief on the EIS investment can be equivalent to 60 per cent – 20 per cent income tax and 40 per cent capital gains tax relief.

Moreover, there is no capital gains tax liability on the EIS shares themselves. You must, however, hold them for at least five years to qualify for the tax benefits.

The scope of the EIS has also been extended to include property-backed businesses such as hotels, leisure clubs and house-building. In addition, schemes may offer a 'contracted exit', meaning that there is a guaranteed return to investors.

This can cut the risk considerably, although any guarantee is only as good as the underlying security – the company could fail and so might its guarantor. You should also remember that investments are locked in for at least five years, even if you are guaranteed an exit thereafter. But if you are a higher rate taxpayer and have money you will not need to access, this is an area worth considering.

Further information is available from:

Local Investment Networking Company (Linc)
0171 236 3000
British Venture Capital Association
0171 240 3846

Enterprise zone trusts

Enterprise zone trusts are based on enterprise zones, which are government-designated development areas around the country that attract special tax reliefs for construction. The trusts offer investors a stake in a portfolio of commercial properties, which should generate an annual income from rents.

Investments can be made during a trust's subscription period, with a normal minimum of £5000 and no maximum. Tax relief is available at your highest rate, but applies only to the portion of money used to buy or build properties, not to acquire the land. The Inland Revenue decides for each trust what proportion relates to land and is therefore disallowed for tax relief; on average, this is about 10 per cent, although it could be up to 30 per cent.

Besides the tax relief, a further attraction is that investments can be funded by borrowing that is itself tax efficient. You can borrow up to 70 per cent of your gross investment and interest on this loan will be set against the income earned for tax purposes. Hence you will need to provide very little, if any, money up front, while the income tax bill on your returns will be substantially reduced.

The income comes from rent on the properties, which is distributed to investors, less an amount to cover the scheme's costs. Several trusts offer a guarantee for an initial period, which will provide a set return if no tenants are found or if the rent drops below a certain level.

But these guarantees should be treated with caution. For one thing, the payments are fully taxable and no tax relief is given against them for interest on money you borrow to invest. Second, the value of the guarantee depends on the financial strength of the guarantor; there have been cases where schemes have collapsed. Third, the guarantee period is generally no more than five years and income thereafter will depend entirely on the rent received, which in turn will depend on the quality and location of the properties.

Enterprise zone investments also represent a long-term commitment, as tax relief is normally clawed back if investors pull out within 25 years. The exception is that, after seven years, the trust may sell a lesser interest in its properties, thereby raising capital which can be distributed to investors.

While returns can look attractive, enterprise zone trusts should be viewed as high risk. The administrative costs can be high and the potential for capital appreciation is becoming more limited, as many zones are nearing the end of their ten-year life and the shortage of new investment opportunities is driving up prices. Hence it is well worth seeking advice from a specialist.

Lloyd's of London

Becoming a member of the Lloyd's insurance market has never been for the faint-hearted. The losses of recent years have only served to emphasise this: in 1989 they amounted to a record £2.06 billion. 'Names', as they are known, have had more than their fingers burned and the market has suffered considerable turmoil.

The primary feature of the market has always been that members have unlimited liability. To become a member, you must have minimum assets of £250,000 and this excludes the value of property which is your main residence. But in the event of losses, all your assets can be at stake, including your home and furniture. Underwriting profits and losses for any given year are not finally assessed for three years so, in the event of a disaster, there can be a long wait to discover the total extent of the damage.

There are currently around 6825 Names, operating in 155 syndicates. The standard procedure for joining has been that, in addition to showing you had sufficient assets, you had to be supported by two existing members and satisfy the committee that you were suitable.

But the recent upheavals brought a radical rethink, as the market needed to put aside its difficulties and attract new

money. In October 1993, Lloyd's members voted to allow limited companies to invest, to provide a back-up for underwriting
syndicates. This has spawned a number of investment trusts,
which provide a means for private investors to participate for as
little as £1000. These are explained in Chapter 8.

A free guide to investing in the Lloyd's market is available
from ShareLink (telephone 0121 200 4610). More information
can also be obtained from:

Lloyd's of London
Lime Street
London EC3M 7HA
Telephone 0171 327 1000

Ethical investment

Ethical investment is about knowing and approving of what
your money goes into.

Although it may sound like a minority pursuit it is worth
remembering that more than £1 billion of funds under management is now directed according to ethical criteria. If you add
church-related pension and other funds whose investment is
ethically guided, the figure may be four or five times that.
Furthermore, the concept is nothing new. Having copied the
idea from post-Vietnam America, British ethical investment
vehicles have been around since 1983.

How to invest

Ethical investment options include unit trusts, pension funds,
endowment policies and PEPs. In its *Money & Ethics* reference
work – which, incidentally, is a must for anyone wishing to
investigate the subject in greater depth – the Ethical Investment
Research Service (EIRIS) analyses 32 funds which are run
according to ethical criteria, as at June 1997. EIRIS lists each of
the funds, appraising them according to no fewer than 23 'corporate criteria'. It is worth listing them just to get a feel for the
subject and whether they would be on your ethical do's and
don'ts list. Those to be avoided are:

- sale and production of alcohol;

- testing of products on animals;
- gambling;
- production of greenhouse gases;
- health and safety breaches;
- operations in countries with poor human rights records;
- intensive farming and meat sale;
- Ministry of Defence contracts;
- production or sale of military goods;
- nuclear power;
- ozone depletion;
- pesticides;
- pornography and adult films;
- road building;
- exploitation of the Third World;
- tobacco production or sale;
- extraction, sale or use of tropical hardwood;
- water pollution.

EIRIS also lists five activities which investors may wish to support:

- provision of positive products and services;
- community involvement;
- disclosure of information;
- good record on environmental issues;
- good record on equal opportunities.

These two groups of issues place ethical investment securely in the twin camps of all that is morally 'right' and 'good' in the fullest, holistic sense and what is best practice in corporate governance. Shareholder power, participation and protest are certainly becoming red-hot issues and some may argue that they are the natural counterweight to the concept of limited liability and corporate short-termism.

Freedom to invest

But how far do you take this in deciding where to invest? Do you avoid all privatised utility stocks, for example, on the basis that you disapprove of the government selling off the family infrastructure silver? Do you avoid a raft of otherwise appealing emerging market investment destinations and the companies which are active in those emerging markets because of alleged or perceived human rights abuses? Would there be any companies or countries left to invest in if you did?

The point about ethical investment is that you are free to exercise your right to invest in those things you approve of and avoid those which you do not. There is an implicit recognition that, beyond financial return, there are other values which should be taken into account when making an investment decision. Which they are is up to you. Of course, each time you set a criterion you narrow the range of investment options open to you.

Screened funds and returns

To take two funds as examples, the largest ethical fund in the UK excludes all but 18 of the UK's 100 biggest companies while another can select from only 400 companies worldwide because of the standards it sets itself. The technical term for this type of selective investment is 'screened funds'. Independent financial advisers and ethical fund investment managers can produce figures to show that this screening does not necessarily impair returns. Performance figures show that ethical funds, like any other, produce mixed results, but the best can match or beat non-ethical funds.

Risk

Depending on a fund's ethical selection criteria it may, however, have a higher risk profile. The argument runs that stringent criteria such as those listed above tend to exclude most, if not all, of larger, FTSE 100 companies. Investments tend to be in smaller and therefore higher risk stocks which can be vulnerable to price fluctuations and public relations accidents, especially if other funds themselves become disenchanted and start to sell their holdings in a significant way, so affecting share prices. This points to the importance of risk spreading within the fund, which, as we have seen, is restricted anyway due to selection criteria: a kind of ethical-financial Catch-22.

There is still a deeply-rooted folk-belief that if you invest with conscience and responsibility you have to accept higher risk and lower returns. However, the spread of shareholder pressure and higher degrees of corporate governance should eventually increase the range of companies which fit ethical criteria and at the same time investors are likely to get more demanding in their performance expectations.

NPI, which runs two ethical unit trusts, has launched the NPI Social Index, designed to measure the performance of ethical investments. The index is made up of 158 companies: 37 from the FTSE 100 Index, 36 from the next tier down, the FTSE 250 Index, eight investment trusts and the rest from the smaller companies sector. The selection aims to reflect the sector structure of the All-Share Index. NPI has tested the index back to 1990 and over that period it has significantly outperformed the FTSE 100.

HSBC is also launching an ethical index, the HSBC Securities Ethical 100 Index. This will comprise 100 of the most ethical companies from the FTSE 350 Index, excluding investment trusts. The constituents will be reviewed every year; new companies may be included if they improve their ethical rating, while any that drop out of the 350 Index will also be dropped from HSBC's.

Ethical banking
Choosing the right ethical fund may require a fairly comprehensive study of all those available, but choosing an ethical bank is a little easier.

The Co-operative Bank led the way in 1990 by nailing its ethical colours firmly to the mast. It says, for example, that it 'will not invest in or supply financial services to any regime or organisation which oppresses the human spirit, takes away the rights of individuals or manufactures any instrument of torture'. Its policy goes on to cover, among other things, the sales of weapons, money laundering, animal experiments, factory farming and blood sports. The bank supplies a range of standard clearing bank services.

In the end, ethical investment is largely a question of what you want it to be. If you are not sure just what would fit your conscience – and your pocket – a good way to start is to contact the Ethical Investment Research Service. It can cut short the process of research and help you to sift through the increasing amount of information which has become available as the concept of ethical investment has gained appeal.

Useful reading
- *The Ethical Investor*, Russel Sparkes, HarperCollins Publishers, 1995, £9.99.
- *Money & Ethics: A guide to pensions, PEPs, endowment mortgages and other ethical investment plans*, Ethical Investment Research Service, 1996, £12.50.

The Ethical Investment Research Service can be contacted on 0171 735 1351. It can carry out an appraisal of your portfolio and tell you which of your holdings may be ethically challenged.

Investing in property

Property has not looked an attractive area in which to invest since the major slump of the late 1980s and early 1990s. Any upward movement in prices has been eagerly hailed as a recovery but it is only now that there seems to be an upswing of any substance. However, with a lump sum to invest, you are well placed to strike a deal.

Domestic property
We all need somewhere to live. It still makes sense to avoid paying rent to someone else and, according to a recent survey, 92 per cent of home owners believe it is better to buy than to rent. Nationwide statistics show that 67 per cent of the housing stock is owner occupied. A lump-sum investor does not need to borrow so, apart from maintenance costs, council tax, insurance and the other usual bills, he can have a roof over his head for free.

The benefit of this should not be overlooked. The purchase price of a four bedroom semi-detached house in good condition and in a reasonably sought-after area in suburban London could be £275,000. To rent a similar property might cost £350 a week. That saving represents a benefit of £18,200 per year or

6.6 per cent of the original purchase price. And there is still the asset of the house which can be sold in due course.

Of course, selling is the off-putting part, with memories of the long slump in the housing market still fresh. Although the market in the south-east, at least, has risen fast, a return to the large quick profits of the 1980s still seems unlikely. Nevertheless, as a cash buyer you stand to get a keen price, which should pay off if you are prepared to invest for some years.

There are still tax advantages in investing in a domestic property although they have slowly been whittled away in successive budgets. Provided it is a main residence, any gain realised when selling the property is free of capital gains tax. Second, for those who are supplementing their lump-sum investment with borrowing, there is still tax relief at 10 per cent on mortgage interest on the first £30,000 of a loan.

Aside from buying a property to live in yourself, you can also buy to let as an investment. Indeed, thanks to the housing slump, many would-be sellers have found themselves becoming landlords instead.

Generally, you will want to set up an 'assured shorthold tenancy' – this is, in fact, what most tenancies are automatically these days. It is a contract for a fixed term, typically six months or a year. Thereafter it can be renewed, but the landlord has the right to repossess at two months' notice.

If you do not wish to manage the property yourself, you can get an agency to do it; many estate agents offer a letting service. The fees are of the order of 10 per cent of the rent to find a tenant and a running cost of 5 per cent to collect rents and manage the property.

Rental income is taxable, but you can claim costs against it, such as insurance, water rates if you pay them yourself and any agency letting fees. If you have a mortgage on the property, you can also offset the interest. In this case, you will not receive the normal mortgage interest tax relief (Miras), but you should be much better off, as Miras is worth only 10 per cent on the first £30,000 of a loan. Some lenders charge a slightly higher interest rate where property is let, generally 0.5 per cent above the standard rate.

Second homes and timeshares

The advantage of not having to pay rent extends, of course, to second homes and timeshares. In the case of second or holiday homes, use of the property is likely to be entirely in the hands of the purchaser throughout the year. The property can be rented out to produce income. Furthermore, it can be nominated as the main residence and exempted from CGT. The switch in nomination between homes is up to the owner in agreement with the Inland Revenue; careful consideration of the best option with a tax specialist is advisable.

Timeshares entitle the owner to the use of a property such as a villa, chalet or holiday apartment for a given number of days or weeks. But most can be exchanged with owners of the same or other timeshares so that you are not locked into taking the same weeks of holiday at the same place for the term of the timeshare. Ultimately, it is possible to sell on the timeshare although the price is unlikely to be predictable. All told, it is worth totting up what you would have paid if you had had to rent other holiday accommodation during the term of the time-share ownership and any profit can be a bonus. It must be said that, as with any other property investment, prices can go down as well as up and there is no telling which way they will go. Lastly, you should not forget to take into account annual main-tenance charges and any other fees which may be payable. These can prove rather costly over the long term.

Commercial property

Although house purchase is the most obvious form of property investment, most of us also invest indirectly in commercial property through pension and life assurance arrangements. The main sectors of the market in which they invest are office build-ings, retail outlets and industrial property.

The factors which are taken into account when fund managers invest can be useful in understanding their investment strategies and in making one's own property investment decision*:

- the position of the property;
- the description of the property;
- the tenure of tenants;

- the lease terms;
- the identity of tenants;
- the amount and timing of rental income;
- the initial purchase price of the property;
- the total yield on the property.

These considerations will be taken into account when the fund manager invests in a piece of property, perhaps as a group of institutions buying an office block or trading estate. At the same time he or she may invest in property companies whose portfolios are made up of a spread of such investments or they may invest in property funds which in turn invest in a variety of different types of property in selected locations.

UK property, along with UK equities, has traditionally been a mainstay of insurance company investment. It has been considered long term and sufficiently reliable. However, confidence was quite severely dented by the aftermath of the property building boom of the 1980s, with projects such as London Docklands' Canary Wharf where boom was followed by bust within a short space of time. In the last year we have seen investors returning and buying in at lower prices. Some of this new activity has been funded by bank borrowings and rights issues. But despite a blizzard of statistics from commercial estate agents and property analysts supporting the idea that recovery is on the way, many investors have yet to be convinced.

Where pension plans allow for individual policyholders to pick which funds they wish to invest in, UK property may appear among the available options. Bearing in mind the above criteria, it is important for investors thinking of looking at the property sector to delve into details of the composition of the fund on offer and what properties their money would be funding, as well as to receive regular updates about broad market trends and reports about the sites themselves.

Unit trusts

Another way of investing in property is through a unit trust. A lump-sum investment can be made from £1000 upwards. There are two authorised property unit trusts investing in commercial property in the UK, of which the larger is the Norwich Property Trust.

According to its latest report, its portfolio is split into five categories (not counting cash): offices, high street retail, retail warehouses, industrial and property shares. This last can be further broken down into ordinary shares, convertibles and convertible preference shares. Of the direct property held, the largest sector (as at 30 November 1997) was offices, at 23.7 per cent, and the largest geographic region, not surprisingly, was London and the south east.

As with any unit trust, the price of units can go up or down, but there is a further caveat, in that you may not be able to sell exactly when you want to; because property itself is not readily saleable, the managers of a trust can delay the repurchase of units. In practice, though, the cash and equity holdings provide a margin which should cover day-to-day transactions, unless there is a sudden stampede to sell. Normally, dealings take place daily and prices are quoted in *The Daily Telegraph* and the *Financial Times*.

13

Charitable giving

Giving to charity may not rank as an investment in the ordinary sense, but it can be regarded as an investment in the future of society. Moreover, with a little organisation – as opposed to simply giving to street collectors – it can be tax efficient.

The simplest arrangement is a payroll scheme, operated by an employer. This allows employees to make gifts directly from their salary, of up to £75 a month. The money is deducted before tax and paid to an approved Agency Charity with which the employer has an agreement. The employees, however, have a free choice of which charities their money goes to and the Agency Charity simply passes it on, although it may make a small charge for administration.

If your employer does not offer a payroll scheme, or you would like to make larger, one-off gifts, you can use Gift Aid. This carries a minimum for each gift of £250, net of basic rate tax, but there is no maximum. You give the charity a certificate which allows it to claim back basic rate tax from the Inland Revenue and, if you are a higher rate taxpayer, you may claim the extra 17 per cent. In this year's Budget, the Chancellor announced an extension to the Gift Aid Scheme – Millennium Gift Aid. Due to start later this year and run to 31 December 2000, it will provide tax relief on gifts from just £100 and upwards.

The Charities Aid Foundation offers 'Personal Charity Accounts' for those giving through Gift Aid or covenants. The Foundation can reclaim tax on the gifts and also provides a 'cheque book' of vouchers which you can make out to your chosen charities.

If you care about the wildlife in our seas and around our coasts

If clean seas and beaches are important to you

- you can help make a world of difference by supporting our vital work to protect the world's oceans

To make a donation, take out a covenant or remember us in your will, please contact:

MARINE CONSERVATION SOCIETY

9 Gloucester Road, Ross-on-Wye
Herefordshire HR9 5BU
Tel 01989 566017 Fax 01989 567815
www.mcsuk.mcmail.com
Registered Charity No. 1004005

INVESTING IN SEAS FIT FOR LIFE

The Marine Conservation Society (MCS) is the only UK charity dedicated solely to protecting the marine environment. Colourful reefs, shoaling fish, dolphins and seals - life around our coasts is as fascinating and fragile as that found anywhere on our blue planet. Yes *blue*, for water covers almost three-quarters of the Earth and it is filled with life of great beauty and complexity.

However, species are threatened the world over by pollution, overfishing and destruction of their habitats - urgent action is needed to safeguard this wonderful marine heritage. As the UK's foremost voice in marine conservation, MCS provides advice to Government, industry and the public. Based on sound research, MCS lobbies for the protection of marine wildlife and to prevent the pollution of our seas and beaches caused by sewage, toxic chemicals, oil and litter.

Just two of MCS's many successes in International Year of The Ocean (1998) were the granting of full protection for basking shark in UK waters after a 10 year MCS campaign, and the publication of the 11th *Good Beach Guide* which highlighted MCS's continuing campaign for clean bathing waters in the UK.

The Marine Conservation Society works to ensure that our seas are fit for life - for wildlife and for future generations.

The **Leukaemia CARE** Society

Last year Leukaemia CARE helped hundreds of families by providing:

● Financial Assistance Grants - Caravan Holidays
● Countless befriending hours

This year Leukaemia CARE will be asked to help even more families. **We** can only help them if you will help us as ever increasing demand is made on limited resources.

A donation or covenant now and a legacy later will make it possible. the Society relies upon volunteers to assist those suffering from Leukaemia and allied Blood Disorders.

If you are able to offer your time and experience to befriend, fundraise, support others etc, please contact the office at:

14 Kingfisher Court (LS98)
Venny Bridge, Pinhoe, Exeter, Devon EX4 8JN.
Tel: Exeter (01392) 464848,
Fax: Exeter (01392) 460331

Registered Charity no. 259483

Further information on Gift Aid is given in the Inland Revenue leaflet IR113 and from the Gift Aid helpline on 0151 472 6038. The Charities Aid Foundation can be contacted on 01732 771333.

Making an investment in a worthy cause

Vicki Pulman
Charities Aid Foundation

Giving to charity may not rank as an investment in the ordinary sense, but it can be regarded as an investment in the future of society. Moreover, with a little organisation it can be tax efficient.

Around 80 per cent of people in the UK make donations to charity. Few, however, are even aware of the full benefits available through the tax system, not just to the charities they choose to support, but to themselves. Overall, government has introduced three schemes for tax-effective giving, enabling both private individuals and corporate donors to make their charitable giving more effective.

Donations made from taxed funds through any one of these shcemes enables the Inland Revenue to repay the basic rate tax of around 25 per cent to the charity. If you are a higher rate taxpayer, you may reclaim the marginal rate of 15 per cent.

The schemes offer three very different methods of payment. These are by deed of covenant, payroll giving and Gift Aid. The *deed of covenant* is the oldest of the three and involves a contractual obligation to make regular donations over a period of four or more years. These payments can be made annually, monthly or in a lump sum, allowing the charity to subtract regular payments on its own behalf. Whichever method is used, tax is reclaimed and added to the total donation, increasing it by roughly one-third, at no extra cost to either you or the charity. There is no maximum amount payable under this scheme, although in order to cover the cost of administration, some charities may require a minimum donation.

Payroll giving was introduced by the government to encourage ongoing and regular gifts to charity. Since 1987, this scheme has enabled donors paying PAYE to make monthly con-

Would you expect a child with a terminal illness in the UK today to receive first class care and sympathetic support?

Although terminal illness in children is relatively rare there are, nevertheless, about 15,000 children in the UK expected to die in childhood. The very fact that they are a minority group means that they are pushed to the margins of the 'caring services' and many families struggle to care at home without help.

ACT is the only national organisation set up to focus exclusively on the needs of terminally ill children and their families. We believe that all such children, wherever they live and whatever their individual condition, should have equal access to specialist care and support, particularly at home. ACT provides a national focus of expertise drawn from its multi-disciplinary membership and has a vital role in co-ordinating and improving care.

We are campaigning vigorously for recognition of their needs and the provision of children's palliative care services throughout the UK. We have published standards of care which are now being used to develop services and the picture is slowly beginning to change. ACT also supports families by putting them in touch with appropriate services and providing information literature.

ACT relies entirely on voluntary contributions - please support our pioneering work and improve the lives of terminally ill children.

Association for Children with Life-threatening or Terminal Conditions and their Families

65 St Michael's Hill, Bristol BS2 8DZ
Telephone (0117) 922 1556 Fax (0117) 930 4707

REGISTERED CHARITY NO. 1029658   EXECUTIVE DIRECTOR: STELLA ELSTON

tributions direct from their pay or pension at source, before tax is levied. The donor then pays tax at the usual rate but only on its remaining income. A donation, for example, of £50 per month made from pre-taxed income, would cost you £37.50 in real terms and only £30 if you are a higher rate taxpayer. The maximum payable through this scheme is now £900 per annum or £75 per month and the real benefit, particularly to the charity, is in providing it with a regular source of income with which to budget and plan ahead.

Gift Aid is the most recent scheme and was introduced in 1991. It is the only scheme allowing single, one-off donations to be made tax effectively. In order to qualify, the gift has to amount to at least £250 but there is no obligation to repeat the donation. As with the covenant, however, tax is reclaimed by the charity at basic rate. This increases the minimum gift of £250 to £333.33 and allows higher rate donors to reclaim the marginal rate of around £50 for themselves.

There is one condition when making donations through any tax-effective scheme: the money has to go to a charity either registered with the Charity Commission or recognised by the Inland Revenue as being charitable. Organisations such as scout groups, places of worship, schools and hospitals, while not being registered charities, are all considered to be 'charitable'. Despite the obvious benefits of these schemes, for many they lack the flexibility and the spontaneity essential when giving to charity. There is a way, however, in which you can respond to a radio or television appeal, send off a few pounds in response to an advertisement or even give to a local street collector – tax effectively.

A personal charity account scheme, operated by an agency such as the Charities Aid Foundation (CAF), enables you to pay your tax-efficient donation into an account rather than direct to a single charity. As a registered charity itself, CAF reclaims the basic rate tax on the donor's behalf and adds it to the amount already in the account, deducting a small administrative contribution. So, on an initial payment of, say, £120, a revised balance of £152 is created at no extra cost to you. Higher rate taxpayers would be able to reclaim a further £24 for themselves.

Once the money is in the account, you are issued with a

The British Federation of Festivals

The British Federation of Festivals for Music, Dance & Speech includes over 300 festivals across the UK and Ireland. Most of these festivals have a wide range of music, speech and dance competitions and workshops, whilst others are more specialist - perhaps choral, theatre or stage dance. Whatever the discipline, they all offer a platform for performance, and in 1997 there were over one million performances, 80% of whom were under 18.

A festival provides many things: the stimulus of preparing for a public occasion; the opportunity to hear the work of others; and, most importantly, the chance to receive advice from a professional ... someone whom that performer may never have the opportunity to meet in any other way. Professional adjudicators give their time to festival work at greatly reduced rates in order to help young people. The British Federation of Festivals forms a unique interface between the amateur and professional worlds. Its educational value is of tremendous importance in the development of young people.

Festivals bring forward the specially gifted and many famous names found their first platform at their local festival. Sir Donald Sinden, Paul Scotfield, Maureen Lipman, Lesley Garrett, Thomas Allen, Dame Beryl Grey, Wayne Sleep, Robert Powell ... the list goes on and on.

But only a few of today's festival performers will go on to become professionals of the future. Meanwhile, the work done with others who will make their mark in other walks of life is equally important. They will enlarge that educated audience who will support the arts for coming generations and the life skills they will learn in preparing for and presenting a public performance will help them throughout their days, from the time they undertake their first job interview onwards.

The British Veterinary Association
Animal Welfare Foundation (BVA:AWF)
The Veterinary Profession's Own Charity

All veterinary surgeons, upon qualification, make a solemn pledge to uphold and promote the welfare of animals under their care. The Animal Welfare Foundation established by the British Veterinary Association (BVA) in 1984, extends this commitment to all animals. It aims to apply the knowledge, skill and compassion of veterinary surgeons in an effective way through a variety of projects and activities.

The Foundation is the veterinary profession's own charity and plays a unique role in animal welfare. BVA:AWF supports specific research projects in which improved welfare is a primary objective. In addition, educational programmes are initiated and support provided to enhance knowledge and understanding of welfare issues.

WORLD LAND TRUST

The *World Land Trust* was set up ten years ago to help protect areas of tropical rain forest which were, and still are, under tremendous threat from commercial and illegal logging, poor management and unscrupulous development.

Market prices for hardwood are certainly part of the problem, but the understandable desire to clear forests to make way for agricultural land in order to support the local economy is also a major cause of the 'slash and burn' activity in recent times. However, generally the soil is not suitable for farming. Once cleared, it is further eroded by wind and rain rendering it useless and barren. Early attempts to restore forested areas often failed. The process was hard to reverse.

The *World Land Trust*, together with distinguished local conservationists, has developed a means of forest management which provides a sustainable future, while, at the same time, providing jobs and a modest but regular income through a controlled harvesting of selected trees and fallen timber. In this way, over quarter of a million acres has been saved which in turn protects the wildlife and, where present, supports the local population. In addition, through careful plant propagation, new acres of forest are being created where they once stood.

To complement this field work, the *World Land Trust* has developed an active education programme. Wyld Court Rainforest Conservation Centre at Hampstead Norreys, Berkshire is a tropical forest with living plants and controlled climate which, last year attracted 60,000 visitors (more than the total number of people to visit the National Parks of Belize in the same period!). Of these, half were school children and a comprehensive education pack aimed at pupils of Key Stage 3 is being prepared so that they can study the forest at school through a range of subjects including: science, geography, history and art.

As a registered charity, the *World Land Trust* relies on the generous support of individuals, companies and grant-making trusts. Investment in the secure future of the world's forests can be achieved in a tax efficient way, through the *Gift Aid Scheme*. For full details, contact the World Land Trust on (01986) 874422.

PLEASE HELP US TO HELP THEM

Mozart was confined alone in a stable for 2¹/₂ years. He was visited only occasionally to be brought food and water. His bed was a build up of his own dung. Mozart's hooves had grown long and twisted, he had lice and was in terrible pain.

When we rescued him he was petrified. He would cower at the back of his new stable when approached. When the door was opened it was many days before Mozart ventured out and he was just as frightened of donkeys as he was of people.

Gradually, with patience and kindness, Mozart is beginning to trust again.

Over 7,600 donkeys have been taken into our care, many from lives of cruelty and neglect. To continue our work, we really need your help - either by direct donation or a legacy.

Please send donations to: The Donkey Sanctuary (Dept. CG98), Sidmouth, Devon, EX10 ONU, Tel: (01395) 578222. Fax: (01395) 579266
Registered Charity Number 264818

Over 7,600 donkeys have been taken into care, many from lives tormented by cruelty and neglect. A donkey is never turned away from our Sanctuary and never put down unless there is no longer any quality of life. We need your help to continue rescuing donkeys and to provide them with a home where they can spend their remaining days grazing peacefully and receiving loving care.

Any donation, no matter the amount is greatly appreciated and our doners' list is carefully guarded - we never release details to other organizations.

Administration costs are kept to a minimum - just 7.4p in the £1. If you would like to receive further information, including a copy of our "Will Making Guide", please do not hesitate to contact us. A legacy is of great value to us in ensuring the future of our large donkey family - many of the donkeys live to 40/50+ years. In return we remember with deep gratitude those who have left us a bequest by inscribing their names on our Memory Wall and remembering them at out Memorial Service held every year on The Feast Day of St. Francis of Assisi.

Please send donations to: The Donkey Sanctuary, (Dept. CG98), Sidmouth, Devon, EX10 ONU. Tel: (01395) 578222. Fax: (01395) 579266
Administrator and Founder Dr. Elisabeth D. Svendsen, M.B.E.

CAMP MOHAWK

Camp Mohawk was originally given to a young leader who worked with some of the most desperately needy families in London's East End Docklands as a place to take young children "out of their Concrete Jungle", as was the fashionable phrase at the time.

There was just a small clearing in the woods with an old and dilapidated woodman's hut.

But the children worked hard and after three years had cleared and developed a children's wonderland.

In 1976 the site was "discovered" by the father of a mentally handicapped boy who asked if his son and his handicapped mates could come.

From then on, over the past 22 years, an ever changing stream of children from Canning Town, Custom House, Beckton and all of the areas surrounding the old Royal Docks, have spent all of their weekends and school holidays caring for terribly handicapped children.

The story was captured in an article in the Daily Telegraph Saturday Magazine of the 19th April 1998 which described the Camp as unique in Europe, and the boys and their wonderful work.

Copies of the article are available on request (0118 940 4045), one of the most moving stories that you will ever read.

But the Camp gets no Government or Statutory help and relies solely on the kindness of its many friends for its support and finances.

No handicapped child ever pays to come to Camp Mohawk. In its way the camp serves three groups. First the children from the East End who find confidence and the ability to love and care for desperately handicapped children who they see as being so much worse off than themselves.

Second, the handicapped children themselves. Children who are so difficult that they are normally kept hidden away suddenly find freedom, joy and laughter, whilst, thirdly, their parents gat a well deserved break from their 24 hour a day "prison" of loving care and attention which their children have to have.

CAMP MOHAWK
"Berkshire's Smallest But Most Caring Charity."

A wonderful children's Spring and Summer Children's Camp in Berkshire where some of the most deprived of East London's

"East End Kids"

give up all of their weekends and school holidays to care for Terribly brain damaged and Autistic children.

Camp Mohawk receives no statutory, Government or Local Authority help and survives on the love, kindness and financial help of its many wonderful friends.

Please help us by making a donation or bequest.

We will help you make it tax effective.

Visitors are always welcome.

Camp Mohawk	The Woodland Centre Trust
Wargrave	(Registered Charity 278681)
Berkshire	
RG10 8PU	Telephone 0118 940 4045

Two thirds of the world's blindness is preventable

Photo by: Colin Jones

With your help

Imagine you had a nine year old granddaughter who is blind.

One day you discover that in a country far away, there is a miraculous cure that will bring her sight back. But you can't afford it.

Sadly, for millions of families the world over, this is reality. Two thirds of the world's 38 million blind need never have lost their sight or could be cured. Human beings have the technology and the drugs. All that is lacking is money.

Will you help?

SEE is a charity which funds research in the UK into every cause of blindness: from childhood injury, to glaucoma to improvements in the treatment of diabetic retinopathy. In Africa and Asia, we support practical work such as eye camps to repair cataract and the treatment of river blindness.

Please help us by a donation, a deed of covenant or a legacy. For just £240 - the price of one eye camp - you could restore sight to a whole village. Including someone's nine year old granddaughter.

Save Eyes Everywhere

SEE (The British Council for the Prevention of Blindness)
Contact: Rachel Carr-Hill
12 Hanover Street, London W1H 1DS
Tel: 0171 724 3716
Reg. charity number 270941

The Causes Of Cancer

Each year in the United Kingdom more than 1 80,000 persons die of cancer. One in three of all persons born in the United Kingdom develops some form of cancer during his or her lifetime.

The suffering of patients and the heartache of family and friends represent a tragic social cost. The agony of patients who develop the disease when their children are growing up represents an intolerable burden.

Cancer is not one disease. It is a hundred or more diseases. It can be induced in experimental animals by the use of chemicals, radiations or viruses.

Inspired by the success with antibiotics in controlling infectious diseases, the public, and indeed cancer research scientists have been concentrating in seeking a cure. It is just possible that for many of the forms of cancer the most practical approach will be to find means of prevention and prophylaxis. Cancer is a preventable disease.

Certain occupations carry a higher risk of cancer development compared to the rest of the population. Cancer of the bladder is associated with rubber, dyestuffs and electric cable industry workers; cancer of the lungs is associated with uranium mining as indeed it is with cigarette smoking; leukemia is associated with excess exposure to ionising radiations; cancer of the mesothelium (tissue lining the lungs) is associated with asbestos workers and miners; liver cancer has been associated with vinyl chloride workers.

Most specialists in the field of cancer research now believe that chemicals present in food and the environment in general are responsible for 80 to 90 per cent of all cancers in humans; the remainder are believed to be caused by radiations or viruses. Current evidence suggests that there exists no safe threshold level for a carcinogenic chemical, Aflatoxin, a natural product and a human food contaminant, can be detected down to levels of one part per billion (ppb). It produces one hundred per cent incidence of cancer in rats when incorporated in their diets at levels of 1 5 ppb. Our knowledge of the action of chemical carcinogens indicates that they act optically when administered as frequent small doses over a period of time rather than as large single doses.

There are basically two @major classes of environmental carcinogens the potent carcinogens, such as the aflatoxin and nitrosamines, which can produce cancer in laboratory animals even in the very low concentrations which have been found in food@ there are also the weak carcinogens such as atmospheric pollutants, a number of pesticides and food additives, with effects that may easily escape detection by conventional biological tests. Because such weak carcinogens are unlikely to be implicated epidemiologically. they may be as dangerous, or possibly more dangerous than the more obvious potent carcinogens. There is a long latent period between exposure to a carcinogenic chemical and the clinical appearance of cancer. There are instances of persons who had been born in the vicinity of asbestos mines developing mesothelioma in their fifties and sixties. A few years ago a rare type of vaginal cancer was observed in young women. who twenty years previously have been exposed to a synthetic female sex hormone, diethyl stilboestrot, (DES), as foetuses when their mothers were treated with the drug. The recent rise in childhood leukemia is attributed to prenatal exposure to endocrine disrupting or other chemicals such as pesticides or petrot additives that program the developing foetus for cancer in early life. There is a fundamental difference between a developing system such as the foetus and a mature system, If one starts giving the synthetic female sex hormone, DES to a month-old mouse and continues throughout its lifetime one never gets any effect. But if DES is given to a pregnant mouse or human. it alters gene expression in the foetus permanently, and causes cancer or other abnormalities in the reproductive tract of the offspring. Adverse effects, such as leukemia in the offspring can be produced by very small doses of some chemicals if they are given at a critical time during pregnancy.

There appears to be additive, cumulative and synergistic effects of combined exposures to environmental contaminants. There is evidence suggesting that smoking enhances the carcinogenic effects of asbestos. There is also increasing interest in the role of chemical carcinogens in activating tumour-producing viruses.

Recent technological developments have introduced into food and the environment in general a variety of chemical pollutants of remarkable potency and diverse actions, whose impact upon the entire population is subtle and unpredictable. These are chemicals to which man has not been evolutionarily exposed and the effects of such pollutants in terms of cancer induction may not become apparent for twenty or more years.

237

Invest in his future...

before it's too late

© J Williams/EIA

The Environmental Investigation Agency Charitable Trust (EIA ct) is dedicated to the protection of the natural world. We work undercover to expose the illegal trade in endangered species and environmental crime. We are a small, highly focused organisation which achieves outstanding results with limited resources. Our ground-breaking work has helped save the lives of thousands of wild animals and their natural habitat.

Recent groundbreaking campaigns have highlighted the desperate plight of the endangered Indian tiger, the smuggling of illegal CFCs across Europe and the devastating effect that illegal logging is having on the Orangutan – arguably man's closest relative.

As we approach the 21st century, more and more species are becoming vulnerable and the world is increasingly threatened by the growth of environ-

mental crime. EIA ct's committed supporters are confident that *every* penny invested in our vital work is an investment in the future of all our children. Please join us.

You can help EIA ct secure a future for our world in the new Millenium by giving us a gift of a donation or a legacy. If you would like to make a donation or you would like a free EIA ct legacy pack please call Mary Rice on 0171 490 7040 or write to her at: **EIA ct, FREEPOST, 15 Bowling Green Lane, London EC1R 1EE.**

environmental **investigation** agency
Registered Charity No. 1040615

voucher book, similar to a cheque book, and a CAF Charity Card, a debit card designed specifically for charitable giving. This helps you to support any charity or cause of your choice and in whatever amounts, either by writing out a voucher in the charity's name or by giving the charity your card details.

Where would your donation go? Take, for example, the balance of £152 used above (which has cost the higher rate taxpayer only £96): £10 could be used to support a local community group, £50 could go to a place of worship, another £50 could go to an international aid agency and the balance perhaps to a local hospice. It is entirely your choice.

An added advantage to using an account is that CAF will honour only those donations made to registered or recognised charities, thereby protecting the money from going to an organisation which is not bona fide.

If you have slightly larger amounts to distribute – a bequest under a will or investments that you wish to give to a charity free of capital gains tax – setting up a charitable trust may be an ideal solution. It can provide enduring support for charities and causes even beyond your lifetime and can help to develop close links with those supported on a regular basis.

Before pursuing this option, however, it needs to be given careful consideration. First, there are legal and accountancy fees to be considered. Trustees need to be taken on, decisions taken over trust fund investment and accounting, separate bank accounts need to be opened and annual reports, returns and accounts all need to be submitted to the Charity Commission. It can take anything from 6 to 12 months simply to get the trust up and running.

By using an agency such as the Charities Aid Foundation, a trust can be established almost immediately and, coming under the guardianship of CAF's own trustees, there is no need to appoint them independently. Another advantage is that there are usually no initial fees or legal charges and CAF will take care of all administration requirements on behalf of the trust holder. Initially, all that is required of the donor is a sum of at least £10,000 – £7,600 plus tax reclaimed (or the commitment to reach that level within two or three years) – a name for the trust which, within reason, is up to the donor and a decision on the duration of the trust.

Once the trust has been established, it operates rather like a bank account. The capital is invested by CAF although the emphasis, such as high income or capital growth, is chosen by the trust holder.

The three investment funds operated by CAF are the Balanced Growth Fund, providing sustained capital growth and increasing growth of income, the Income Fund, which maximises income return with an element of capital protection, and the CAF Cash Deposit Fund, which pools investments to create a high rate of interest. The three schemes are designed exclusively for charities and trusts in a tax-effective way and are used by thousands of such organisations.

As with tax-effective giving, when it comes to distributing funds from the trust, donations may only be made to registered or recognised charities either by using a voucher book or standing order. Capital can be added to the trust at any time, and tax effectively, and all rights and responsibilities of the trust can be passed on at any time to a successor of the trust holder's choosing.

Under the current schemes, it has never been easier to support the charities of your choice tax effectively, whether you give in a sustained and regular way, make your donations spontaneously and with flexibility, or whether you simply want to ensure that both you and the charities you support gain the maximum benefit from your donations.

Further information on Gift Aid is given in the Inland Revenue leaflet IR113 and on the Gift Aid helpline on 0151 472 6038.

For further information about the Charities Aid Foundation's Charity Account Scheme telephone 01732 771333; or to find out more about the trust service contact 01892 512244.

Payroll giving and voucher accounts

With a cache of money to dispense or save as you please you may wish to consider opportunities to give regularly to charity either as and when you like or through your salary. Payroll giving is a tax-free way to give from your pay. The voucher account system offers a versatile and flexible way to give to charity. Both schemes are administered by the Charities Trust.

THE ROYAL COLLEGE OF PSYCHIATRISTS
17 Belgrave Square, London SW1X 8PG

THE ROYAL COLLEGE

LET WISDOM GUIDE

OF PSYCHIATRISTS

HELP IS AT HAND

Mental health problems are common and can affect most families. They cause great distress to sufferers and those close to them. The Royal College of Psychiatrists produces a wide range of 'Help is at Hand' leaflets for the general public on mental health problems. These have proved to be enormously helpful to those trying to understand and come to terms with mental illness and more than 4 million have been distributed on demand.

We have to obtain funding for every project we undertake. We are currently seeking funds to reprint some of our most needed leaflets on Panic Attacks and Anxiety, Phobias, and Anorexia and Bulimia.

Every donation, however small, will be much appreciated and put to very good use.

If you would like further information about the materials we produce please ring the External Affairs Department on 0171 235 2351. extensions 131, 127 and 259. E-mail: cgear@repsych.ac.uk. Ref: DT/CG.

SHIRE HORSE SOCIETY
EAST OF ENGLAND SHOWGROUND, PETERBOROUGH, PE2 6XF
Registered Charity No. 210619   Telephone: Peterborough 01733 234451

The Shire Horse Society was established in 1878 to improve the breed and to promote the breeding of English cart horses - later to be called Shire horses. At one time, the shire horse was the major means of motive power in the United Kingdom. In the late 1950's and early 1960's, there were only a few hundred Shire horses in England and Wales. Through the determined efforts of a handful of dedicated breeders and the Shire horse Society Council, a resurgence of interest was established not only in the United Kingdom, but throughout the world.

The Society has exhibited at two Overseas Exhibitions in the last four years. In 1996, the Society organised and staged the First World Shire Congress.

Funds are urgently needed to continue with the Society's active breeding policy, promotional activities and to help with the investigations into the future use, care and welfare of Shire horses.

SHIRE HORSE SOCIETY
Patron: Her Majesty The Queen

The Society has been responsible for over 100 years for the promotion of the Shire horse and the maintenance of the Stud Book. In more recent years the conservation and development of the breed - part of our national heritage - has become a greater priority.

The Society actively encourages the breeding and use of Shire horses throughout the country. There are Shire horse classes at over 180 affiliated Shows.

As a result of the Society's endeavours the Shire horse is currently enjoying an upsurge in the iunterest among overseas buyers, particularly in Europe and the United States.

Further information can be obtained from:
TONIE GIBSON, OBE, Secretary
Shire Horse Society, East of England Showground, Peterborough, PE2 6XE.
Tel: 01733 234451   Fax: 01733 370038
Registered Charity No. 210619   Company Limited by Guarantee No. 12383

Charities Trust is incorporated and registered as a charitable company to operate as a payroll giving agency in accordance with Sections 505 and 506 of the Income and Corporation Taxes Act 1988. Charities Trust aims to provide a high quality payroll giving service, which is non-profit making. The trust acts as a clearing house, sending donations to the chosen charities. Money is taken directly from the donor's pay with the benefit of tax relief. Any one of a quarter of a million causes can benefit. All contributions have to be distributed within 80 days of receipt and the interest obtained on deposit during that time helps to offset costs.

The administration fee is designed to cover the cost of the processing of the donor's requirements and the distribution to the selected charities. The fee is currently 5 per cent or 30p per donor per month, whichever is the greater. The breakdown of a single donation of £10 would be as follows: agency charge of 50p, cost to taxpayer of £7.50, charity receives £9.50.

How the payroll giving system works

A maximum of four charities per person is permitted. The minimum donation per charity is 25p per week or £1 per month. Donors can vary their choice of charity or stop giving at any time. A statement of donations can be provided to employers on request at the end of each tax year.

Employers provide to employees a facility for a pre-tax deduction for charitable donations. Employers send those donations to Charities Trust monthly together with a list of donors. It is recommended that the donor code used is the employer's payroll number or National Insurance number. Donations are sent before the 19th of the following month in line with PAYE.

Employers should note that to achieve maximum tax benefits, they need to enter into a contract with an Agency Charity and register with the Inland Revenue. Charities Trust can undertake this on their behalf. Donors leaving a company's employment are entitled to request from the employer a statement of their contributions made during the tax year.

Employers may elect to match employee donations and/or pay their administration fees. To ease administration, personnel

CSW
Christian Solidarity Worldwide

"With CSW we see first-hand the suffering of victims of persecution and repression. We often reach forgotten people in forgotten lands and try to be a voice for those who have no voice. Please help us to help them."

(Baroness Cox)

We are working for a world free from religious persecution

CSW, PO Box 99, New Malden, Surrey KT3 3YF   Tel: 0181 942 8810   Fax: 0181 942 8821

We can easily take freedom for granted - but for millions of Christians across the world, freedom is only a hope. At this moment, many thousands are suffering - imprisoned for practising their faith, tortured for preaching the gospel, punished for speaking out against injustice.

Christian Solidarity Worldwide (CSW) is a Christian human rights organisation which aims to defend the rights of Christians everywhere, through prayer, campaigning and practical action.

And we need YOUR help.

The many faces of persecution

Suppression: In many countries, the law is used to restrict Christian life and witness. Churches may be forced to register with authorities which forbid open evangelism or the distribution of Christian Literature. In Islamic countries, for example, even becoming a Christian is made an offence punishable by imprisonment or death.

Imprisonment and torture: Accusing Christians of wrong doing is an effective means to get them out the way. For simply practising their faith, speaking out for justice or befriending the poor, many find themselves locked up in squalid prison cells, where routine physical and psychological abuse can wreck a person's health for life.

"Ethnic cleansing": Persecution on a grand scale is taking place in little- known civil wars around the world. Whole communities of Christians face assault, bloodshed and possible annihilation, with any attempt at reconciliation ignored or prohibited by governments hostile to peace.

PRAY

Prayer paves the way for all CSW's work. Those we've helped testify to the power of prayer in bringing comfort, swaying decisions and empowering action.

ACT

As individuals or in groups, we can do a great deal.

Be a CSW Supporter

Fill in the form and receive regular updates on CSW campaigns and advice on how you can help. Alert your MP to the latest developments, or send off our preprinted postcards to register your protest with the relevant ambassador or Head of State.

Be a Church Representative

Supporting the CSW on a church-wide basis can help to maximise the impact of our campaigns. As well as handing out extra copies of all our regular publications, you can be in charge of local fundraising, organising prayer groups and special meetings to help spread the message.

GIVE

Our fellow Christians pay for their faith in everyday abuse, discrimination and danger. CSW campaigns cost only money - to track down the facts, organise campaigns and keep our supporters in touch. We don't charge for membership, but gifts of any size are welcome (standing orders and covenants can increase the value of your donation).

● Campaigning

Grass-roots activity is essential to the international work of CSW. Supporters make their mark by sending their MPs, foreign ambassadors and other key officials written protests against specific cases of abuse or injustice. Where it is safe to do so, letters are sent to prisoners themselves, letting them know the're not forgotten.

● Lobbying

CSW representatives in both Houses of Parliament raise the issue of Christian suffering with government and foreign embassies, United Nations and European Union decision-makers regularly hear from CSW board members with strategic insight into issues of global importance.

● Being there

Fact-finding missions help CSW make a practical response "tailor made" to identify needs around the world. Where no other organisations are working, food, medicines and other essential supplies are sent in to relieve communities devastated by war, prejudice or persecutions. Where individuals are facing trial on unjust charges, CSW sends delegations of Christian lawyers to act on their defence.

● Spreading the news

CSW plays a major role in keeping the media up-to-date on the issues surrounding individual cases of Christian persecution. While international journalists and film makers travel with CSW on overseas missions, publicity at local level includes country profiles, regular newsletters and a prayer calendar, detailing what's top of the CSW's current agenda.

243

departments are advised to produce easy-to-follow forms to input for submission to Charities Trust and use constant donor/employee reference numbers. Inland Revenue regulations prohibit the return of any money withheld from employees.

Voucher accounts

Alternatively, you can open a voucher account. The minimum monthly donation is £120 per annum – £10 per month. The maximum individual donation is £900 per annum. With the tax advantage, a £10 donation would cost only £7.50. The scheme gives you the flexibility to give to whomever you want, whenever you want.

The money is paid into a 'pot' and whenever you wish to make a donation, whether it be to the local hospice or a TV extravaganza, the money is paid out. A book of vouchers or a charity cheque book is issued to you to enable this to happen.

A group voucher scheme runs alongside the individual voucher scheme. A 'group' is considered a minimum of five individuals. These contribute to a 'pot'. The minimum and maximum donations by the group are the same as for the individual's scheme: £120 and £900 per annum respectively. One employee is nominated to complete and return a group voucher account registration form to Charities Trust. An account number will then be issued.

In addition, each employee donating to the group completes a Charity Choice Form but nominates the group account number rather than a specific charity. Once the group or individual account is established, a book of vouchers will be supplied.

The vouchers are completed at the individual's discretion like a cheque book and forwarded to the charity. The charity will complete its section and return the voucher to Charities Trust for processing. Please remember that the charity must be or become registered with Charities Trust. A statement of account is provided on a quarterly basis to the account holder(s). Statements show donations made (less an administration charge of 5 per cent maximum), vouchers issued and balance available to use.

Charities Trust can also offer personal advice to companies on how employers can save time and money, how voucher

english touring
OPERA

'It is wonderful, and would be if it were opening the Salzburg Festival or the season at La Scala.'
THE SPECTATOR

Perhaps you've seen us in Preston, Truro, Lincoln, Yeovil - or in one of the 28 towns and cities we visit each year. If not, you might like to know that we:

♦ Produce acclaimed, accessible full-scale operas in English.

♦ Work with young people, elderly people, people with disabilities, in schools, communities and hospices.

♦ Provide unique opportunities for the best young singers.

If, like us, you think English Touring Opera is a vital visitor to a theatre near you please help. Any contribution - great or small - can make a crucial difference. And, if you support us through Gift Aid or by covenant, we can claim a tax rebate, increasing the value of your gift by 30%.

Please ring Lucy Anderson Jones or Amelia Clarke on 0171 820 1131 if you would like to talk about ways of supporting English Touring Opera.

Please help us to keep touring.

Funded by
THE ARTS COUNCIL OF ENGLAND

245

Firefighters fight for you. Will you help us fight for them?

Firefighters wear their yellow helmet badge of courage when they fight for you. Will you help us fight for them?

They can risk injury and death every time they are called to duty for us.

Their great skill and courage save us from serious physical and financial disaster everyday of every week.

Their total dedication and professionalism, all too often, results in their loved ones being left in distress or severe hardship.

The Fire Services National Benevolent Fund meets these deserved cries for help from firefighters, their loved ones and dependents by:

- **Relieving both physical and financial hardships**
- **The provision of rehabilitation and therapy**
- **Residential, nursing and convalescent homes**

We rely heavily upon contributions from the public - Please Help Firefighters fight for you. Help us fight for them. A donation now and a legacy later will show your appreciation.

**To: Fire Services National Benevolent Fund, Marine Court,
Fitzalan Road, Littlehampton, West Sussex BN17 5NF Tel: 01903 736063**

FIRE SERVICES NATIONAL BENEVOLENT FUND

Investing In Health

Since you are reading this, the chances are you have a lump sum to invest, but you may also have decided to donate to a charity. But how do you decide which charity?

Medical research offers the same thrill and gamble as stock-market investment. It requires a vision of the future, assessing the potential risks and opportunities. Seed funding one project could lead to a scientific breakthrough, a new surgical technique, the potential Nobel prize. Like stock-market investment, it requires a long-term commitment to see the real rewards. But these could be ones from which you directly benefit - without your health, what use is all the money that you will make from this book?

Like any medical charity, St Peter's Trust for Kidney, Bladder and Prostate Research can recite the scary statistics: kidney disease is the fifth largest cause of death, and yet by the time you present symptoms of kidney disease to your doctor, 70% of your kidneys will have been destroyed; renal-stone disease affects up to 12 % of men and 5% or women by the age of 70; by 60, 50% of men will have developed benign prostatic hyperspalsia with its associated incontinence, and by the age of 80, the figure has reached 80%. The charity also recognises that people tend to give to medical causes that directly affect them. So you may already be intrigued to learn more about it. But the tragedy is that you might be completely unaware of your need for its work.

St Peter's Trust is probably unique in this country, in that it supports research throughout the urinary tract - from kidney to urethra. And it has a long history (27 years) of supporting scientific breakthroughs. The projects are undertaken at the Institute of Urology and the Division of Nephrology, University College London Medical School, and the St Peter's Hospital at the Middlesex Hospital.

For an 'investment' of £2,250 you could have provided a year's consumables for one researcher, Guiping Sui, and be involved with a truly unique cutting-edge project involving culturing human bladder cells. No one else in this country has mastered the technique of using these cells with the intention of making material for transplants. A £38,250 grant to support Guiping Sui has made the possibility of continence control, without drugs, following bladder recontructive surgery a closer reality.

For 40% of 60 year-old men benign enlargement of the prostate means incontinence, and even renal failure. Given this statistic you might have thought there would be a wealth of research on this topic. However virtually nothing is known about the biological process which make the prostrate muscle relax. If this could be understood, then relief from incontinence would be greatly advanced. So the Trust has just given Neal Appleton a grant to do this. His research may eventually lead to better drug treatments, without the side effects of those currently available. But this is in the future.

By supporting these projects, St Peter's Trust shows the type of long-term vision that you would expect of anyone managing your money. In effect that is what the Trustees do. £500 or £1000 donations can only have an impact when they are invested together. In the 1997-98 financial year, the Trust spent £100,000 on new research, trying to ensure that you and your grandchildren can enjoy good health in the future. It could easily have spent more, had it had the money.

FOR PEOPLE WITH CEREBRAL PALSY

Scope is the leading charity in Britain for people with cerebral palsy and associated disabilities. It works with local support groups, volunteers and staff to supply and improve services which respond to the real needs of people with cerebral palsy, their families and carers. Cerebral palsy is a wide-ranging term and can encompass people with barely noticeable movement problems through to those with very severe disabilities affecting all four limbs.

A few weeks ago I visited a Scope training centre called Thorngrove, where people with cerebral palsy are taught horticultural and agricultural skills to use in the outside world. As I watched them learn, I cast my mind back to when I joined The Spastics Society, now Scope, some 20 years ago.

Things were so very different then. At this time, the main focus of our work was the provision of residential care for people with cerebral palsy. Any thought that those very same people would ever be able to lead full lives in an unprejudiced society seemed - to me at least - to be mere pipe-dreams.

How wrong I was. In just ten years the whole emphasis of our work had changed. Our pioneering campaigns had led to ever greater independence for those with cerebral palsy, and we were actively fighting discrimination. The possibilities seemed limitless.

Today, a further ten years down the road, Scope's work is transforming the lives of many thousands of people with cerebral palsy. The progress we've made is incredible, and can be seen everywhere: in hospitals, in schools, in the workplace - and in the very way disabled people are regarded by society.

But now we must turn our thoughts to the future. 1,500 new babies each year develop cerebral palsy, and Scope must be there for them - not just next week or the year after that, but in 15, 30, 50 years' time. Scope must exist for as long as its work is needed. We must provide practical and emotional support at every stage in life - advice and guidance for parents at the time of diagnosis - school choice and emotional support for the family throughout the early years - later on, access to employment and residential care for the many thousands of people with cerebral palsy disabilities.

We need your financial support.

Helping Scope is easy. You could make a specific gift of cash, stocks or shares - or consider leaving a legacy in your Will.

Please do call or write to me to discuss these issues. Your concern and help could make all the difference.

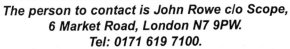

The person to contact is John Rowe c/o Scope, 6 Market Road, London N7 9PW. Tel: 0171 619 7100.

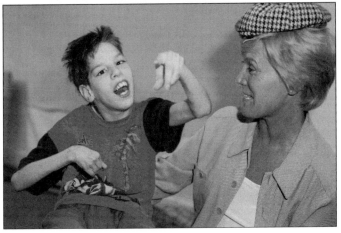

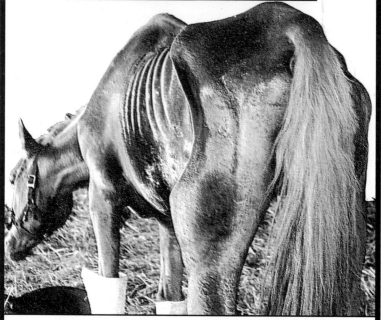

PROVIDING FOR THE FUTURE?

Many of us, for a variety of reasons, put off making a Will as it can appear a somewhat complicated and protracted business. It is, quite simply, something about which we have good intentions, but never quite get round to doing.

However, your Will is so important in protecting your loved ones and ensuring that their future needs are met. If you are no longer around to provide for and look after them, you could leave your family and those you care about facing uncertainty as well as bereavement.

Making a Will need not be an expensive minefield of red tape and, once completed, you have the assurance that your loved ones will be provided for as you would wish. Making a Will is also a wonderful opportunity to consider your favourite charity or charities - a legacy is perhaps the largest donation you could give to a cause you believe in.

THE ILPH - WORKING FOR EQUINES WORLDWIDE

Founded in 1927 by Norfolk born Ada Cole, the International League for the Protection of Horses (ILPH) is the world's leading international equine welfare charity. Its early work centred upon the cruel treatment of horses exported from England to the Continent for slaughter where continental slaughter houses still used terrible, inhumane methods for dispatching horses.

Miss Cole was appalled by the indescribable suffering and cruelty she witnessed and, through her extraordinary energy and efforts, one of the first achievements of the ILPH was the Exportation of Horses Act 1937 which put a stop to the export from this country of aged and work-worn horses for slaughter. Since that time, the ILPH has achieved much with regard to the welfare of equines throughout the world, and today, has 90,000 members and supporters and runs five farms in the UK, all of which are dedicated to the rest and rehabilitation of equines.

The charity, which relies entirely on donations and legacies, also works throughout the world, believing that education and training (in saddlery, farriery, veterinary care and nutrition) are of fundamental importance in ensuring long term improvements in equine welfare.

For a free copy of our new Legacy Pack Remember the Past, Protect the Future, please contact Tracey Woods, our Legacy and Trust Officer on 01953 498682.

Royal College of Art

The world's only wholly postgraduate university of art, design and communications, the Royal College of Art teaches its students how to invent and innovate.

Do you drive a Bentley Continental R, an Aston Martin DB8, a Hyundai or a Land Rover? Have you ever admired the work of John Bellany, Peter Blake, Barbara Hepworth, David Hockney, RB Kitaj, Henry Moore, Eduardo Paolozzi? Do you have a coin of the realm in your pocket? Do you know who designed the typography and layout of most of today's quality newspapers in Britain? Have you ever sat in a polypropylene stacking chair? Do you have a Ballbarrow in your garden, or a Dyson vacuum cleaner in your house? Do you wear a Philip Treacy hat, a Zandra Rhodes original, a David Emanuel design?

The answer to these questions, and hundreds like them, is that they are creations that have come from the hearts, hands and minds of the students, graduates, staff and associates of the Royal College of Art.

You can help us to continue to mix the skills and talents of the most gifted applicants from all over the world with the finest electronic tools and technology, by investing in the future of the men and women who will create the next century.

Royal College of Art
Postgraduate Art & Design

For more information about endowed and named student Scholarships, Professorships, and our plans dramatically to improve our public and teaching facilities, please contact:

Sally Mason
Director of Development
Royal College of Art
Kensington Gore
London SW7 2EU
England

Tel: +44(0)171 590 4111
Fax: +44(0)171 590 4110
Email: s.mason@rca.ac.uk

The Royal College of Art was founded in 1837; in line with Prince Albert's sentiments and, indeed, with our Royal Charter granted in 1967, the College maintains close and consistent connections with the professions and industries we seek both to serve and stimulate.

We are the only exclusively postgraduate university of art, design and communications in the world, with the authority to confer Masters and Doctoral degrees; the most concentrated community of young artists and designers to be found anywhere.

The College demonstrates, almost daily, that it is at the cutting edge of developments in art, design and communications. The chances are that you have sat on the classic polypropylene chair designed by Robin Day, a design student at the RCA in 1935. He is currently designing the new seating for the London Underground, two of whose stations were decorated by David Gentleman and Sir Eduardo Paolozzi – respectively, a graduate of Graphic Arts in the 50s and a current Honorary Professor. Those who travel in more upmarket style might do so in the latest Bentley Continental R, designed by Ken Greenley, Professor of Vehicle Design and John Heffernan, a Visiting Lecturer to the course. If you decide to send a letter instead, College alumni such as John Piper and David Hockney may well have designed the stamp. The clothes you wear, the vehicles in which you travel, the exhibitions you visit or the household items you buy are as likely as not the work of Royal College of Art graduates. They, quite literally, designed your day.

Structured into six Schools, the College undertakes a wide range of postgraduate activities: from Painting to Industrial Design; from Architecture to Visual Arts Administration; from Jewellery to Graphics – we currently operate over 20 postgraduate courses. Our research and development activities are also becoming increasingly important, where both education and industry are concerned. The Helen Hamlyn Research Centre, an action/research centre within the College, will in future be researching lifetime design, responding to the 'grey' population explosion. Green issues are the focus of the Environment Programme, which also provides a perspective on each course: at the Royal College of Art we have a commitment to engaging in debate over sustainable development within the College itself, and between the College and the international academic community.

But our most important effect on the environment takes place far from the College and beyond its control: it is the result of decisions made by graduates who will exert a powerful influence throughout their careers. Recent research into the destinations of our graduates between 1992 and 1996 revealed startling results: an average of 92.5% of graduates across all disciplines – art, design and communications – have gained employment in the subjects for which they were educated at pre-professional level at the RCA, and at the right level.

But we are far from complacent about these results. We cannot stand still. The RCA is a people place and also, as a result, an ideas factory. A factory housing a series of studios and workshops with the capability of handling the traditional and historic activities of printing, glass-blowing and casting bronze; the capability of prototype-making and digital production; the capability of shaping the interactive electronic environment of information technology now racing towards the 21st century. We also have exhibition galleries and lecture theatres, a central Library (containing a unique collection of works on Colour) and an ongoing requirement to update the equipment made available to students in our workshops. Our plans for radically improving our public and teaching facilities will cost £12 million, in addition to our ongoing need to attract endowed Scholarships for our students, many of whom are not eligible for grants, and to finance the College's world-class teacher-practitioners.

For further information about how you can invest in the future of art, design and communications, please contact:

Sally Mason
Director of Development
Royal College of Art
Kensington Gore
London SW7 2EU

Tel: +44(0)171 590 4111
Fax: +44(0)171 590 4110
Email: s.mason@rca.ac.uk

Please invest in the future
of disabled people and their families.

Please help RADAR.

In the UK 6.5 million people, including 300,000 children, have a disability.

45% of people aged over 60 have a disability.

1 in 4 households have some experience of disability.

£5 helps us to answer five Helpline calls.

£250 pays for RADAR to visit and advise a disabled person or group for the day.

We rely on your support. Thank you.

Invest in the future.
Support RADAR.

RADAR's services are available to all disabled people in the UK. Over 20,000 people contact our unique Telephone Helpline every year and many hundreds of thousands of people have benefited from our specialist publications since we were formed in 1977.

RADAR promotes good practice and legislation to ensure that disabled people can live independently and participate fully in the community.

RADAR values the contribution of our supporters. As a supporter you will receive our quarterly newsletter and regular feedback reports about our progress.

Your support is vital to our work.

Please feel welcome to contact us if you would like more information about **RADAR's** work.

**12 City Forum, 250 City Road
London EC1V 8AF**

**T. 0171 250 3222   F. 0171 250 0212
Minicom 0171 250 4119**
Registered Charity Number 273150

Serving 6.5 million disabled people in the UK.

Skill: National Bureau for Students with Disabilities

promoting equality in education, training and employment for disabled people

In 1997 Skill:

- gave advice to nearly 6,000 individuals
- opened offices in Scotland and Northern Ireland to promote awareness
- highlighted the needs of disabled young people in transition from school
- set up schemes to promote and value disabled volunteers

Your gift will help us to create more opportunities for disabled people.

To make your gift tax efficient please contact Skill's fundraising department at:

4th Floor Chapter House 18-20 Crucifix Lane LONDON SE1 3BB
Tel: 0171 274 0565   e-mail: SkillNatBurDis@compuserve.com

Registered Charity No 801971

Skill: National Bureau for Students with Disabilities was established some 24 years ago to promote opportunities to empower young people and adults with any kind of disability to achieve their potential in further, higher and continuing education, training and employment throughout the United Kingdom by providing individual support, promoting good practice and influencing policy in partnership with disabled people, service providers and policy makers.

Discrimination is still legal in education. Even when students and trainees do enter education or training, they are often prevented from achieving their potential by lack of access, support or information. Skill's policy staff work with key policy makers & Government to change the system.

Getting information early on helps ensure that education is a positive experience. Skill's information staff give individual advice by phone or letter to support disabled students, trainees or job seekers. The Information Service also offers leaflets and publications that answer the questions that disabled people regularly ask.

Skill receives a small annual grant from the Department of Education and Employment but has still to raise in excess of £400,000 from voluntary income.

Your donation can make a real difference to the lives of disabled people, ensuring that they have access to the same opportunities others take for granted.

Contact Skill's fundraising department today and we will tell you how you can maximise your gift to help a disabled student.

Your £23 will change lives

There are six million people in Britain today who care at home for those who cannot manage without help. They care for a child with a terminal illness, a frail neighbour, a youngster with severe learning difficulties, a partner disabled in a car crash.

Whoever they are, whatever their circumstances, The Princess Royal Trust for Carers makes sure they don't face the struggle alone. Through our national network of Carers Centres we provide help, advice, comfort and support to around 35,000 of Britain's carers.

Yet millions more are attempting to cope by themselves. Your £23 gift will give hope to carers with nowhere else to turn.

Your help can make a difference. Just tick the box below indicating the amount you are giving (or write it in) and send it with the coupon to **The Princess Royal Trust for Carers, FREEPOST, LON11215, London E1 8BR.**

The Princess Royal Trust
for Carers

I would like to help the carers of Britain.

Ms/Mrs/Miss/Mr _____ First name _____

Surname _____ Address _____

_____

Postcode _____ Telephone _____

Here is my donation by Cheque/Visa/Mastercard/CAF Charity Card

£12 ☐   £23 ☐   £36 ☐   £50 ☐   £100 ☐   I would prefer to give £____

Credit/ Debit card number ☐☐☐☐ ☐☐☐☐ ☐☐☐☐ ☐☐☐☐

Expiry date _____

The Princess Royal Trust for Carers is a registered charity. Registered Charity Number CR 43968/PLB.
Photo courtesy of Jenny Matthews/The Princess Royal Trust for Carers.

She can't call 999

But **you** can help by supporting the world's first marine wildlife rescue ship. *(The 5th emergency service).*

- **EarthKind is a UK - based environmental and animal welfare charity with an emphasis on education via Ocean Defender, the world's first wildlife rescue ship.**

- **Remembering EarthKind in your Will can help us to ensure a better future for humans and animals alike, for generations to come**.

For more information contact:
Katy Hemmings, EarthKind,
Avenue Lodge, Bounds Green Road,
London, N22 7EU.
Tel: 0181 889 1595 Fax: 0181 881 7662
e-mail: info@earthkind-uk.web
www: earthkind-uk.web

Registered Charity No. 260708

EarthKind

EarthKind is one of the oldest UK charities, set up in 1955, working to protect both animals and the environment through humane education, conservation and marine wildlife rescue.

Every year, thousands of tonnes of oil, effluent, rubbish and chemicals are dumped in our seas, killing wildlife and putting Britain's shore line at risk. EarthKind's Ocean Defenders project is a world first and, without it, our fragile marine environment would have no 'lifeboat'.

The impact of overfishing, pollution, sewage and over 600 oil spills each year pose a very serious threat to our seas and oceans. Equipped with a unique on-board marine wildlife treatment unit, Ocean Defender and her crew played a vital role in saving the lives of hundreds of oiled birds during the Sea Empress oil disaster of 1996.

EarthKind is committed to practical, long term conservation of the environment, and we believe the role of education to be essential in the fight to create a better world for humans and animals alike. When not attending to marine disasters, the ship tours the UK coastline bringing EarthKind's vital conservation message to people all over the British Isles.

Ocean Defender's volunteer crew consistently demonstrate unrivalled dedication and commitment to the environment, as they sail around the UK coast educating British schoolchildren and raising awareness of the role we must all play to preserve the world's resources for future generations.

Naturally, EarthKind prefers to plan for the future as far as we possibly can. Our vital work is funded entirely on the generosity of our loyal supporters, and the long term commitment associated with Legacy bequest is essential to ensure EarthKind's future.

If you would like further information, a Legacy pack, or to speak to someone in confidence about leaving us a lasting gift in your Will, please contact Katy Hemmings at EarthKind on 0181 889 1595, or write to EarthKind, Avenue Lodge, Bounds Green Road, London N22 7EU

Your actions can help shape the headlines!

Finding vaccines against all the different strains of meningitis takes precious time and resources. Every second counts because every day someone, somewhere is struck down by a disease which can kill within hours.

The National Meningitis Trust is leading the search for vaccines, funding research into every facet of this deadly disease. But we can't do it alone. We need **your help** and we need it **now!**

Investing in one or more of the National Meningitis Trust's current research projects would turn the promise they hold, into the reality of vaccines and treatments against all forms of the disease.

When drawing up your plans, make the National Meningitis Trust part of your investment portfolio. You'll be playing a special role in bringing the day closer when everyone is protected from this deadly and devastating disease.

NATIONAL MENINGITIS TRUST

Fighting Meningitis through Research, Awareness and Support

Registered Charity Number 803016

Call or write to us now.
Contact:
Jason Blackburn, Corporate & Trust Manager,
National Meningitis Trust, Dept LSI,
Fern House, Bath Road,
Stroud, Gloucestershire GL5 3TJ

Telephone: 01453 768000.   Fax: 01453 768001
E Mail: support@meningitis-trust.org.uk
Web Site: http://www.meningitis-trust.org.uk

Marie Curie Cancer Care
50 Years of Dedication

The Marie Curie Golden Daffodil Appeal marks 50 years of dedication since the charity was founded in 1948. As well as commemorating half a century of cancer care, Marie Curie is also looking ahead to the Millennium and beyond in order to meet the ever increasing demand for it's services.

Marie Curie Cancer Care is working for people with cancer by:

- offering a unique service, with a network of Marie Curie Nurses across the UK giving practical nursing care at home to people with cancer, free of charge.

- providing specialist care in eleven Marie Curie Centres for people with cancer and offering day care and home visits for outpatients.

- investigating the causes, prevention and early detection of cancer through research.

- improving the quality of cancer care through the education and training of healthcare professionals.

Marie Curie Cancer Care depends on your help.
Contact Mike Flynn, Marie Curie Cancer Care,
28 Belgrave Square, London SW1X 8QG
Tel: 0171 235 3325
www.mariecurie.org.uk

will power

1 in 3 people get cancer. Where there's a will there's a way to help them. For a copy of our leaflet **'Fight Cancer With Your Will'** contact Helen Smith at Marie Curie Cancer Care, FREEPOST, 28 Belgrave Square, London SW1X 8YZ.

Freephone **0800 716 146**

NURSES • SPECIALIST CANCER CARE CENTRES • RESEARCH
THE DEDICATIONS NEVER ENDING

www.mariecurie.org.uk

Charity Reg. No. 207994

50 Years of Dedication

Looking Forward to a Bright Future

and helping make dreams come true...

With the Proceeds of a Children's Tax-Exempt Savings Plan

Why not give YOUR CHILD a flying start in life with a Children's Savings Plan?

Whether you are a parent, grandparent, godparent, or just a friend or relative, you can pay for a Children's Savings Plan to provide a child with a tax free cash sum just when it will be needed most.

How much does it cost?

As little as £10 a month (max £25), or £100 (max £270) a year. We also offer a single payment version (minimum £1000), which many grandparents find attractive, as they know that even if they were not around to pay the premiums at some time in the future, the plan will continue to completion. As a guide, the maximum single payment for a child under the age of 1, maturing at age 18, is currently £3206.25. The Plan matures at either age 16,18 or 21 – the timing is your choice at the outset. With the concerns regarding the future costs of higher education we find that the majority of people are electing for the plan to pay out at age 18. However for this to be the case the child must not be older than age 8 next birthday at the outset so the plan can run for a full 10 years. Plans for children aged 9 to 11 next birthday must run to age 21. The exact maturity value will depend on the addition of bonuses to the plan which cannot be guaranteed. If you were to cash in your savings plan at any time before it matures, but especially in the early years, you may not get back the full amount of your original investment.

Why National Deposit?

Firstly, as a Friendly Society we have no directors or shareholders, the Society being run by a committee of Management consisting of Members (policyholders) elected by their fellow Members – people just like you – for the mutual benefit of the entire Membership. Secondly, all surpluses are passed back to Members by way of enhanced benefits and bonuses on with-profits policies.

Ask us for a free illustration

– It must be worth a look – and while you are about it, why not ask for one for yourself. Anyone in good health from age 12 to age 70 next birthday can have an adult version of the Children's Plan.

The full written terms and conditions of the plan are available on request.

Phone us FREE on 0500 418 559

(Monday to Friday 9.00 am - 5.00 pm)
and give us the details – or write to us at:-

Head office: 4-5 Worcester Road, Clifton, Bristol BS8 3JL.
Incorporated and Registered Friendly Society No. 369F.
Regulated by the Personal Investment Authority.
Member of the Association of Friendly Societies.
This advertisement relates only to the packaged products of the Society.

NATIONAL DEPOSIT
Friendly Society Limited

accounts can be set up, enabling irregular donations to be made to an assortment of charities. The trust is the second largest payroll giving agency in the United Kingdom. It currently handles over 800 employers and more than 100,000 donors. Funds are distributed to over 2,000 charities.

For further information contact: Charities Trust, PO Box 15, Liverpool L23 0UU. Telephone: 0151 949 0044.

Wills, legacies and charitable giving

Making wills is an age-old occupation. It is quite impossible to say when the first will was made, by whom and under what circumstances. There are of course copies of ancient wills still in existence or records of what they contain. The purpose of wills has, however, never changed as it represents the inalienable right of people to leave their lifetime possessions to whomsoever they wish. For some it also provides an opportunity to speak from beyond the grave and throughout history all manner of people have used their wills to express unflattering observations about their kith and kin. Equally, some of the sentiments expressed in wills about friends, relatives and reasons for leaving money to charity are loving and heart warming and depict the best features of human nature.

The style and nature of wills has of course changed down the centuries. Here is an example of a will by Joshua West of the Six Clerks' Office in Chancery Lane, made in the eighteenth century. He wrote:

> Perhaps I died not worth a groat;
> but should I die worth something more,
> then I give that, and my best coat,
> and all my manuscripts in store, to those
> who shall the goodness have
> to cause my poor remains to rest
> within a decent shell and grave.
> This is the Will of Joshua West.

With the passage of time the collection and storage of wills became more regularised and a system evolved whereby probate matters in England and Wales were dealt with by a mixture of almost 400 ecclesiastical and secular courts. Some of these,

273

including the Prerogative Court of the Archbishop of Canterbury, were situated at the famous Doctors Commons near St Paul's Cathedral and it was there that the Principal Probate Registry was first located.

In 1857 Parliament passed The Court of Probate Act which established the Principal Probate Registry and 40 District Probate Registries in England and Wales with effect from 12 January 1858. In October 1874 the great collection of wills stored in old Doctors Commons was transported through the streets of London in vans and wagons to Somerset House in the Strand into offices vacated by the Admiralty in the previous year. One hundred and twenty three years on, Somerset House remains the central repository for wills proved in England and Wales.

The case for challenging a will

In most respects the law in England and Wales provides the greatest freedom of choice for will makers in comparison with other countries. In other words, anyone from the age of 18 onwards can make a will disposing of their worldly goods in any way they choose. This of course can and does lead to injustices and where this occurs claimants have a right to challenge the will under the Inheritance (Provision for Families and Dependants) Act 1975. The basis of any claim is failure by the deceased to make reasonable financial provision for any person or persons who had some degree of financial dependence upon them prior to death. In other words, the plaintiff can claim compensation for the loss of benefit out of the estate.

The legal position is that claims should be made within six months from the date of grant of representation (probate) but the court can extend this time limit in very special circumstances. In order for the Act to be applied the deceased must have died domiciled in England and Wales. Currently the classes of persons who may challenge a will under the 1975 Act are:

- wife or husband of deceased;
- former wives or husbands of deceased who have not remarried;
- a child of the deceased;
- any person (not being a child of the deceased) who, in the

case of any marriage to which the deceased was at any time a party, was treated by the deceased as a child of the family in relation to the marriage;

- any person (other than those above) who immediately before the death of the deceased was being maintained, either wholly or partly, by the deceased;
- for deaths on or after 1 January 1996, a new category: persons living with the deceased in the same household and as the husband or wife of the deceased, during the two years immediately prior to the date of death (Law Reform (Succession) Act 1995).

The first Act of this kind was introduced in the 1930s since prior to that date a will in England and Wales could only be challenged on the basis that the legator was not of testamentary capacity – in other words they were not considered to be of sound mind, memory and understanding. This was a very unsatisfactory state of affairs since in order to gain redress for any injustice created by the will the plaintiff could only in effect allege that the deceased was of unsound mind. This could be deeply distressing when the testator or testatrix was a loved relative. It still remains a fact that wills are occasionally contested on the basis that the deceased did not have testamentary capacity, but in most cases wills are now challenged under the 1975 Act.

In Scotland the position is markedly different. Under Scottish law a will can be challenged on a number of grounds – for example if the person were insane when it was made, if children were born after the will was made, if the person had been improperly influenced by another person when making the will. The 1975 Act referred to earlier does not apply to Scotland in that there are inbuilt rights to protect the immediate family. Basically, whatever the will says, a surviving husband, wife or children can if they wish, after 'prior rights' have been satisfied, claim further 'legal rights' to a proportion of any property excluding house and land.

The amounts designated under 'prior rights' are changed from time to time but the current provision is as follows.

Prior rights
These are the surviving husband's or wife's rights to (a) the house (up to the value of £110,000); (b) furniture in the house

(up to £20,000); (c) a payment of £30,000 if there are children, £50,000 if there are not.

Legal rights

After prior rights have been dealt with, a surviving husband or wife and children have certain 'legal rights' to a proportion of the 'moveable estate' – that is, all things such as money, shares, cars, furniture and jewellery.

Where there is an intestacy (no will) and any prior or legal rights have been dealt with, the remainder of the estate is given to surviving relatives according to a strictly laid-down sequence – for example, any children have first claim; if there are no children, half goes to the parents or parent and half to the brothers and sisters; if there are no children or parents, all goes to the brothers and sisters and so on. In the event of there being no qualifying relatives in the case of an intestacy, the estate will pass to the Crown.

Because of the complexities in the law relating to claims and contested wills, it is imperative that plaintiffs, defendants and lay (non professional) executors seek legal advice from qualified solicitors.

Having set out the ways and means by which disputes over wills can be resolved, it is important to remember that the overwhelming majority of wills create no problems at all and the intended beneficiaries receive their bequests as the will maker intended.

Why make a will?

Let us now consider the reasons why people make wills. As already stated, anyone over the age of 18 in England and Wales is eligible to make a will, whereas in Scotland girls from the age of 12 and boys from the age of 14 are able to make wills. Some people make a will at quite an early age, perhaps because they are involved in a dangerous job, pursuit or hobby or serving in Her Majesty's forces. Long-distance travel or going abroad as a family often motivates people to make a will. Another strong reason for making a will is marriage or partnership or buying a house. It is also very important for people to make a will when their children are born, both to provide financial security and deal with guardianship issues. Divorce does not totally invalidate a will except where it affects the provisions made for the former husband or wife. As life moves on, the marriage or partnership of children may motivate parents to make wills, as may the birth of grandchildren. The problems associated with the ageing process are often the main reasons for making wills such as illness, the death of loved ones and the general desire to put one's affairs in order. Experience of dealing with an intestacy is another strong motivator for making a will. Moral – don't make life harder for the loved ones you leave behind.

Above and beyond all else, it is important for people to realise that the only way to ensure their worldly possessions pass to the beneficiaries of their choice is to make a will. It is often presupposed that there is no need to make a will because the immediate family will benefit anyway, which is to some extent true where the estate is of modest size. In the case of high-value estates, it has been known for husbands or wives in particular to find that the provisions under the Intestacy Rules do not sufficiently cater for their needs and it may then be necessary in England and Wales to seek further and better provision under the 1975 Inheritance Act.

Tax considerations

For some people tax planning is important and anyone wishing to make special arrangements to reduce or avoid tax should seek expert advice. Bequests to a surviving husband or wife are totally exempt from inheritance tax as are gifts through wills to charities. Other beneficiaries, such as children, are liable to pay tax on any inheritances they receive in excess of the inheritance tax threshold. With effect from 6 April 1998 the inheritance tax threshold was raised to £223,000 from the previous level of £215,000. This will clearly release quite a few more estates from tax completely. For estates over £223,000 a flat rate tax of 40 per cent is levied on the excess unless it passes to exempt beneficiaries as mentioned earlier.

There are other ways of reducing the burden of tax on estates but because of the unique nature of each person's affairs it is always advisable to obtain professional advice on the legitimate ways in which this can be done. While many solicitors have knowledge in this field, it is sometimes better to consult accountants who probably have the greatest skills in this area of tax planning.

At the moment, for instance, we have what is generally known as the seven-year rule. This relates to any personal gifts made during a person's lifetime in excess of the annual or other specific exemptions, such as gifts on marriage known as 'potentially exempt transfers'. These transfers are subject to inheritance tax only if the person who makes the gift dies within a seven-year period from the time of making the gift. Tax is reduced on a sliding scale depending on how many years have elapsed before the donor's death as shown below:

Years before death	Percentage of full tax charge
0–3	100
3–4	80
4–5	60
5–6	40
6–7	20

The wealth factor

It is impossible to say how many people place a high priority on tax planning when making their wills but, looking at the wealth statistics produced by Smee & Ford, the vast majority of people who die each year do not leave large estates. For instance, in 1994 there were approximately 544,000 adult deaths in England and Wales. Of these fewer than half (247,491) left estates worth over £5000. The probate value of these estates was £17.66 billion; 53,409 or 21.6 per cent died intestate, the cumulative value of their estates being £2.02 billion. The 194,082 will makers together left £15.64 billion. Furthermore, detailed analysis indicated that 85 per cent of the will makers had estates worth between £5000 and £125,000, suggesting that the great majority could be described as cash poor but asset rich. In other words, for most of them their house would have been their most valuable possession. Just under 15 per cent of will makers had estates valued between £125,000 and £1 million. People leaving estates in excess of £1 million totalled 690 or 0.4 per cent of all will makers. Fourteen millionaires died

Leave the gift of life

Include Blue Cross in your will

This 2-week-old kitten was thrown over a wall into a building site and left to die. We called him 'Everest' because he climbed so many mountains in his battle for life. He was just one of the thousands of animals saved by Blue Cross last year – animals that were rescued, adopted, nursed back to health and rehomed.

We couldn't save even one without our supporters. Especially those who care enough to include Blue Cross in their will. *You* can help us save lives. If we are to keep our pledge never to turn away an animal in need, we desperately need to find new supporters. Find out how you can help by filling in the coupon. It could mean 'the gift of life' to another defenceless animal like 'Everest'. **BLUE✚CROSS** *We save lives*

Blue Cross has been helping animals in need for nearly one hundred years, and today is one of Britain's larger animal charities.

The Blue Cross veterinary service is provided for animals' owners who cannot afford private veterinary fees. We have three Animals Hospitals and a Clinic, which give over 60,000 free treatments annually, and perform over 6,000 lifesaving operations.

Every year, loving new homes are found for over 8,000 cats and dogs, through the eleven Blue Cross Adoption Centres which take in unwanted and abandoned animals. We believe no healthy animal should ever be put to sleep simply because it has no home.

This promise can only be kept if we have your support to provide care for the many animals at risk.

intestate and of course their estates would be distributed in accordance with the Intestacy Rules.

Professional involvement

Although available evidence indicates that relatively few will makers take financial advice from accountants when making their wills, it is very important that they consult a solicitor who will be able to give sound legal advice, particularly when complicated provisions are required. The research carried out by Smee & Ford reveals that the majority of will makers still appoint lay executors only but in most cases these executors engage solicitors to obtain the Grant of Probate and carry out the subsequent estate administration on their behalf. Many will makers appoint non-professional executors because they believe it will reduce the cost of administering their estates but, for the reasons stated above, legal charges are incurred by the employment of solicitors who will require a written undertaking from the lay executors that their proper professional fees will be deductible from the estate. When solicitors are themselves appointed executors their charging clause will automatically be written into the will. All the main banks provide a will making and probate service but have only a very tiny percentage of the executorship market, possibly due to the fact that their charges are for the most part higher than the fees charged by solicitors.

It is of course quite feasible for people to make home-made wills or use the standard forms which can be obtained from stationer's shops. Providing people observe the basic legal requirements, such wills are perfectly valid and raise no problems in implementation. Even so, the best advice is to consult a solicitor who will be prepared to give prospective clients a quote for making their will. The cost of a solicitor-made will is not nearly as high as some people believe. In some cases it can be less than £50 with special deals for joint wills made by husbands, wives or partners.

Legal requirements

The basic principles for making a valid will are that it must be in writing and must appoint executors. The attestation clause must follow the legal requirement that the testator and two witnesses be together and sign the will in the presence of each other. In the case of Scotland, only one witness is now required, but there the testator is required to sign each page of the will, whereas in England and Wales the testator need only sign the attestation clause on the final page along with the two witnesses. Although it is possible to have up to four executors, one is sufficient, but on balance it is preferable to choose two people such as a solicitor and a younger adult relative or close friend. Remember, a will may be declared invalid if it has not been signed and dated by the testator in the presence of the witness or witnesses who must also sign the will. Witnesses do not need to know the contents of the will they are witnessing nor should they be beneficiaries, since being a witness or a spouse of a witness could invalidate any gift bequeathed to them if the will is made in England and Wales. In Scotland it is preferable not to have the will witnessed by a beneficiary but this will not invalidate the attestation or (as in England and Wales) the gift. On the other hand, an executor may be named as a beneficiary in any will.

As indicated earlier, the sole purpose of making a will is to dispose of one's lifetime possessions and to decide on the list of beneficiaries who are to inherit your estate. There are three main types of legacy. The first is a specific gift such as a car, house, item of jewellery or other household effect. If at the time of death the gift described in the will cannot be found or identified, it will fail. The second type of legacy is a pecuniary (cash) gift of any size (for example £1000). The third type of legacy is what is called a residuary bequest, which is all or part of the balance of the estate after all debts, taxes, expenses and other legacies have been paid. With the passage of time, pecuniary legacies will lose value because of inflation and legators may therefore wish either to index-link their cash gifts to family, friends and charity or divide the whole estate into shares or percentages so that all classes of beneficiaries will gain if the value of the estate increases between the will being made and the time of death.

Charitable giving through wills
Despite the growing incidence of divorce and the increasing numbers of people who live alone, the strong allegiance to family and other loved ones is still reflected in the provisions of wills, but there have always been a minority of legators who make charitable

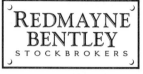

The British Veterinary Association
Animal Welfare Foundation (BVA:AWF)
The Veterinary Profession's Own Charity

All veterinary surgeons, upon qualification, make a solemn pledge to uphold and promote the welfare of animals under their care. The Animal Welfare Foundation established by the British Veterinary Association (BVA) in 1984, extends this commitment to all animals. It aims to apply the knowledge, skill and compassion of veterinary surgeons in an effective way through a variety of projects and activities.

The Foundation is the veterinary profession's own charity and plays a unique role in animal welfare. BVA:AWF supports specific research projects in which improved welfare is a primary objective. In addition, educational programmes are initiated and support provided to enhance knowledge and understanding of welfare issues.

bequests. Although this amounts only to about one will maker in seven, Smee & Ford estimate that in England and Wales alone charitable will makers collectively leave £1 billion to their favourite causes each year. It is the second most productive form of voluntary income for charitable organisations and any diminution in this source of funding will have very serious implications for most of the United Kingdom's leading charities. To illustrate this point further, the following charities among many others receive over 50 per cent of their total voluntary income from legacies: RNLI, Imperial Cancer Research Fund, Cancer Research Campaign, Guide Dogs for the Blind Association, Barnardo's, RNIB, Salvation Army, RSPCA and British Heart Foundation. A number of smaller charities are also heavily dependent upon legacy income including the Dogs' Home, Battersea which every year receives more than 90 per cent of its income in the form of legacies.

It may well be that far more people could be influenced into leaving charitable gifts, bearing in mind the tax benefits to both the giver and the receiver. Charities have been influential over the years in promoting the concept of will making since there is no provision for charities under the Intestacy Rules. No will equals no charitable bequest.

It is to be hoped that with the passage of time and continuing growth of individual wealth more people will see the wisdom of making a will and not allow the law to have the final say in their affairs. I began this article by quoting an ancient will and I will end with a few lines from a very recent will:

O, grant me, heaven, a middle state,
Neither too humble, nor too great,
More than enough, for nature's ends,
With something left to treat my friends.

Bernard Sharpe is Director of Consultancy with Smee & Ford Ltd, having previously worked in the charity sector for over 20 years, promoting and administering legacies for the RNLI and SCOPE.

14

Where to Go for Professional Advice

One question often asked by investors is where to go to get reliable financial advice. In practice, there is no shortage of people or organisations willing to offer advice, from stockbrokers to solicitors and accountants, banks and various kinds of intermediary. The services offered also cover a wide range, from advice on specific types of investment, such as life assurance plans or stocks and shares, to overall financial management, including tax planning and long-term strategies as well as day-to-day affairs.

As well as scope, services differ in terms of independence, cost and the type of client they are aimed at. Traditionally, for example, stockbrokers, merchant banks and accountants focused on the top end of the market, so-called 'high net worth individuals', while smaller investors dealt mainly with insurance brokers and agents or the local bank manager.

These two extremes have now come much closer together. The top end has spread downwards, as stockbrokers have made efforts to enlarge their appeal and appear more user-friendly. Some are even advertising on commercial radio in order to spread the message to a wider audience. At the same time, smaller firms of advisers have been expanding the range of services they offer, moving up the scale from simple life assurance into the realms of investment and, in some cases, tax planning.

There are perhaps three main reasons for these changes. In the first place, the substantial growth in home ownership before and after the Second World War has meant that far more people are now inheriting property. In many cases, they already own their own homes, so the inheritance translates into a sizeable capital sum – even despite the 1990s' fall in property prices. This creates a need not only for investment advice, but also for tax planning; the nil rate band for inheritance tax of £223,000 can easily be surpassed where the estate includes a house.

Redundancy, sadly, is another source of increased demand for advice. Again, there are two sides to this. First, the redundancy payment may be a sizeable sum that needs careful investment, particularly if the redundancy happens fairly late in life and the person is not expecting to find another job, or not at the previous level. Second, the tighter job market has encouraged younger people to set up their own businesses, with a consequent need for advice on matters such as tax and pension arrangements.

Third, the spate of privatisation issues over the last few years has enticed many first-timers into the stock market, some of whom have then caught the bug and gone on to other share dealing. A good number, of course, have not stayed in the market, particularly as some issues gave exaggerated opportunities to take a quick profit. But this in itself encouraged the growth of cheap share-dealing services; while the issues could be bought very easily through application forms in newspapers, selling was more of a problem and 'no-frills' services sprang up as a convenient solution.

The Financial Services Act

In addition to these social changes, a major influence on the development of financial services, and the cause of much upheaval, has been the Financial Services Act, which became law in 1988. This is founded on the principle – which has been much questioned ever since – of self-regulation by the industry rather than statutory control by the government.

Nevertheless, it has still spawned a substantial amount of bureaucracy and one suspects that vast acreages of forest must have been expended on producing rule-books, which are continuously needing to be updated for amendments, and which are so complicated that further reams of paper are devoted to clarification of what it all might mean. If there has been one growth area during the recent recession, it has been the compliance departments of financial services companies, which are responsible for ensuring that all these rules are followed.

At the top of the regulatory tree is the Financial Services Authority (FSA). At the next level down are the Self Regulatory Organisations (SROs), which take their authority from the FSA and carry out the day-to-day tasks of regulation. Prior to 1994, there were four of these bodies: the Financial Intermediaries, Managers and Brokers Regulatory Association (Fimbra); the Life Assurance and Unit Trust Regulatory Organisation (Lautro); the Investment Management Regulatory Organisation (Imro); and the Securities and Futures Authority (SFA).

In July 1994, a new SRO came into operation: the Personal Investment Authority (PIA). This is responsible for retail investment services and is in effect an amalgamation of Fimbra and Lautro, plus Imro members who deal primarily with private clients.

The PIA was originally conceived as an answer to funding problems experienced by Fimbra, particularly in relation to the Investors' Compensation Scheme. It was felt that a single regulator would be more cost effective and financially sound; it would also offer a measure of control to life assurance companies, which had been repeatedly asked to subsidise Fimbra while having no say in how it was run. The creation of the PIA was also seen as an opportunity for raising regulatory standards.

In addition to the SROs, there are also Recognised Professional Bodies (RPBs). These cover professionals who offer investment advice and management services as part of their business, such as solicitors, accountants and insurance brokers. The Law Society, the Insurance Brokers Registration Council and various accountancy bodies act as RPBs.

The FSA was set up in 1997 as a replacement for the Securities and Investments Board (SIB), which had previously supervised the whole show. It is intended that the FSA will eventually become a 'super-regulator', taking over from all the others, but there is no final date for this as yet.

Anyone who gives financial advice must be authorised through one of these various organisations. The PIA covers independent financial advisers, life assurance companies and their agents and unit trust groups, while investment managers dealing mainly with institutional clients continue to come under Imro and stockbrokers are governed by the SFA.

Anyone who offers financial advice without being authorised is breaking the law, unless it is on a casual, one-off basis and unpaid. This was once explained to me by a regulator as follows: if you are in the pub one evening and a friend asks you for some advice, you may obviously offer your opinion. But if you hold court at the bar every night, offering advice to all and sundry and perhaps accepting a few drinks in return, that would, strictly speaking, be against the law.

Polarisation

Authorised firms must display on all their literature, stationery, business cards and so on which of the regulatory bodies they belong to. In addition, they must make it clear whether they are offering advice in a wholly independent capacity, or as the representative of one particular company.

This distinction, which is known as polarisation, was one of the main planks of the Financial Services Act when it was first drawn up. Before then, it was quite common for some advisers to recommend products supplied by more than one company, but without professing to cover the entire market. For example, they might limit their suggestions to just a handful of companies because they lacked the resources to research all of them. Alternatively, they might act in the main for a single company, but occasionally recommend others if the required product was not offered by that one company.

The powers that be decided that this could prove much too confusing for the customer, who would not be sure whether the advice he was getting was genuinely free range or in fact limited to a small sector of the market. So they came up with the principle of polarisation, under which an adviser must be either completely independent and able to offer the products of any company in the market, or tied exclusively to one company and barred from offering the products of any other. Since then, there have been occasional proposals to modify the principle; for example, to allow 'multi-ties', under which an adviser could represent several specified companies, but so far it has not been changed.

To be independent, the cardinal rules laid down were 'know your customer' and 'give best advice'. The former still holds: advisers must complete a fact-find on their clients, covering circumstances such as age and tax position, the range of their financial needs and other relevant factors such as attitude to risk.

The 'best advice' principle has since been toned down to 'good advice'. The adviser is not expected to have a crystal ball to show which product will produce the best results at the end of the day – which could be 20 years hence – but he must select the most appropriate for his client from all those available, in terms of both the type of product and the track record of the company on charges, past performance and so on.

In practice, this means that the adviser may focus on particular companies if they are seen to be the market leaders. For example, if he identifies one company as being good for endowment policies, there is nothing to stop him recommending it to several different clients, but he must be prepared to justify his choice to inspectors from his regulatory body, who will make periodic visits to check that the rules are being satisfied.

While this is basically a sound concept – and what any good adviser should be following anyway – there are certain drawbacks in practice. First, advisers may be tempted to stick to big name companies, the choice of which would not be queried, rather than face having to justify a recommendation which might be based on gut feeling as much as hard facts.

Second, the considerable costs and pressures of being independent have meant that a large number of advisers have simply given up and become tied, so the availability of independent advice has shrunk considerably. It is arguable that the quasi-independent advice that existed before, for all its faults, at least gave investors a degree of choice.

Those tied to one company may work as part of a direct salesforce or be self-employed but acting as an appointed representative. Either way, they can offer only the products from that one company's range but, within that, they are still expected to recommend the most appropriate product. The obvious drawback is that the company may simply not provide the type of product that would best suit the client, in which case he may be persuaded into a poorer substitute.

In practice, the competition between companies to attract and retain good quality representatives does influence the product range, although it is still true that any single company is unlikely to be a market leader across the board. Naturally, both independent advisers and representatives will argue fiercely for their own merits: the former point out that they are free to select the best product on the market for any given need, while the latter claim that the closer relationship they have with the company can work to the client's advantage. The truth is that there are good and bad in both sectors; what really counts is honesty and competence.

For banks and building societies, polarisation presented a difficult problem. On the one hand, they did not want to give up offering independent advice, as that might mean losing their more discriminating (and more valuable) customers, but on the other, the branch network represented an excellent outlet for business from an associated operation.

Midland, Barclays and Lloyds already had associated life and assurance and unit trust companies and a number of others have set up subsidiaries since: among them, NatWest Life, Abbey National Life, Woolwich Life and Halifax Life. In fact, 'bancassurance', as it is known, is becoming a growing force in the market and represents considerable potential competition to traditional operators because of the huge opportunities afforded by high street outlets.

Of the major banks, National Westminster was the only one to retain independent status at the outset, which it has now given up, while among the top ten building societies, only Bradford & Bingley offers independent advice. To some extent, though, banks and building societies have cut across polarisation by offering tied advice through their branches and independent advice through a separate arm. But where they have associated operations of their own, these would not normally be recommended through the independent side; the rule for that situation is that the recommendation would have to be 'better than best advice', which in practice would be almost impossible to prove.

With so many developments in the market, it is difficult to be categorical about what sort of advice is available from where. What follows is therefore just a basic guide to current sources and the services they offer.

Merchant banks

Merchant banks still tend to operate very much at the top end of the scale, offering investment services mainly or wholly for six- and seven-figure portfolios. These would be based on UK equities and gilts and also on overseas investments, either directly into equities or, particularly for smaller markets, through the medium of unit trusts and other pooled funds.

Commonly, they provide services on a discretionary basis, which means that they will take the decisions without previously referring to the client. You do, of course, have the chance to specify your aims and requirements; for example, whether you are primarily seeking income or capital growth and the degree of risk you are prepared to take.

The firm will take care of all the paperwork, but you will be kept informed of all the transactions and in addition will receive regular reports and valuation statements. The management fee will generally be based on a percentage of the portfolio value on an annual basis.

Stockbrokers

At one time, stockbrokers were generally regarded as inhabiting a rarefied world of high finance which had little to do with the man in the street. In recent years, though, the mystique has been all but dispelled. For one thing, Big Bang brought greater potential for competition between firms, stimulating the wider publicity of their services. For another, potential clients are no longer just the upper classes whose families have placed business with the same broker for generations. With privatisations, all kinds of newcomers have been drawn into share-buying and most stockbrokers are keen to attract this new business.

As a result, where choosing a broker was once largely a matter of personal recommendation, a number now advertise their services and provide information on what they offer. For example, the Association of Private Client Investment Managers and Stockbrokers produces a directory in which members set out brief but alluring guides to the facilities they provide. All this is very welcome, as it makes the choices much clearer.

Most brokers offer a range of services, from the very basic to the fully comprehensive, as follows.

1. *Dealing or execution-only service.* This is for people who simply want the broker to buy and sell shares, generally without any advice being given. Because there are no added frills, this is generally much cheaper than management facilities.

2. *Discretionary or portfolio management service.* This is suitable for those who have an overall idea of what they want, in terms of income or growth and degree of risk, but do not want to take part in the decision process. The broker will take full responsibility for managing the investments, but the client will be kept informed of the transactions carried out and will receive regular valuations and reports. While some brokers only offer this type of service to wealthier clients, many are happy to take on quite small portfolios and there may be no fees above the dealing commission.

3. *Advisory service.* This may cover dealings in individual shares or the whole of your investment portfolio. Unlike the discretionary service, the client takes responsibility for decisions; the broker will offer advice, based on the client's needs and objectives, but no transactions will be carried out without reference and express permission. Although some brokers specify a minimum portfolio size, which might be anywhere between £20,000 and £75,000, others are happy to consider any amount.

4. *Comprehensive financial planning.* In addition to investment management, this would include advice on any other financial needs; for example, retirement planning, school fees, tax planning, mortgages, life assurance and general cash management. In fact, it could go right down to advice on bank and building society deposit accounts and some brokers also offer banking facilities themselves.

Now that standardised commission scales no longer exist, costs can vary from one firm to another. As a rule, those based in the provinces are likely to be cheaper than those in London, simply because they have lower overheads, and with modern communications technology, location should not have any impact on the quality of service. If you are using an advisory service, it may be more convenient to choose a local firm; for a discretionary service, this is not particularly necessary, although you may need to make the occasional visit to update your objectives.

Accountants and solicitors

Traditionally, accountants have focused on tax affairs, while solicitors have touched on financial matters only indirectly, through business such as conveyancing and wills. Nowadays, however, the distinctions are becoming blurred and accountants in particular may offer overall financial planning services, generally on a fee basis.

Solicitors are becoming more involved in investment business and there is now a trade association for those who specialise in giving financial advice – the Association of Solicitor Investment Managers. A directory of members can be obtained free by telephoning 01892 870065. Work is undertaken on a fee basis, as solicitors are required by the Law Society to disclose and repay any commission earned.

Independent financial advisers

Independent financial advisers will generally come under the auspices of the PIA, but that, and the fact of independent status, are more or less the only things that any one may have in common with any other. In other respects, this group has enormous diversity, ranging from one-man bands to large firms and offering a wide variety of services.

In the first place, there are different categories of authorisation, depending on the type of business carried out. At the lower end, the adviser will not actually handle your money; you simply make out your cheque direct to the company supplying the product. Firms that do handle clients' money have to undergo more rigorous checks designed to ensure that they are not likely to make off with it.

New entrants to the industry must undergo 'Stage 1' training before they are allowed to give any advice. This includes passing an examination, commonly the first paper of the Financial Planning Certificate, which tests knowledge of regulation and products. They may then give advice under supervision as part of Stage 2 training. To become a 'competent' adviser, a person must obtain Stage 2 qualifications such as the second and third papers of the Financial Planning Certificate.

Once qualified as competent, advisers must undertake a minimum amount of ongoing training as continuing professional development. There are also additional examinations that are required for certain specialist activities, such as discretionary portfolio management, broker fund management and dealing in options and warrants.

The Financial Services Act has led to greater costs for independent advisers and a considerable burden in time and money to comply with the morass of rules. One response has been the establishment of networks, linking together anywhere between a dozen and 1200 advisers. Through either centralised or decentralised administration, a network can take over much of the burden of compliance with the rules, leaving advisers to concentrate on their main business, and may also offer technical support and training. Generally, network members will deal with their clients in the normal way, but they may also cross-refer for specialist products, which may be an advantage for the investor.

The range of services offered by independent advisers can include any or all of mortgage arrangements and related products, life assurance, pension planning, school fees planning, unit trusts and investment trusts. In the last two categories, some firms provide portfolio management facilities on a discretionary as well as an advisory basis. However, they do not normally offer advice about individual stocks and shares or get involved in sophisticated tax planning techniques.

The majority operate wholly or mainly on a commission basis, but some are fee-based or may offer the client a choice. The organisation IFA Promotion runs a telephone service which can supply investors with the names of three independent advisers in their local area.

Insurance brokers

Insurance brokers are members of the Insurance Brokers Registration Council (IBRC). In addition to general insurance, such as motor and household, they may also deal with life assurance, pensions and a certain amount of investment business. In the case of those who are authorised only by the IBRC, this last is currently limited to a maximum of 49 per cent of total business, but a number of insurance brokers are also members of the PIA, and hence are not subject to this restriction.

Choosing an adviser

In addition to the above categories, financial advice is also offered by banks and building societies, although, as mentioned above, the majority of these act on behalf of one particular provider and can only offer its products. Similarly, the appointed representatives and direct salesforces of life assurance companies can offer advice within the range of the company they represent. Unit trust groups may also offer portfolio management services within the scope of their own trusts.

All advisers must clearly notify the investor of their status, whether they represent one company or act as an independent. The Securities and Investments Board maintains a central register of authorised firms, so if you are in any doubt, you can check whether a firm is authorised and the types of service it is allowed to provide. The information can be obtained by telephone or through Prestel.

In principle, independent advisers offer the widest choice, because they can select any product on the market. But if you are happy to deal with one particular product supplier, a tied agent can offer equally valid advice and, by virtue of his relationship with the company, may be better placed to sort out any problems that arise.

Types of service
Discretionary
With a discretionary service, you are effectively handing over all control to the adviser. At the outset, you will, of course, set out your basic requirements, your investment aims and the degree of risk you are prepared to accept in trying to achieve them. But thereafter you must trust the adviser to carry out your wishes faithfully and effectively.

On the other hand, there is the advantage of speed of action. Since the adviser is not having to refer decisions to you for approval, he can act immediately on opportunities which might otherwise be missed.

Advisory

Advisory services give you complete control, while you still have access to professional advice. Of course, if you are simply going to agree to everything the adviser suggests, you may as well give him discretion and have done with it. But an advisory service can also provide a useful learning process, so that you gradually come to take a more active role.

Since every transaction will require your prior authorisation, it is important that you should be accessible to your adviser. Equally, he should be readily accessible to you whenever you need advice or to deal.

Execution-only

Execution-only services are aimed at those who are confident that they know what they want and do not want to pay extra for added frills. Since no advice is being given, the choice may be largely cost-based but, if you plan to deal actively, you need to be sure that you can place an order easily and that it will be carried out quickly. Also, some execution-only share-dealing services do offer a few additional facilities, such as company reports or recommendations, and may also deal with the paperwork; for example, looking after share certificates and providing composite tax vouchers at the end of the financial year.

Commission versus fees

The commission versus fees issue has always been a sensitive one and has become more so lately. From the start of 1995, all independent advisers and insurance company salespeople have had to disclose what they stand to earn from a product sale before the client signs the application form. This includes not only commission but, for company salespeople, any relevant additional benefits provided by the company.

As there is no longer a maximum commissions agreement, companies are free to pay whatever levels they choose, which means there is the potential for advisers to be biased in their recommendations. In practice, rates are still based on the old scales and the differences between providers tend to be small. A more important issue is possible product bias, as products with similar functions may carry quite different rates of commission. In particular, if an adviser has spent considerable time checking a client's circumstances and requirements, he may be reluctant to recommend something like National Savings Certificates which carry no reward.

Commission disclosure, however, will not prove whether a product is good value for money. That depends on a number of factors, including the overall level of charges, the service provided and the total returns one might expect. To judge impartiality, an investor would need to know not only the levels of commission on all the possible alternative products, but also their relative merits in different circumstances; without that knowledge it would be difficult to prove a case of commission bias.

The obvious solution would be to move to a fee basis for all advice. But while this would increase independence, it is no guarantee of good advice. There is also the key question of whether people would be prepared to pay realistic fees. For those who are, there are a growing number of advisers who work on a fee basis or offer clients the choice. But this route is likely to prove more expensive for small investors, for whom percentage commissions can offer very good value.

Making complaints

If you feel that you have been badly treated by a company, or given inappropriate advice, the first step should be to take it up with the company itself, explaining why you are not happy and what action you expect. Always keep copies of any correspondence and also make a note of any telephone calls – when they were made, who you spoke to and what was said.

If you are not satisfied with the response, the next stage is to take your complaint to the appropriate SRO. Advisers and companies must indicate which SRO they are authorised by.

If you believe you are entitled to compensation, and this is not forthcoming from the adviser, you can take your case to an ombudsman. There are now ombudsmen covering each sector of the financial services market: banks, building societies, insurance, investment and pensions, plus a PIA ombudsman.

However, just as the FSA is to become the single regulatory body, it is also proposed to create a single, centralised ombudsman. It will have compulsory membership and be regulated by the FSA, and is expected to come into force in 2000.

This should avoid the current problem investors have of not knowing which of the eight ombudsmen to take a complaint to. It will also mean equal powers in all areas, whereas the current ombudsmen may differ, for example, in the amount of compensation they can award.

But there are drawbacks. A 'super-ombudsman' could become a bureaucratic monster compared with the smaller, more user-friendly offices there are at present, with long delays and backlogs of cases. The new scheme will also be more formal in its procedures, with hearings that can be attended by lawyers, and this may scare off the very people it is intended to protect. Finally, it will cover only the firms that are regulated by the FSA, which could exclude some mortgage lenders, for instance.

In some cases, you may be able to make a claim from the Investors Compensation Scheme. Claims should be made within six months of a default being declared and the maximum for any individual claim is £50,000. The main criteria for eligibility are that:

- you are a private investor;
- the firm involved is fully authorised;
- the firm cannot pay out claims;
- the firm owes money or was holding investments on your behalf;
- your claim relates to business regulated by the Financial Services Act.

But the Scheme cannot help in the following cases:

- the firm is not fully authorised;
- the firm has gone into liquidation but has not been declared in default;
- the firm is still in business;
- the business was conducted before 18 December 1986.

Bear in mind, too, that you cannot claim compensation simply on the grounds of bad performance if you have been fairly advised and warned of investment risk.

The various ombudsmen publish guides to their services, which are provided free of charge to investors. Product providers – whether life assurance companies, unit trust groups, banks or building societies – can also supply information on their complaints procedures, but if you have any doubts, further guidance is available from the Public Information Office at the SIB.

Useful contacts

Investment Management Regulatory Organisation: 0171 390 5000

Personal Investment Authority: 0171 538 8860

The Securities and Futures Authority: 0171 378 9000

The Financial Services Authority, Central Register: 0171 929 3652; Public Information Office: 0171 638 1240

The Banking Ombudsman: 0171 404 9944

The Building Societies Ombudsman: 0171 931 0044

The Insurance Ombudsman: 0171 928 7600

The Investment Ombudsman: 0171 796 3065

The Pensions Ombudsman: 0171 834 9144

The PIA Ombudsman: 0171 216 0016

The Investors Compensation Scheme: 0171 628 8820

IFA Promotion: 0117 971 1177

Cancer Prevention Research Trust

Purpose and programme

To carry out biomedical research into the prevention of cancer.
To provide funds for research to combat cancer and the human suffering it causes.
To help sustain critical research programmes.

Broad objectives

1. Develop the means to reduce the effectiveness of environmental agents (carcinogenic chemicals, viruses, radiations) for producing cancer.

2. Develop the means to educate the public (e.g. that restriction of intake of calories reduces tumour incidence) in order to minimise cancer development.

3. Develop the means to prevent the transformation of normal cells to cells capable of forming cancer.

4. Develop the means to prevent and control the progression of precancerous cells (polyps and other innocent tumours) to cancers, the development of cancer from precancerous conditions and the spread of cancers from primary sites.

5. Develop the means to achieve an accurate assessment of the risk of developing cancer in individuals and in population groups as well as the presence, extent and probable course of existing cancers.

6. Develop the means to treat cancer patients and to control the progress of cancers.

7. Develop the means to improve the rehabilitation of cancer patients.

Cancer Prevention Research Trust Cobden House, 231 Roehampton Lane, London SW15 4LB

For donations, in memoriam gifts, bequests
Registered Charity No. 265985

Guidelines to help you avoid cancer

1. Avoid rigid diets or rigid lifestyles. Variation in a person's daily habits is desirable, when feasible, to avoid the unconscious continued application of unsuspected carcinogens.

2. Limit consumption of highly seasoned food, black pepper, curries etc.

3. Limit consumption of herbs and herbal remedies. Some herbs have been found to be carcinogenic. Most herbs have not been tested for carcinogenicity.

4. Avoid a high animal fat diet and limit red meat consumption. Eat fish, chicken, turkey.

5. Limit consumption of charcoal-broiled or smoked meat or fish.

6. Limit consumption of nitrite/nitrate treated food: ham, bacon, sausages. For bottled water check the label for nitrate content; the lower the better. If possible use glass-bottled water.

7. Avoid iron tablets and food with added iron; low blood iron helps protect you from cancer as well as from infections.

8. Avoid excessive exposure to the sun; some of the ingredients in sun-screen lotions are suspect carcinogens.

9. Avoid exposure to bleach/chlorine fumes.

10. Limit frequent use of hair dyes; they have been associated with ~~~~ ~~~~~.

~~~~~ ~~~~~~ ~~oid exposure to passive smoke.
~~~~~ ~~egetable, fruit or other
~~~~ ~~ots, cabbage etc. Do not

13. Eat bran, oat-based cereals, reduced fat cottage cheese, broccoli, cauliflower, red cabbage, watercress, walnuts, apples.

14. Eat vegetables and fruit rich in beta-carotene and other carotenoids such as carrots, apricots, Cantaloupe-type melons, mangoes, paw-paw, pink grapefruit.

15. Eat fresh fruit rich in folic acid, e.g. blackberries, clementines, oranges, grapefruit, raspberries. Folic acid has been shown to protect against the risk of cervical cancer. It may also protect against prostate cancer.

16. Eat one or two Brazil nuts periodically for their high selenium content.

17. Drink green tea. Epidemiological studies have shown green tea to have cancer-preventive effects.

18. Use stainless steel or glass cooking utensils.

19. Women to completely avoid the use at talcum powder around the lower abdomen or near their private parts; it has been associated with ovarian cancer.

20. If you are pregnant do not keep any pets, especially cats; they have been associated with childhood leukemia.

21. If you are pregnant do not expose yourself to petrol fumes such as when filling up the petrol tank.

22. Hormones have been associated with breast cancer, hepatitis B or C viruses or alcohol with liver cancer, high salt intake with stomach cancer, asbestos or tobacco smoke with lung cancer, excess animal fat and low calcium with colon cancer.

~h Trust Cobden House, 231 Roehampton Lane, London SW15 4LB

For donations, in memoriam gifts, bequests
Cancer is a preventable disease
Registered Charity No. 265985

The **Leukaemia CARE** Society

Last year Leukaemia CARE helped hundreds of families by providing:

- Financial Assistance Grants - Caravan Holidays
- Countless befriending hours

This year Leukaemia CARE will be asked to help even more families. **We** can only help them if you will help us as ever increasing demand is made on limited resources.

A donation or covenant now and a legacy later will make it possible. the Society relies upon volunteers to assist those suffering from Leukaemia and allied Blood Disorders.

If you are able to offer your time and experience to befriend, fundraise, support others etc, please contact the office at:

...fisher Court (LS98)

Pinhoe, Exeter, Devon EX4 8JN.

1392) 464848,

01392) 460331

301

Registered Charity no. 259483

Index

References in *italic* indicate tables

Index

Index of Advertisers

Index of Advertisers